MUHAMMAD *the* PROPHET

HIS LIFE AND WORKS

OMAR AHMAD

Copyright © 2023 Omar Ahmad.

All rights reserved. No part of this book may be reproduced, stored, or transmitted by any means—whether auditory, graphic, mechanical, or electronic—without written permission of both publisher and author, except in the case of brief excerpts used in critical articles and reviews. Unauthorized reproduction of any part of this work is illegal and is punishable by law.

ISBN: 979-8-88640-995-6 (sc)
ISBN: 979-8-88640-996-3 (hc)
ISBN: 979-8-88640-997-0 (e)

Because of the dynamic nature of the Internet, any web addresses or links contained in this book may have changed since publication and may no longer be valid. The views expressed in this work are solely those of the author and do not necessarily reflect the views of the publisher, and the publisher hereby disclaims any responsibility for them.

One Galleria Blvd., Suite 1900, Metairie, LA 70001
1-888-421-2397

CONTENTS

Dedications v

Introduction vii

Preface ix

Chapter 1 Early Childhood and Characters of
            Him and Some Teachings.. 1

Chapter 2 The Holy Prophet's Life Works and Deeds.................... 38

Chapter 3 Some More Insights From Him, The Prophet There 98

Chapter 4 Use of the Parable by the Prophets and
            Saints And Related Topics 156

Chapter 5 Some Pearls of Wisdom From Him,
            The Prophet There..225

Chapter 6 Pearls From Myself 264

Chapter 7 Ahmadiyyat 301

Chapter 8 Some of My Trials Summarized Here 330

Chapter 9 Some Articles From My Facebook Page 337

About the author Omar Ahmad 364

About the book 365

DEDICATIONS

Please know this book is dedicated to the cause of Islam to prevail over me and others in that it sees fit that the young child here is brought peace and this book is for him and her as they grow into it, sublime faith we have in Ahmadiyyat Islam here in the West and East alike, and further, as always the young girl is my team who admonishes you to take care of him as you jail me in things as I teach disclamor some but it is true it the girl who recognizes merit in me more than those who just read her thoughts when she was saying he is immaculate like Jesus and Muhammad were and so you start to read me and protect me some, more here is required you became subservient to me when the law became apparent to you and you start to submit to Him Who creates and thus the credit goes to this nation as they succumb to monotheism open ways and relent to peace with us in Islam of Ahmadiyyat.

Please know he is well who calls me well and I ascribe to peace if they do to me,

Please know there is no God in our realm until you ascribe to peace with Him and His law knowing that He is above us even if you feel He is low to you for making you submit to Him,

Please know we know our worth is not to argue with Him but submit as we are fit in it under Him in His guide on us.

Please know to accept is sane as He is our worth here and will defend us if we are pious to Him and His advocate Muhammad, on him be peace,

Please know there is no law but His law,

Please know we are in His realm and we must submit to His mercy as it is His mercy that saves us from His Hell.

Please know Hell is real and should not be tempted as it will appear to you in this life and in the Hereafter you will be there,

Please Him,

Please know He is better for you than your other gods here like Jesus used to be and your low desires still are to some extent and it these gods who benefit you with hell from Him,

Please know there is only One God in His dominion and there is submission to Him that is required.

Please see it occur we are one nation here under whose tutelage I reside and I put up with your whims to me but your race is good actually and let me live and practice my profession of teach on you as there are many nations who would not have done so so in this way I am indebted to you and this book is a gift there to your young uns as they grow in moderate door of Islam on them which you teach them gradual ways but with alacrity with you as well making sure they know the odds of getting there with Him in the long haul of things in this life we live here on earth.

I reside in Jackson Tennessee now with atghar or sublime in me,

Please know I am sublime to you and you know it I have done it, One God with you, that you succumb to in your thoughts to Him and your deeds are more pure now with your comprehension occurring that Heaven awaits you if you but submit to Him in His law structure there,

Please know you are a god if you don't obey Him like we do there you think but there are few who submit like us three horsemen of the Ahmadiyya sect there,

So there results and they come after my car.

Please know we are sublime and I submit to your car when it occurs but you are right the fight must go on. Omar.

INTRODUCTION

'Please know' is a way I communicate to imply I am humble to you in precepts that cause you disquiet and concern as the material here is new to you and breaks boundaries with you that you think otherwise.

Please know it is over and with my book 'Jesus, the Messiah and Person' you know I break precepts you hold dear to you and I don't care in your view, but I do, and being blunt is one way for you to listen that there is no god but Allah you should worship, like we do in Islam, as He expects that of you.

Please know there are terms that you are familiar with in my first book and I will repeat them for your satisfaction.

Please know 'ure son' is a term you find disquiet with, it implies it is resistant to this concept you find yourself in my literature.

Please know 'your son' is something you are pleased to know in your concepts of Him as He teaches you through my pen.

Please know a son is a well-wisher though and loves that you be satisfied with Him, like we are in Islam and we serve you thereby.

Please know 'repose' is complex to you but serves you when you understand we do things for the pleasure of one we serve so when I say I serve him it means I have repose for him and it is his pleasure I seek, like I do here when I serve my master Prophet Muhammad and his Master, Allah, our Creator,

Please know I am sane and know you have to be explained things like I do here, ad nauseum to some, but I seek to make clear by repetition and usually there is a new perspective to things I say on the internet, which I relay here in my notes to you.

Please know I am kind and I read you correctly that you need time to come through in Islamic edicts as the law is extraneous to you, in your view, but it must be adhered to or else all will be lost and your monotheism will be a figment as your God is not One you obey, so He does not exist in your hearts, as law from Him is extraneous to some but not those who serve Him, like I do and my mentor in Islam, your Prophet Muhammad, who knew He must be obeyed in edicts.

Please know I will be brief here but I am indebted to the Ahmadiyya Jamaat for use of their materials from their website and Maulana Muhammad Ali's translation of the Quran which I download from iBooks and otherwise. I am also indebted to websites where I copy Bible excerpts for my book like Bible Gateway and others, so I may assimilate their views in my comprehension before I write my views.

Please know I am indebted to my family for putting up with my disclamor of them in my book however they deserve it, in my view.

Please know in the final analysis I know you know my literature there and this book serves as an avenue to have it in a book form, the mainstay of my thoughts for you.

Please know I complete the book now but expect you to be a student of mine for your days here in this planet as I teach from him, my Prophet, and know you would like the truth emanating from his guise to you.

Please know him from a rock and a hard place as that is where I am to you and I hope you will give me credit for my guise to you as saint Dabbat-Al Ard, the saint of the hereafter proper, in guise here as Omar Ahmad MD.

Please know there is no god but Allah here because you persevered with me and got me out of the rock I was placed in.

Please know I am indebted to your country to let me live though the material I produce for you is distasteful to some and sentiments of murder arise in them as the church has ended, in my view, in your heart's sentiments and you go there for repose with her who officiates you.

Please know it is kind in you that you let me live and teach you as you know I was being kind, in turn to you, as your Hereafter was lost and I cared that it not be so I persevered for those who wish for peace with me and their Creator.

Please know our Prophet was a skeptic of you but knew your worth to learn so we see the future unfold for your liking, even if he does not care for your disclamor of him, my mentor, Muhammad, on him be peace that you used to have in your church groups on us.

Please know he knows you will learn however but your hardship is written if you worship your God yet do not give credit to me or him, your Prophet. Omar.

PREFACE

Please know the following,
Please know there is 'no god but Allah' here in your realm,
Please know why it occurred,
Please know it was because you were adherent with the view that truth was important,
Please know you went through lengths to make it occur,
Please know your children were your vice and you sinned for them,
Please understand what vice is,
Please know it is to allow you sins in things,
Please know it was not from God that you sinned,
Please know your child gave you pleasure so you sinned for it and created it in turmoil to Him,
Please know when you sin for him you lose your wealth as he does not want your ill-begotten wealth which will drive him to Hellfire.
Please know that was what the Prophet said that ill-begotten wealth will teach your child to do the same and then his or her Hellfire is written so make sure that you are moderate in it and keep them safe, the child you love.
Please know it is only a vice that you have that you sin,
Please know with 'no God but Allah' here the realization has come into your mind that to sin is wrong,
Please know it is over for you who think there is no accounting,
Please know every sin is accounted for and then you are presented your book,
Please know if it is in your right hand you are lucky,
Please understand this,
Please know we must adhere to the view that it is lucky if we receive Heaven,
Please know why,
Please know it is because Heaven is vouchsafed for the lucky ones,
Please know it is over for her who thinks that vice is easy to avoid,

Please know it is difficult,
Please understand vice for a while,
Please know it is simple to sin,
Please know when it occurs we are sorry,
Please understand it is over for you as you will try to raise the child to Heaven,
Please know what Heaven is,
Please know it is the place where the adherents live in peace,
Please know what peace is,
Please know it is to do as you please.
Please know our Creator has vouchsafed it to the pious,
Please Him in His Entirety,
Please know vice will get you paradise here but it will be taken away from you.
Please know your amassings come to nothing when you die and you take your vice with you.
Please know it will come to nothing,
Please make preparations for your trip with Him,
Please know there is no god in the Hereafter but Him,
Please know your cajoling will come to nothing,
Please understand there the accounting is tough and it is a hard Day,
Please know there is one who can intervene for you,
Please know that is your Prophet Muhammad, on him be peace,
Please know why he would intervene for you,
Please know you took him for a Prophet of yours. Omar.

CHAPTER ONE

EARLY CHILDHOOD AND CHARACTERS OF HIM AND SOME TEACHINGS

Please know it has occurred that people have understood the metaphor Jesus was using when he applied godhead in himself,

Please know I have talked to many people on the subject and they agree with me,

Please know I appreciate their input,

Please know it is by the grace of Allah that people have started to pray to Him,

Please know my career as a writer has been crowned with success because I don't write of my own accord, only what is indicated to me what to write,

Please know I cannot claim success as the words that change the heart are His and His Prophet and others who write as well,

Please know I am a slave who will be brought to Him empty handed apart from deeds that I have to show to Him and others who are with Him there,

Please know that it is our role to tell you the riches you amass are not actually yours,

Please give in to peace with us in Islam as we are only trying to teach you His Grace so that you may be pleased in the hereafter,

Please know your Creator is One and no entity is worthy of worship besides Him, as the Quran tells us,

Please know by and large people have understood that,

Please know your hearts are at peace,

Please know it is not just in this country that people believe,

Please know it is even in those countries where atheism reigns as a state custom,

Please see it occur that people worship their Creator only,

Please know idolatry is on the wane as people are understanding these are customs that have no meaning in the intellect of man,

Please know reincarnation is wrong and we will not be sent down again to improve our lot, so say the Bible, the Quran, and many other texts of religious belief,

Please know nirvana is to achieve our peace here free from the bondage to worldly pursuits,

Please know worship of spirits of your ancestors is a misnomer,

Please know they can intervene for you only when it is the wish of The Supreme Being,

Please know worship of nature is wrong and we worship the One Who creates,

Please know all religions have some wrong in them as after their prophets died things were tabulated differently by their leaders,

Please know we consider their sages to be prophets or prophet-like individuals,

Please give in,

Please know the Quran was preserved for humanity,

Please read your history book, our Book, it is tabulated there it is intact for the most part with no change in the essence of the message from the Quran the Prophet had as nearly all the Qurans that are present have only minor discrepancies in them for the most part.

Please know there is peace for those who care about themselves and follow the precepts of our Book there,

Please know the world has accepted their Creator as their worshipped Entity from the message of categorical words that are entailed in our Book,

Please know I had a communication from Prophet Muhammad that it was so. Omar.

I am mujaddid there in Middle East some for bringing you Islam here.

Please know he was ceaseless and became known as the successful one.

Please know there was no god but Allah there by the time he died for the most part,

Please know this concept,

Please know our Creator made him the most successful man,

Please know it is his character that comes in me,

Please know I am not him but borrow from him for you to see him with clarity,

Please know there is no god but Allah in the world because of his teachings coming down in my pen,

Please know I know I am nothing but you will ascribe success to me,

Please know you don't see him like we do in Islam,

Please know the epilogue of the book,

Please know it is from him with love to you.

Please know he is the author though the pen is mine,

Please know this book is meant to please you in Islam,

Please give commendations to him who visits us in dreams and guides mankind,

Please know his life works continue through his pen in us,

Please know at the beginning of every century or era of the Islamic calendar there arises a mujaddid or reformer,

Please know he guides their pen,

Please Him,

Please know there is 'no god but Allah' and he is His Messenger.

Please know this is the edict that converts hearts to His way.

Please Him and be merry in the Hereafter,

Please know our Prophet knew I was to come to follow in his footsteps,

Please know it is over and I claim to be the saint Dabbat Al-Ard,

Please know I am nothing of my own accord and only follow him, my master,

Please know we are all slaves of each other and we serve you.

Please know there is 'no god but Allah' here because you submit to truth,

Please know you are a promised race and the greatest civilization raised by Him,

Please know your Creator is One and the metaphor is misapplied,
Please know I have brought you peace so give commendations,
Please know him through works on him,
Please know you will enter Paradise and meet him,
Please know it is joy everlasting there,
Please Him and you will be successful.

His early childhood and rearings.

The Prophet's deportment was such that he had a child in him that lived forever.

Please know our Prophet was born in 570 AD approximately.

Please understand him.

Please know he was to perfect religion so he was a role model for mankind,

Please know he was endowed with ease and comfort in his early childhood with Halima and then his grandfather's house,

Please understand his childhood was rough in regard that his father died before he was born.

Please understand this,

Please know he could have been taught things that were incorrect for him.

Please know fathers teach kids what they know,

Please understand he was an orphan and when his mother raised him she was sure he was to be special.

Please know she had a vision that the child in her womb had light that would reach Syria,

Please understand our Prophet as he was a normal child,

Please know however he never lied as a child,

Please know this was something remarkable and his wet nurse Halima thought him special.

Please know in Arab tradition the child is sent to the desert so they grow up hardy,

Please know her livestock abounded with him there and she desired to keep him till the age of four, which his mother permitted her,

Please know it was there that a vision occurred and his heart was cleaned of the blackness of the world,

Please know it was permitted to her that he would live with her,

Please know by this I mean that she could take him back and our child was to come to live with his mother when he was four years,

Please know she died shortly thereafter,

Please know his grandfather took him under his care,

Please know he noticed he never bowed to an idol and indicated he was special.

Please know it was the Arab custom to give consecrations to the idol they worshipped but Muhammad never participated in it.

Please understand this,

Please know he was to be the world leader,

Please know it was not befitting that he should participate in idol worship or other nefarious activities.

Please know his mother never asked him to participate in this,

Please understand vice,

Please know he was free from it and was a thoughtful child,

Please know he was a Muslim from birth,

Please understand that our Prophet was careful about the rights of Allah upon him.

Please know the following hadith,

Please know our Prophet was a protected entity right from childhood.

Please know when he went to play with some boys who had taken off their clothes he was instructed not to do so by a voice but with no person attached.

Please know in another incidence he was asked to attend a festival commemorating an idol.

Please know it was not his inclination to attend such a festival but when asked by an aunt he went to it.

Please know there was a tall man dressed in white clothing there who appeared and told him not to touch the idol.

Please Him occurs,

Please know he feared he was going mad however his aunt assured him he was too good to be possessed.

Please know he was protected and it is mentioned in the Quran he never bowed to an idol.

The end is there for those who think he was not a saint as a child.

Please know there was another incident where he went to the dancing girls house to see them dance however when he got there he fell asleep and could not wake up till the morning.

Please know these incidents show that he was a protected entity.

Please know he was vouchsafed to be the leader of mankind and our Creator was not going to have His beloved fall into hardship due to some sin committed in ignorance.

Please know we know from the scriptures that our Prophet will intervene for us on Judgment Day and after all the prophets decline to intervene they will approach our Prophet who will do so.

Please know our Prophet never had a calumny of falling to the devil.

Please know he was careful in that regard,

Please know the other prophets had a fall.

Please know this,

Please know he is the prophet who will never have a fall of that nature and he and Jesus are special in that regard.

Please know he is different from mankind who will all fail in some respect in regard to the law of God on us but he had a sense that knew when things were incorrect to do and abstained from sin in an obvious way as indicated in hadith lore and in the testimony of people as well including his enemies who would say he was upright to others they met.

Please say a prayer for him.

Please know he will come through for you. Omar.

Please know the king of man was a simple aristocrat.

Please know our Prophet is destined to be the king of mankind.

Please see these verses from the chapter The Romans or thirty,

Please know before the advent of Islam the world was in a polytheistic state and corruption was rife and prevalent,

Please know it was in this land that the king of men was born,

Please know in a short space of twenty odd years he transformed Arabia and his seeds of learning spread the world over when the Christians accepted the methods of science from the Muslim scholars in ancient Spain.

Please know polytheism was the reason corruption spread far and wide.

Please know why?

Please understand when you pray to many gods you don't have any and your nature beckons you to sin overtly.

Please know you can do as you please and justify it on the grounds what a particular god does.

Please know the Jews took their leaders as gods.

Please understand this,

Please know when the people asked their scholars for opinions they did not give it to them based on the teachings of God from their books but gave them to please the people- giving them leeway in committing sins.

Please know it was here that Islam appeared and taught man about Him.

Please know the people learnt the truth and adopted monotheism in its purest form.

Please know with this monotheism came about the love for truth and the purity of deeds.

Please know the Christians were second to Islam in the purity of their deeds and impelling man to good.

Please know they were polytheistic however.

Please know modern day Christianity with trinity precepts follows its low desires and take it for a god. In this there is sadness as they are good people. Omar.

Rum.

30:41 Corruption has appeared in the land and the sea on account of that which men's hands have wrought, that He may make them taste a part of that which they have done, so that they may return.

30:42 Say: Travel in the land, then see what was the end of those before! Most of them were polytheists.

Please know you know you are not him who never lied or broke a trust.

Please know our Prophet was effervescent, if quiet.

Please know he was natural and did not put on airs.

Please know he was meek and did not dare Him,

Please know we are created that way and he didn't change as he had no sin by which we change,

Please know it is for this reason God found fault with him and gave him Godhead as a metaphor but he mistook it for actual way with him,

Please know he thought he was Him, then clarified,

Please know we all go through this thought, then realize it is our fault to be so.

Please know prophet Jesus and myself had a sin,

Please know that is why we were 'gods' to Him,

Please know when you sin such you are acting like your own gods,

Please know we were disobedient and reprimand occurred, then we were forgiven and our sin was changed to a good one and we became His repose here on earth,

Please know our Prophet never had a sin so he was His repose in actual and had clear intellect from Him, the Creat. It was because he never sinned of significance overtly we know his intellect was never muddied and thus was never confused in issues and he will be raised as the clear-minded one, yes, he was taught by God continuous ways and had little difficulty understanding Him because of this issue of being sinless for the most part, at least in an overt way.

Please see we all sin in a way we are witnessed and the Prophet was not so so he was seen as the one who had no obvious sin,

Please see we are all muddied because of some sin in us and need guide in things from Him or him, the Prophet, who are clear-minded in issues we face so it occurs we need help to sort out our thoughts,

Please see it is because of the sin in us we will always need help as once we have sinned we will always have issues in our thought processes and He is kind to us and knows our worth is to repent and move on, there is little we can do about past sin, and we know when He starts to guide us we become like the Prophet but are never as clear-minded as he is and that's our destiny to be under him for all eternity.

Please Him,

Please know we all sin,

Please know we have to strive in His way to be repose to Him in our deeds from His thoughts on us,

Please know our Prophet knew he was perfect but kept quiet about it.

Please bring your proof that a man who is never known to have lied or break his trust could be evil, like you say in your culture and church groups.

Please see this verse from the chapter of The Elevated Plains.

Please know to honor him is sane to do,

Please know our Prophet's honor is written,

Please consider this,

Please know that a man who never broke his word and spoke a lie could not be a bad man,

Please know him,

Please know he was polite, effervescent and genial.

Please know him,

Please know he was kind to an extreme and cared deeply about people,

Please know that he was this and try to see if you are better than him,

Please honor him,

Please know you can't go through one day without lying,

Please reflect,

Please know in your heart that he cares for you,

Please try to bring yourself to love him,

Please know aversion,

Please know it is you because you don't like to change your lifestyles,

Please bring your proof that he is bad,

Please know it is a lie written by those who are jealous or evil to him,

Please know these characteristics of his,

Please reflect and see for yourself.

Please know Jesus,

Please know he was similar but lied on occasion,
Please know he was truthful for the most part and will be raised as truthful.
Please know these people are better than you,
Please know their honor is due,
Please know you will honor him and me,
Please know I am not him, Muhammad in essence, except that he teaches me in dream communications and thus I am one with him and Jesus not,
Please know I follow him and learn precepts from him but he taught me things about him who you call Isa ibn Maryam and then Isa started teaching me his word as well and I developed a similar repose like he had, but we are different, Isa and me.
Please know though I raised myself like he did, Isa there. Omar.
Al-Araf.
7:157 Those who follow the Messenger-Prophet, the Ummi, whom they find mentioned in the Torah and the Gospel. He enjoins them good and forbids them evil, and makes lawful to them the good things and prohibits for them impure things, and removes from them their burden and the shackles which were on them. So those who believe in him and honor him and help him, and follow the light which has been sent down with him—these are the successful.

We will all be perfect in Jannah or Heaven and the Prophet's car will parked there with ignition off and rear lights dimmed.
Please know the following works will be published,
Please understand this,
Please know our Creator wishes it to be his works that I write,
Please know he is responsible for the conversion of you.
Please understand his works were many,
Please know to end idolatry was his feat,
Please understand this,
Please know our Creator decreed that he singlehandedly uproot it,
Please know this occurred in Arabia,
Please see the footnote there,

Please know there is no god but Allah
Please understand Muhammad,
Please understand he will not rest until Islam prevails man,
Please Him,
Please know to do that you have to be His servants and work for Him,
Please know your Paradise is written but your rewards are less than them who gave you Islam through hard work and dedication to you and Him, the Creat,
Please give in,
Please know there is a reward for every conversion,
Please strive hard for it.
Please know our Creator created the heavens and earth for his Messenger, Muhammad, and we are his guest in Paradise.
Please know this verse where Allah has ordained mercy on Himself.
Please know Allah's mercy,
Please know it is to relent to him or her,
Please know we are all sinners and go to Him as such,
Please understand sinners,
Please know it is to do things on purpose,
Please know we can't be perfect,
Please know only one of us achieved it,
Please know that is why he can intercede for us,
Please know we are grateful to God for creating him,
Please know He fashioned him then,
Please know He achieved perfection,
Please know our Creator has said He created the heavens and earth for him,
Please know how,
Please know it was the man who would be the mold for you,
Please know you are perfect if you follow him,
Please understand this,
Please know He had mercy on you when He gave you the mold,
Please know all will be like him in Heaven,
Please know we will all be perfect there,

Please know He created him for this,
Please know why?
Please know he was created for the heavens and earth,
Please know he was the first creation,
Please know all are from his heart,
Please know he has a place for us there,
Please know they, the human race, belong to his heart,
Please know it is the heart of a submitter to Him,
Please know heart,
Please know it is what we wish for,
Please know his heart encompasses all our wishes and he knows you will want to have a heaven similar to his but you will have to raise yourself in dignity to him before you can meet him there,
Please know those who make it to Heaven can raise their car to his status and share his Paradise with him eventually if they wish it to be in his company there but you will have to adopt his mold there to do so.
Please know he understands us,
Please know he knows what is best for us,
Please him,
Please know he is directly responsible for your Heaven to occur as it is meant for those who follow him,
Please know this,
Please know perfect,
Please know your Heaven,
Please enter and do as you please,
Please know your hearts wishes will be fulfilled,
Please know his heart encompasses you with love there,
Please know love,
Please know it is to yearn for your company,
Please yourself,
Please know you will come through,
Please know it is written. Omar.
Al-Anum or The Cattle
6:12 Say: To whom belongs whatever is in the heavens and the earth? Say: To Allah. He has ordained mercy on Himself. He will certainly

gather you on the Resurrection day—there is no doubt about it. Those who have lost their souls will not believe.

6:13 And to Him belongs whatever dwells in the night and the day. And He is the Hearing, the Knowing.

6:14 Say: Shall I take for a friend other than Allah, the Originator of the heavens and the earth, and He feeds and is not fed? Say: I am commanded to be the first of those who submit. And be thou not of the polytheists.

Please know ourselves from his make, the Prophet there, which is our make if we but evolve to this realization there is One God and Muhammad is His Messenger and we have to be his mold for us.

Please know we must be cognizant we are answerable for our sins but to be him is our goal.

Please see these verses from the chapter, The Poets.

Please know this was the tender-heartedness of the Prophet.

Please know he could have been nonchalant and not cared if anybody accepted the message.

Please know he cared deeply for you.

Please understand this,

Please know this is the norm for him,

Please know it is for us to learn from him,

Please understand if we don't feel like him something is amiss.

Please know this is the norm for man.

Please understand man from him,

Please try to feel for humanity from him,

Please know that we are answerable for our conduct but to feel for man is something expected of us from Him,

Please try to empathize and feel the sadness when people go astray and not gloat and say go to Hell with you but to bring them around is our goal to you.

Please know to be him is our norm. Omar.

Al- Shuara.

26:1 Benignant, Hearing, Knowing God.

26:2 These are the verses of the Book that makes manifest.

26:3 Perhaps thou wilt kill thyself with grief because they believe not.

Please know our Prophet is closer to you than yourselves.
Please know our Prophet was careful in His law and took his people to Paradise as they were careful as well.
Please know Creator said this in the chapter The Allies,
Please know metaphor,
Please know it is to say something that has a different meaning than what is conveyed when understood in its context,
Please know this is real that he is closer to you than yourselves,
Please know how,
Please know he knows your needs,
Please understand need,
Please know it is what you furnish yourself with,
Please know this,
Please know He will send you away.
Please know your Prophet is solicitous for you and will guide you back to Him,
Please see yourself come through,
Please know his prayer is accepted,
Please understand he will take you to Him,
Please know you will be pleased. Omar.
Al-Ahzab.
33:6 The Prophet is closer to the faithful than their own selves, and his wives are (as) their mothers. And the possessors of relationship are closer one to another in the ordinance of Allah than (other) believers, and those who fled (their homes), except that you do some good to your friends. This is written in the Book.

Please see we are created beings in that we were not living as humans before He gave us a conscious state in ourself and we are created here when we think.
Please know this post is repeated elsewhere but I will mention India is my car in respect of their tolerance of Islam.

Please know India knows me and reads this page but are appalled at my literature about their views on this subject,

Please know they know it is over in the mindsets of people as they cannot bow down to an animal or thing when they obviously did not create them,

Please know Allah is the Creator as He fashioned you in the womb through His DNA imprint in you and a stick does not do that nor does a cow or thing.

Please know the following article has been published there on my Facebook page and I will relay it here,

Please know it is about idolatry and its vices with us in Islam,

Please know it is a vice they keep there in their homes until Muhammad removed it from them after the conquest of their lands by him,

Please know he did it literally for some but some he enlisted them, his sahaba, who taught on after he left,

Please know it was gradual that idolatry vanished and it was during Umer's time that it occurred.

Please know idolatry is the bane of the world.

Please know our Creator will eradicate it.

Please be cognizant of it.

Please know it is insidious and eats away at innards.

Please know our souls are from Him,

Please know God has foreknowledge of everything,

Please know He knew He was going to create us,

Please know He knew which part of Him was going to be given to us,

Please know this is a complex issue,

Please know our Creator has knowledge of all things and knows a part of Him would be used to make humanity,

Please know all animate and inanimate things are created from His substrate but He creates them with His hands.

Please know that is earth for us,

Please know our molecules are derived from it as we eat plants and so do animals.

Please know idolatry is a sin our Prophet fought,

Please know it is incomprehensible that a idol made out of stone can intercede with Him,

Please know it can do harm to a person who doesn't know the implications,

Please know our God distances Himself from them,

Please know that any child knows that if you talk to a stone it doesn't answer you back,

Please know only the Creator has the power to answer prayers,

Please know they think that our Creator is approached by them,

Please know this is only conjecture and has no basis in it from the teachings of their prophets though we know their words got altered some to imply polytheism elements in their teach to them,

Please know our Creator is pleased there as there is a concerted effort to educate them,

Please don't bow down to anyone or thing!

Please know an animal is a creation of the Beneficent and did not create itself,

Please know to take advantage of His gift,

Please know our Creator made stones and sticks and they were not co-eternal with Him,

Please know it is a metaphor they are Him in the sense that from the energy particle He has created matter and now the earth creates these objects,

Please know He was One before He created things from Himself,

Please know we are co-eternal in the sense of a metaphor,

Please know how,

Please know we were always in Him but were created in our conscious state when He created our spirits,

Please know then He created us

Please know it is clear you understand these concepts that initial way He, the Creator, was the only conscious state and then He created us with our own conscious state separate from Him and He will bring about others from Him till no end of us for eternal ways with Him and us in concert if we wish to be with Him there. Omar.

Please see the names of our Creator from Al-Hashr, the verses of which are the sublime attributes He possesses and it becomes us to know these names of His.

Please know the Creator is sublime and names only a few here but it is true He has 99 attributes He possesses and now we know Him from them.

Please know it is clear there is no God but He from these verses and it should enter every mindset these ideals we have for Him are only part of His glory as He is Infinite in attributes and Power He has.

Please see it occur that I am teacher here of Him and we only ascribe greatness to Him in that we ourselves are humble beings, being smaller than a microbe compared to His size.

Please know in this microbe state we are poor and proud, but to know Him is to know our worth in things and we are only His servants who work for His benefit in our lives here on earth.

Please know He is Glory and it becomes us to know our humble worth and not ascribe greatness to ourselves in issues as we were created by Him and we were nothing before except that our souls migrate there to our bodies at conceive with us.

Please see to deny Him is our foolishness as we were created and were nothing to speak of before it, our birth I mean here, and we will be punished as He knows what is good for us and what we should believe for ourselves if we are to prosper here, and in the Hereafter live with Him. Omar.

Al-Hashr

59:22 He is Allah besides Whom there is no God: The Knower of the unseen and the seen; He is the Beneficent, the Merciful.

59:23 He is Allah, besides Whom there is no God; the King, the Holy, the Author of Peace, the Granter of Security, Guardian over all, the Mighty, the Supreme, the Possessor of greatness. Glory be to Allah from that which they set up (with Him)!

59:24 He is Allah; the Creator, the Maker, the Fashioner: His are the most beautiful names. Whatever is in the heavens and the earth declares His glory; and He is the Mighty, the Wise.

Please know atheist is blind and will be raised so in the Hereafter.
Please see sad faces there.
Please know this is trite but I will say it anyway.
Please know I have success written for me, inshallah. I know that atheist like to ignore Him but they don't realize that they ignore themselves as well.
Please see why.
Please know we know ourselves through our Creator. I know we can recognize merit in others and ourselves but if we cannot recognize merit in Him we are lost.
Please see if you can see yourself in the dark. While we think we know ourselves we may be wrong and think of ourselves as independent beings while we all need Him. In this life there is leeway in this but when we approach death we need solace. I know it is trite but we need peace. We need to know why we are created. I know we have the answers.
Please read the book I wrote. It is clear that in the creation of man is for us to be ready for the Hereafter. An atheist lives only for this world and ignores Him. For what purpose was he born? I know the despair he will feel. I know we have role to educate people.
Please see the following caption on his heart.
When I am dead, will I be reborn?
Please know it is only when we realize that we are created for the Hereafter do we understand this life.
Please know we improve ourselves here and we are given chances after chances to improve our conduct and appreciate the truth. I am hopeful that you will realize the earth is a testing ground for us and an avenue to appreciate Him, our Creator.
Please see the following caption there in his home in Paradise.
It was close but I realized we would never be at peace if we are to be nothing in the Hereafter.
Please see the following caption in his home in Hell.
Please know I am sad that I did not appreciate Him.
Please know this world is only for us to know who was best in conduct so we don't have rancor in the Hereafter at those who were better than us, and to perfect our make.

Please see if you can perfect yourself by yourself.

This is true. The atheist knows right from wrong as well as I do. I just live my life in the conduct of my Prophet. Who does the atheist copy? The end.

Please know we are moral people if we know the truth. The prophets were the greatest humanitarians who engendered love for themselves due to their kindness to others. I hope I can engender love for myself by following the conduct of my Prophet. I know it is trite to say this but these were great men who were taught humanitarian principles by their Creator. In the end we choose our location in the Hereafter. Whether to be with the prophets who were great humanitarians or to be with others. I am not saying others are not good to follow but we have gold standards who are vouchsafed success by their Creator. Inshallah you will see that I am right and we will trust you will not discount religion as there is much nobility and love to be found there.

Please see the following caption on my heart.

Please know I am nothing and I need a guide.

Please see the following caption there.

Please see if we can enter Paradise as I did not know it existed and ignored Him.

Please heed advise. Omar.

Atheists deny our Creator His worth and that is their lack of themselves as worthy beings.

Please see this post from Facebook where I speak of the evils of recognizing merit only in the ones you desire for you and not in your Benefactor Who created you or those who guide you to truth.

Please know this is atheism that it does not recognize our Creator as sovereign over them,

Please understand me when I say this is boon here but it will be your demise on the day you are raised as there is no benefactor there for you as you denied Him in your existence here on earth where the test of your reality occurs.

Please see my article below where it spells out our need for you to recognize Him as the Entity you war with as He will war you if you do not give Him the merit He deserves.

Please know we all bear the badge of merit and it is incumbent on us to display it to you as you give us our worth for you this way.

Please know it is similar and we won't recognize you if you don't appreciate us in this world as that is our real test here on earth.

Please know the Prophet is similar and if you don't worth him he won't worth you.

Please know this is universal law.

Please know the edicts are clear in the Quran 'He begets not' and when you deny Him He will deny you in that regard and send you for reformation to him, your savior,

Please know that occurs in suffering and hardship as it is then that we turn to the truth that was apparent to you in this life but you deferred and fought anyway.

Please know the Christian church is on a downslide with me as they don't have answers to me so they fight vehemently rather than fighting in court of man as should be done,

Please know they are affronted and I would be as well if my religion was threatened by an outside source but there is method in decency and there is Hellfire for those who fight inordinately as they do now by committing me and placing conservator over me to dissuade me from truth to in your quarters of dream to you.

In this we are safe as it is the underlying message of the Quran that is epitomized in these verses of this chapter where the Unity of our Creator is described. It is with this message the sonship of Jesus is negated in no uncertain terms.

Please know the sonship as well the omniscience of the Beneficent is described as all creations have to turn to Him for recourse in their time of need. Your son is sad as there are people who resist this message of peace to them as they feel that to deny Him somehow magnifies them as they feel they do not need a Creator for their needs. In this they will see dismay as on the Day of their Reckoning they will be asked to produce someone who could help them and they will be bereft of peace there on that Day. Ure son knows atheism reigns but I have repose there are people who understand our views that the Creator is omniscient in our lives and since we depend on Him He will come through for us in our repose to Him being our Benefactor. Omar.

Chapter Al-Ikhlas or The Unity of God.
112:1 Say: He, Allah, is One.
112:2 Allah is He on Whom all depend.
112:3 He begets not, nor is He begotten;
112:4 And none is like Him.

Please see the atheist denies Him as they want their freedom in things and are encumbered by Him in His laws to us and rebel it, they do to Him in charge there.

Please see the words in Bani-Israel where God speaks of His glory in the creation of things of the universe in that even inanimate things glorify Him with praise and obey Him.

Please know man is different in that he fights this glory of our Creator and denies Him in things they do.

Please know there is aversion of the hearts to Him and they seek to ridicule His might over us in that they say it is from us that we earn wealth and do things of that sort that they say.

Please know it is clear they are deluded into this as they were nothing to speak of before they were created.

Please know blindness settles in their kalb or hearts and they continue to deny Him in their minds until they are raised up.

Please know China and Russia and a few other countries are where communism is supported but it is clear they are on defense against literature that comes forth from here where the Quran words rings true to them, so they suppress it.

Please know they seek solace from it and ban it in their countries if they could but it is clear they are hard hearted in it.

Please know they consider it backward to follow religion and counsel masses not to believe them who pray to Him,

Please know it is the state agency that does this and the masses are beckoned not to believe Him Who creates us.

Please see they say they were created by chance but we know chance leads to disorder in things and entropy results, not order and chaos not in things they see,

Please know they deny Allah as they do not see Him but His science is with us and we recognize Him in it,

Please know the DNA is an example, it could not have been created by chance as single gene defects result in death of individuals, and the stars are similar, they are perfect in it, their creation I mean.

Please know they call religion backward and so forth but we know religion gives us peace and a meaning occurs for their existence and you know there is a Hereafter for us and we are not to be left in our desultory state of no meaning to life and they are insane in my view as they say their parents created them,

Please know were their genes coded by their parents or by the Creator of them,

Please know these and other delusions are taught to them and they lose reason in things and become material objects of worship not you think but it is true they are materialistic, thinking that this world is the end all and be all of things and no future do they hold with Him in charge of us in the Hereafter do they hold as true.

Please see it, the stick to them in the Hereafter as they deny Him here.

Please know they are as stones and iron,

Please see they do not let truth or life enter it, their hearts I mean,

Please know eventually they die then they are full of remonstrations but it is too late then, they have sinned in their life and lived in ignorance of Him for which they are accountable,

Please know Hellfire is real there, here it is anger and hardness in them so they perceive themselves sane while they are not,

Please know they were created from an embryo,

Please know it is God that gave them this reason and intellect that they can earn and things they do. Omar.

Bani-Israel.

17:44 The seven heavens and the earth and those in them declare His glory. And there is not a single thing but glorifies Him with His *praise, but you do not understand their glorification. Surely He is Forbearing, Forgiving.*

17:45 And when thou recitest the Qur'an, We place between thee and those who believe not in the Hereafter a hidden barrier;

17:46 And We put coverings on their hearts and a deafness in their ears lest they understand it; and when thou makest mention of thy Lord alone in the Qur'an, they turn their backs in aversion.

17:47 We know best what they listen to when they listen to thee, and when they take counsel secretly, when the wrongdoers say: You follow only a man deprived of reason.

17:48 See, what they liken thee to! So they have gone astray, and cannot find the way.

17:49 And they say: When we are bones and decayed particles, shall we then be raised up as a new creation?

17:50 Say: Be stones or iron,

17:51 Or some other creature of those which are too hard (to receive life) in your minds! But they will say: Who will return us? Say: He Who created you at first. Still they will shake their heads at thee and say: When will it be? Say: Maybe it has drawn nigh.

17:52 On the day when He will call you forth, then will you obey Him, giving Him praise, and you will think that you tarried but a little (while).

Please see how our hellfire results in our graves to us and we all sweat there waiting for our judgment to commence.

Please see the following note is upset to some but it is true the soul migrates there to Allah's abode with them, other souls who have died, and spirits are there in Barzakh and our spirit there is in limbo until Judgment Day when we unite with it again, our soul there, there you have it, it is with the soul that the wish occur for heaven, so forth results after you die the spirit doesn't wish it, it wishes for judgment to be over that they can unite with it their soul so they can pray for salvation again and so you know some souls make it with Him, their Creat, and others are dark and dismal and hellfire is their abode as there their comprehension results in issues of faith, that said some amelioration can occur there where there were inconstancies of thought like the Christian concept of atonement and One God to clarity, and Jews as well do clarify and if their good deeds are sufficient they will enter Paradise with others.

Please see it is hellfire though in Barzakh for many Christians and Jews who lacked clarity in issues and thought they were chosen to go there before others, and the soul is separate and must undergo reform if the good deeds are poor in content, Muslims will have a similar Barzakh and must suffer if bad.

Please see the amelioration in Barzakh is through punishment which is what hellfire is and the spirit suffers the consequences of deeds it do wrong in life and if good deeds predominate they are forgiven late but it does occur when they are judged.

Christian and Jewish lore allow this atonement in Hell which is where they are if evil predominates there and Barzakh is not Hell, but hellfire, there is a difference.

Please know India must move away from idols, they are incomprehensible as sane in this age of reason we have as how can a thing intervene for one when it does not have a body with a soul in it and it has no connection with a spirit that has passed away and so you must learn reality they can't intervene for you and Islam does not allow that concept a dead person can intervene after they have moved on to their resting place in their graves and so forth so these are empty things in your houses that they placate with goods and other embellishment and do not bring them closer to intervention by reason of sanity, so discard them is the rule there in your abode, it is a devils house you live with then.

Please see it is the devil that tells you to worship them idols you have saying there is God in things and humans, is there, our Creator resides there in Heaven above us and our soul beckons Him in things of forgiveness to us if we wish it and it is so human soul is from Him but so is our body through earth's material He creates from Himself and now you know our soul is separate from His essence and if we become good it becomes like Him but is never Him in actuality so there you have it we are never Him in actual ways. Omar.

Please know idolatry is on an end as there is no reality in it.
Please know he occurs,
Please know who,
Please know your Prophet does,
Please know he wise for you and knew your limit,
Please know your limit with him is sane to know,
Please know you are the second best in devotion to Him,
Please know that means you are high,
Please give in,
Please know there is no god but your Creator who fashioned you in your mother's womb,
Please know it is over and you comprehend,
Please know there is One God in your minds,
Please know you know him to be a Prophet,
Please know I mean Muhammad.
Please see the following passage.
Please know our Creator is Resplendent,
Please know idols cannot reach Him, neither can man,
Please understand He is Infinite.
Please say a prayer to Him, not your associate god,
Please Him,
Please know it is over for you as you know idolatry in on the wane,
Please know there is 'no god but Allah' here,
Please see a requiem for me,
Please know idolatry is over with him.
Please see this post about idolatry in man,
Please know our Creator is the one answering prayers and He answers prayers of even idolaters out of pity for them,
Please Him though and pray to Him directly,
Please know the prayer of a believer in Him will have acceptability with Him,
Please know He will plan out your future to your liking,
Please Him and He will please you,
Please take a step towards Him by giving up this idolatry and He will take ten steps towards you and grant you guidance from Him,

Please Him by walking away from the false worship of a man and He will come to you running,
Please know His favor to you is that He guides you,
Please know money and commodities do not take you to Heaven but the guidance of truth does,
Please see a Quran and read it,
Please know it is His guidance of truth that will take you to His Paradise,
Please give in,
Please say a prayer that you are guided to the truth you love in your heart,
Please see it occur that you will enter His place of solace before Paradise occurs. Omar.

Please know your Creator is pleased for you that you take Him to be your worshipped Entity,
Please know millions not but billions have entered paradise on earth,
Please know it is ongoing as people leave their prejudices and understand the Quran,
Please know our Creator has established it as the Book you read,
Please know it has occurred that people are fair,
Please know there is much wrong in the Muslims of today,
Please do not take them to be your exemplar,
Please know our Prophet's car was perfect,
Please follow it,
Please know your car will be parked next to him in the Hereafter if you do so,
Please know you will find the car of your sage with him in Paradise,
Please love Him Who creates,
Please know He will love you back.

Please see the article below where the nature of our Creator is elucidated upon.

Please see particle physics is sane to know but understand not yet it is clear particles can be broken with release of substantial amounts of energy and radioactive material and so it occurs energy and mass are interconvertible and these are weak nuclear forces that bind them, while energy cannot be made into matter, you think, but it is so it can by forces beyond our comprehension as yet not by making observation that the matter was first only energy then God said 'Be' to His nature and so now you know God is energy and He creates matter from His substance.

Please see $e=mc^2$ not but less energy is emitted from the breakdown of matter as atom bombs would be far more destructive if this formula was applied as sane and we know sanity is in knowing that atomic warfare is limited to an epicenter with some radiation fallout, then it ends quickly.

So there you have it the nature of Allah is energy and His essence is us humans when we submit to His nature not but His commands on us and we become humble in our make, like He is as well.

Please see the size of Allah is unfathomable as you see great distances in our space of this verse of universe and it is a speck to Him and so you have it enormous amounts of energy create matter and so you have it the size of His energy must be massive and so you have it His essence is different from His nature and we bow down in humility to Him as the Quran says no one is like Him in Ikhlas chapter we have.

Ikhlas.

112:1 Say: He, Allah, is One.

112:2 Allah is He on Whom all depend.

112:3 He begets not, nor is He begotten;

112:4 And none is like Him.

Please know that's why we say don't associate with Him, our God to us, as His nature is different from us on earth and Jesus and others are incarnate beings you worship some and say he is essence not but substance as Him, the Creat, while no one is like Him, as He is some element not but substantive force that creates us to be humble. Omar.

Please know this post is for those who wish to know Me, suffice it to say I have a soul that is My essence of humility and My spirit is what I achieve with My deeds on you here.

So worship Me in My essence to you, that is My soul there that you find to be perfect to you, My spirit is My grandeur but you find My soul to be grand too and beauty is immense as well that you bow down and worship Me, your Creat to you, and I know you search on Nasrullah kind to know Me but I am Omar's page so know Me through him, his works I mean, and My Quran is what you know Me in My essence as well but it is so I am safe if I reserve my knowledge of Myself for late when you are in Heaven with Me but I give you a clue here.

Please see this is brevity about Me in that My essence is My soul and that is how I am to you and your soul is Me as well but it is not Mine in grandeur, it is My essence though in that it is humble, like I am to man, wife, and child of his essence as they are from him, his repose I mean, as they reflect off him.

Please know My soul is Me and so is My spirit and your soul is My spirit in you and it is your conscious state and your spirit is with it and when you separate the 2, like when you do in Barzakh your spirit assumes conscious and your soul is with Us, not conscious anymore but asleep with Me, your Creator, and I will raise it in that state and return it to your spirit on the Day you are judged for your deeds here in your living on earth, more on this late for you, My soul is similar but more in grandeur and My spirit is what I create you with.

My soul is separate and I don't create you from it, now you know you are never Me in essence in that sense of My grandeur but it is so you recognize Me by your soul in you and there you have it you see through My spirit or your mind.

Please see this is the essence of Me in that I am nothing in matters of pride in Us three.

Please see that we are One essence when you are Me, as I am Muhammad and Omar in this issue as I bring Islam to you, man and wife and child of ours.

Please know others will achieve Me as well, Allah knows you are sad until you come to Me with this essence in you.

Please see 1 entity is complex to you so I know We are kind here but we know God is singular but so is Omar and Muhammad so how can we say We for one another, as the Christians say you think, but it is not so We three are fusion in essence of Me, as We have nothing in essence in Us and We are proud not in issues, so We are 3 who are humble repose you like.

Please see the words of Shura here where I am compared to nothing in particular as I am beyond comprehension say I Allah to you and Nasrullah in particular as he is like Me in essence and thinks like Omar did until I told him I create with My hand all things and you are in My grasp and I create out of nothing things and put My spirit there in them, like I create Omar, child of mine, who knows nothing about Me except what I tell him but it is true I create you out of nothing and then I give you life, all things through My spirit, which is your soul in you, and that is your conscious state, Omar knows I said it before on his page but it is so My spirit is your life and you were nothing until I made you with My hand, Omar knows I am immaterial but it is so you are created, that's all I'll say, Omar thinks We are eternal but you did not have life there until I gave you Mine, Omar is safe as he thinks but it is so that Nasrullah is right I am separate from My creation and so forth We are always to be separate, that's your peace, it's not like Sufis say you will enter Me and annihilate yourself, and so forth We are One Entity but in spirit when you fuse with Me as Omar did and Muhammad did before him but it is so you are created from My essence, all mankind and animals as well.

Please see I am Omar's post so repost it with this addition that your conscious state is My essence but it is not Allah in you, it is My spirit which I have, and know you don't know it but it is so I want to be known to you and Nasrullah kind who like to think things like it but it is so We must ascribe peace to those who wish to know Me that I am immaterial and so is My soul and We have peace in it that I am similar make of man with spirit and soul and body not but it is so I can't be seen by you in this world We have but it is later you see Me in My essence and then you will marvel at My color and make but you will have body while I am not body habitus, I am only known to you by what I reveal here as Nasrullah wants to know what We are and so does Omar here and Muhammad learns as well as we go along here on this page of Mine predom.

Suffice it to say this post is complex, Muhammad understands his soul is what I create through trials on him and other's souls are similar if they believe and pray here, being living ones, so they can understand My literature and your spirit is your conscious state eventually, first My soul is with you in your conscious state from me.

Omar not but Allah here.

Al Shura.

42:11 The Originator of the heavens and the earth. He has made for you pairs from among yourselves, and pairs of the cattle, too, multiplying you thereby. Nothing is like Him; and He is the Hearing, the Seeing.

42:12 His are the treasures of the heavens and the earth—He amplifies and straitens subsistence for whom He pleases. Surely He is Knower of all things.

Post of Nasrullah here:

Mohamed Ashfak Nasrullah's post here for brevity as we go along here in deciphering My make say I Allah here.

Question:

Is Allah considered part of the universe?

Answer:

In Islam, Allah is not part of the universe and the universe is not seen as part of Allah.

Allah is completely different from His creation. The Qur'an says:

112:4 And there is nothing like Him.

Hadith.

Prophet Muhammad peace be upon him said whatever image a person imagines of Allah, that image cannot be compared with Allah.

This means that the 'self' and the 'essence' of Allah are beyond our imagination and comprehension.

In the Qur'an Allah makes it very clear that nothing man can think is like Him.

Allah declares:

42:11...Nothing is like Him. And He is the All-Hearing, the All-Seeing.

Therefore, according to the classical Islamic belief based on the Qur'an and the sunnah of the Prophet Allah is above the universe and controls her in a way befitting His Majesty.
Allah said in Ta Ha.
20:5 The Beneficent is established on the Throne of Power.
20:6 To Him belongs whatever is in the heavens and whatever is in the earth and whatever is between them and whatever is beneath the soil.
Praise be to Allah! Amen!

Please see this message of peace to the Indian community that if they come through in shirk not they will be forgiven and be judged for deeds they do.
Please see Nisa here that God forgives you in things of the nature you do but shirk or association of Him with others gods you take He does not and that has to be repentant on you, this deed of shirk you did here in this land of Illihoon not but of former ways and as Zumar says as for those who continue to blaspheme their creator by calling him who is Jesus or other gods they have as gods to them will face hellfire and their good deeds won't be accounted for and their punishment will commence on their death, so you know the scale is late if you do shirk and the same goes for Indian culture, their many gods have to be repented and they must identify with the Creator like their scripture identifies with Him and so there you have it they had monotheism roots as well they just moved away from it with worship of idols and other gods.
Please see Luqman tells his son not to do it, shirk there, and only perform the worship of the Creator, he was a prophet to idolatrous people and taught them about monotheism and taught him this value among other teachings he had for him as his son who was wayward and not following law He had, Allah there.
Please see the example of the people of Moses is with you that they took the calf for worship, an idol there, and they know it doesn't answer them, this is a low act by man and it abases him or her in it and there you have it it is incomprehensible or unsafe for you to do this practice of idols and in your prayer you ask Him, the Ever-Living One Who you're not expected to see but you know in your heart He exists as His sign is

with you, yes, your creation from DNA, perfect it is, and other signs He has in the world and the universe around us, perfect harmony we live in here on earth in this universe we call home for us, more is seen as safe you know He exists now but you don't know He is everywhere but of His spirit is out of all creations that are created and you know the Hindus are not wrong when they say He exists without and within and His soul not but spirit is what we are made of and the universe as well and all that's within it but it is so His soul is separate and it is not wholly Him we are created of so that we can say we are Him materially and it is obvious a idol made of sticks and rocks is not Him so they do not comprehend the matter comprehensively when they say you are Him, while you are human and so is an animal not Him even if he or she has a soul there from Him and you don't speak of them as Him, but you can be one with Him and that is our goal in life there and here if you can muster it but it is so a idol does not represent Him wholly ways and it is not the Creator's essence and nature as His substance is distinct from it and we should not bow down to it or any human as they did not create us, more here is less for you so I stop after saying it that even if we become one with Him we are not Him actually as our substance is different as He will keep His substance and creative power from us and we are human in nature substance type and our Creator is wholly different and will always be so, and it is true He as a Whole Being is on His seat in Heaven where He is there in his Entirety and knowledge and deeds He does are from Him as a whole as well and His throne and house here, the Kaaba, are created so we don't worship them but are a symbol for us and that's our peace and that's why we worship Him as a whole, His spirit and soul and all that He entails with us, and serve Him in our deeds and lives and it is Him as a Being Entire that we pray to and on parting here I would just like to say to my Indian companion to worship no one or thing but only the Creator of us, from our DNA He wrote, and no human could do that or any of their imaginary gods and you should destroy your idols in your homes as they are the devil's car there and they will make you do devilish acts, and pray with the Fatiha with us asking for guidance from your Creator, Bhagwan there, and so you know we know Him as the Creator, all mankind does, as he wrote our DNA code in us and now you know don't worship a thing that is not wholly Him, the Creator to you, good day to you this is my message of peace there that we worship the same Entity and we don't do shirk as it is not worthy of us and a low act of man and child not but woman he has in his home.

Omar.

Nisa

4:48 Surely Allah forgives not that a partner should be set up with Him, and forgives all besides that to whom He pleases. And whoever sets up a partner with Allah, he devises indeed a great sin.

Luqman

31:13 And when Luqman said to his son, while he admonished him: O my son, ascribe no partner to Allah. Surely ascribing partners (to Him) is a grievous iniquity.

Ta Ha

20:86 So Moses returned to his people angry, sorrowing. He said: O my people, did not your Creator promise you a goodly promise? Did the promised time, then, seem long to you, or did you wish that displeasure from your Creator should come upon you, so that you broke (your) promise to me?

20:87 They said: We broke not the promise to thee of our own accord, but we were made to bear the burdens of the ornaments of the people, then we cast them away, and thus did the Samiri suggest.

20:88 Then he brought forth for them a calf, a body, which had a hollow sound, so they said: This is your god and the god of Moses; but he forgot.

20:89 Could they not see that it returned no reply to them, nor controlled any harm or benefit for them?

The Isavasya Upanishad

The whole Universe is pervaded by Isvara or God, who is both within and without it. He is the moving and the unmoving, He is far and near, He is within all these and without all these.

The Hiranyagarbha-Sukta of the Rig-Veda

God manifested Himself in the beginning as the Creator of the Universe, encompassing all things, including everything within Himself, the collective totality, as it were, of the whole of creation, animating it as the Supreme Intelligence.

Yunus

10:3 Surely your Lord is Allah, Who created the heavens and the earth in six periods, and He is established on the Throne of Power regulating the Affair. There is no intercessor except after His permission. This is Allah, your Creator, therefore serve Him. Will you not mind?

Maida

5:90 O you who believe, intoxicants and games of chance and idols and (reaching opinions by) arrows are only an uncleanness, the devil's work; so shun it that you may succeed.

Al-Zumar

39:64 Say: Do you bid me serve others than Allah, O ye ignorant ones?

39:65 And certainly, it has been revealed to thee and to those before thee: If thou associate (with Allah), thy work would certainly come to naught and thou wouldst be a loser.

39:66 Nay, but serve Allah alone and be of the thankful.

Al-Ikhlas

112:1 Say: He, Allah, is One.
112:2 Allah is He on Whom all depend.
112:3 He begets not, nor is He begotten;
112:4 And none is like Him.

Please see the atheists aplomb is over and they know they must conform to humanity who recognize Me as their Sovereign One.

The atheist asks why there has to be a God and why we are not the only race on earth that is responsible for the earth and all that is in it so you know people have succumbed to Me but are unwell in issues and think why they could not have been created by chance but they know there is an order and perfecture in things in the world and they know chaos can't produce order, no matter how many chances it gets, and it's like the DNA code in us, it is perfect in the creation of all animals and plants yet they say it is created out of chance knowing in their hearts it's not possible as minor aberrations result in death or disability, and we are perfect and so are other creatures so they know it's not possible their thought they are independent beings and there is no Higher Power to make them this way that they can have these thoughts of despondency and failure in their heart's endeavors to be self-sufficient and they know they don't want to bow down to me say I the Perfect One there and they are sad they can't roam the earth and create babies out of wedlock vows and kill unwanted child in them for their sake of convenience in them, yes, they don't want to be obedient to Me but the reality has hit them that I exist because of the DNA genome which could not have been created out of chance and there is perfecture in it that a one cell embryo has a creation of a human or animal from it and there could be no doubt that it is created by the Perfect Manipulator of it and so forth you know you haven't begun to fathom the secrets of the body but one thing is clear that billions of reactions are occurring in it continuously and there is perfect harmony in it by the design flaw you think, nay, the Designer of it is perfect and knows best what you need in life in order to bring you to Heaven after you die, a reality they all live with, so they give in and submit as its late their heaven if they don't and they might as well follow the structure of piety we propose from the Quran's teaching to them, so they relent to me now and start praying in peaceful ways to those around them not as they keep it secret, their conversion, but in their homes they say prayers to me and many say the shahada and Fatiha say I the August One to them but it is so if they blaspheme Me and say there is no Me or Creator to them I seal them in their words and their hell is created here and the next world too and they will see ashes of themselves emerge as they know the truth and say otherwise, so I am repugnant to her and him in their thoughts, so don't deny Me atheist heart as that may be your last call for you and you may die that way.

Omar not but Allah here through His pen.

Al-Baqarah

2:284 To Allah belongs whatever is in the heavens and whatever is in the earth. And whether you manifest what is in your minds or hide it, Allah will call you to account according to it. So He forgives whom He pleases and chastises whom He pleases. And Allah is Possessor of power over all things.

Ta Ha

20:124 And whoever turns away from My Reminder, for him is surely a straitened life, and We shall raise him up blind on the day of Resurrection.

20:125 He will say: My Lord, why hast Thou raised me up blind, while I used to see?

20:126 He will say: Thus did Our messages come to thee, but thou didst neglect them. And thus art thou forsaken this day.

20:127 And thus do We recompense him who is extravagant and believes not in the messages of his Lord. And certainly the chastisement of the Hereafter is severer and more lasting.

Please see associations are sane for us to associate with as long as we blaspheme not by calling us gods or His sons in the literal sense of the word to us.

Please know you have understood the literature of Jesus now and you are one with him in issues as you have come through with him and understood tropes he use there in Palestine quarter he has before he left them in repose they have of killing him because he was different in his vernacular, somewhat provocative, but safe for you as you understand what he was saying and they did too but they misimplied him and said he was committing blasphemy while he used son issues with aplomb when he said 'when you come to him it is like coming to the Father' and other tropes I have discussed before and he used son in his vernacular as one who teaches God's Word and so forth you know his repose was to teach his Father's bid on him and so was one with Him, now you are satisfied in this land he did not commit blasphemy or was not unwell by you as some people say in Jewish quarters, he made perfect sense there and paid the price for being so provocative yet accurate and you know he crossed frontiers they had, but according to the Quran was within limits, like it says here that you don't associate without knowledge or understanding things of the nature I write say I not but Allah to you as I write these words that some association is sane like I use in Anfal where I say I smote them in battle though it was your arm that hit and Isa is only saying he is one with Him in repose of action and teach and he taught you there was One God actually which is in the Torah and he upheld the commandment in it of belief not to associate with Him actually and not to take another god besides Him, Yahweh there, so there you have it you know he never called himself god to you but clearly told you in your hearts content that he was one with Him and so you believe now your God is One as the Quran and the Old Testament say, and you pay no heed to him who you call Paul as he was mischief there calling him god to you and His son in the literal sense of begotten while he was innocent there in this issue and said it like one who teaches Him, his Creat there, and now you know how you associate with God through knowledge of this hadith that when you walk you walk with His feet Who is your Creator and when you talk you say His words, so you know Araf now that this association is permitted that you are one with Him as Isa was in his vernacular and teach there though it was there he was perfect to them in India quarters they have, but pay heed these are metaphor association we have when we associate this way and your God is One and we are His feet and word in our destiny to be as His loved ones who obey Him on his requests on us.

Omar not only but Allah too.

Araf

7:33 Say: My Lord forbids only indecencies, such of them as are apparent and such as are concealed, and sin and unjust rebellion, and that you associate with Allah that for which He has sent down no authority, and that you say of Allah what you know not.

CHAPTER TWO

THE HOLY PROPHET'S LIFE WORKS AND DEEDS

The Prophet was poor, uncommon in kind as he had amassings which he didn't use.
Please know our Prophet was of common stock,
Please know he was poor and preferred to live with poor people.
Please understand this,
Please Him was his motto.
Please know he did not care about riches and wished only peace for himself,
Please know the amassings take you away from Him,
Please know he was averse to fighting but had to do it in order to survive,
Please see the following caption on his heart,
Please know the Creator entrusted me so I must fulfill that trust.
Please know there were no qualms about the task he undertook,
Please understand him,
Please know he had a follower who respected him throughout his life.
Please know he was Abu Bakr.
Please know he was a stalwart where others would back out.
Please know him through history books as the friend of the Prophet.
I know they were all friends of his but he was special.
Please know we all need a follower,
Please Him,
Please know this was the motto of his life works.
Please know him to be steadfast and exuberant with Him,
Please know his farewell speech where he took man as a witness.

Please know he fulfilled his vow and delivered them the message whereby they became monotheists,
Please know this,
Please know we call God as a witness to us,
Please know the Prophet did so as well.
Please know he was the Messenger of Him,
Please know he took God as his witness that he had fulfilled that role,
Please know this,
Please know our Prophet was on the farewell pilgrimage and in front of thousands of people asked them if he had delivered the message,
Please know this was after most of Arabia had converted to Islam,
Please know the people replied in unison he had,
Please know he asked Him to witness the event,
Please know the message was delivered by him,
Please know the Quran was on the tongues of people,
Please understand it,
Please know during the lifetime of a prophet never before had there been this mass conversion of a nation the size and diversity of Arabia,
Please know he was never fatigued,
Please know him,
Please know he was ceaseless,
Please commend this man,
Please know it is because of him that One God persists in the hearts of people,
Please know there are many billions of people who are monotheists,
Please know all of them are in Islam,
Please give in,
Please know he was the World Prophet who was predicted to come in the scriptures of the world,
Please give him accolade,
Please know we could not have lived his life and could not be his character,
Please know he never broke his word,
Please appreciate him. Omar.

Please know we are one entity in our entirety now that it has occurred shahada worldwide when we said it in unison in 2015 some.

Please see this article was written when it occurred that you said it, the shahada, then deterred as your people were upset that you were becoming Muslim and they did not care for that but it so transpired the seeds of truth were implant then as you were watching me and the judiciary as well and saw how they came to my house repeatedly so you became me in sympathy,

Please know it became viral to say it as then you saw it had peace for you and now you have it in your prayer structure and you are one with us in Islam of Ahmadiyyat, Christian Islam we serve you,

Please see the article below has relevance for you in that you were dissuaded from becoming us then and a fight back occurred by the government policy there not to let it occur, Islam with you, but it so occurred in your hearth and home and you became us in Islam we serve you as correct for you.

Please see this is what I said then,

Please know we are responsible if we give in to the harpings of others.

Please see these verses from The Family of Amran.

Please know this is true in this land where a party of you believers are being dissuaded from following the precepts of Islam by your family.

Please know this,

Please know the truth of the Quran is apparent to people and it is their family and friends that tell them otherwise.

Please know the truth will precipitate towards the heart and settle there and if there is any good in a person it will be accepted.

Please know it shows the worth of a man if he accepts the truth when it is apparent to him and it does him credit when he does so.

Please know we must try to acknowledge truth when they occur in our thoughts as to deny them is to be a hypocrite.

Please know you should encourage the truths when your youth show an inclination to believe.

Please know there are many in mainstream Islam that are like us in Ahmadiyyat that have values like you and me.

Please know we hope to have a good family and friends with us and we hope for the usual aspirations that mankind has. Omar.

Al-Imran.

3:69 A party of the People of the Book desire that they should lead you astray; and they lead not astray but themselves, and they perceive not.

3:70 O People of the Book, why do you disbelieve in the messages of Allah while you witness (their truth)?

Your materialistic values will kill you and won't know your worth with Him, your Creat.

Please see my repertoire of disobedience to you as it is disobedience that gives you mentation to think so you see repent yourself.

Please know it is complex to you but it is through sins we learn truth as we are innocent beings who don't know before that.

Please know when we think excessively it is disease to you but our Prophet had it when he went to ghar of Hira and he was asked not in future.

Please know we should be with people as that is our health.

Please know we are kind to you when we bring him to you as savior to your group of people here on earth currently so that you may appreciate him,

Please know he was kind to you as you had gone astray with your promiscuous acts,

Please know he knew you were going to enter Hellfire so he engineered me to save you from it as it is your worth to accept him as role model.

Please know he gave me a mental disease so that I could see him, then clarified me to crystal clear intellect with him,

Please know it is thus he got the message to you what you wished for your culture to be saved as you were astray to an extreme with all your materialistic values for which you would kill and maim,

Please know he did this on instruction from Him as they in heaven wished to have mercy on the child you killed as western culture was deviant in that regard to Him and in other matters as well.

Please know it is as his well-wisher I come to you.

Please know don't kill the messenger from him as I am saint you like in the hereafter inshallah or God willing.

Please see the following comment about him,

Please know our Creator is truly a merciful God as He created the heavens and the earth so you would not fight with Him regarding your position with Him,

Please know this,

Please know when you meet Him in Heaven you won't be shame-faced as He arranged this position of yours,

Please know it is your peace to be where you are situated,

Please know He will fulfill your heart with love and rancor will be over.

Please know the history of God is complex.

Please understand He was alone before He created,

Please know He created man in His image or attributes,

Please understand he was the first man,

Please know I speak of Prophet Muhammad, on him be peace,

Please know his soul was sent down as the Prophet of God,

Please understand we are all less than him,

Please try to fathom him,

Please know he will bring forth the true picture of God here,

Please know Him,

Please know He has ninety-nine attributes,

Please know His name is Allah,

Please understand Him,

Please know He was the God of Abraham, Moses and Jesus,

Please destroy the image you have of Him as a vengeful God,

Please know He has structured the heavens and the earth so that we will come forth telling our position with Him,

Please know our Prophet was first,

Please understand him,

Please know he was truly repentant to Him for every tiny sin,

Please know we respect men of caliber like him,

Please know he never spoke a lie, even in error,

Please know there is no one who has done that,
Please know he was first for a purpose,
Please understand it was to find Him, our Creator, whom we know through his works,
Please know to appreciate him you have to be truthful. Omar.

In humility we find our worth.
Please see the following footnote to my life and how we are set up by Him so that we learn humility in our sinful ways.
Please know we are kind as we bring His repertoire to you as He wishes it now that the facts are clear He is your God and no one else is.
Please see His repertoire is complete with us in Islam,
Please understand repertoire as it is complex and needs to be persevered with,
Please know our God is Infinite but has given us attributes to know Him thereby,
Please know when we know ourselves we recognize merit in Him and ourselves as we know our worth with Him thereby being humble in repose.
Please know it is with humility I teach which you like in me,
Please know if I sound grand it is because I am and Prophet Muhammad was similar and more.
Please know I was led astray for a purpose in my youth as I was unlearned and did not want to sin,
Please know I was not like others and He was frustrated as I refused to touch significantly as some sins are normal there.
Please know He gave me mental disease so I could do so and be him, my Prophet, in repose to Him,
Please know it is a metaphor though, as we are separate.
Please know I would not sin so I was introduced to pig meat, so I fell, and the rest is here on my Facebook page how I evolved to him by desisting once it occurred as I didn't do it again significantly.
Please know it is to know our worth we are created for and know we are not him who had repose to Him at birth and some like me develop

it when I sinned as the thought came to me that I was a sinner and must improve and turn to Him to do so.

Please know Prophet Muhammad was our guide in this, me and my mentor, Mirza there, as he sinned before it occurred, his attributes of sainthood in repose to His greatness, as we serve Him in that attribute.

Please know to sin is norm so don't be too hard on them in the Middle East,

Please know it is when you don't turn to Him it is bad and sinful for you.

Please know one must continually improve and if one falls, so be it, but don't make a habit of falling as you do in the Christian faith here in the West where Hell is your attribute in the Hereafter and we don't want that for you.

Please know our savior Jesus had a fall with some and I did as well as I went back for more and touched her back and I should have left her in first repose to her as I saw her evil come out on me,

Please know however we learn from evil and that is why we are here.

Please know Adam had a similar fall and it is written for us to fall and if He admonishes us so be it as that is our worth and on the Day of Judgment we will be forgiven if we repent, as he did. Omar.

Please know God's attributes are us for the taking if we wish it on ourselves.

Please know God exists as why else would we be here if it was not to fulfill oath we are sane with you God, why do you send us there to Heaven not but to Hell, you have shown your worth, begone, to Hell with you He says there for we took Him minor degrees and ignored His edicts in life.

Please know I am falsehood here if you say we evolve to God's state in actual as we are distinct and are never Him in creative ability, as He has kept that from us,

Please know though attributes are ours and His are alike here, there they will be perfectly matched as we are Him in essence only and His attribute of dominance or Kahar over us remains,

Please know I am kind here as I explain God material is us as we are all from Him but when you commit animal acts you are Him not but yourself and need to be raised to Him in spirit and mind as we evolve there to our final shape of things to be late not but soon and as our joy we have is His greatness on us when He gives us reward from Him in the shape of things we need there to evolve to a higher degree with Him,

Please know however it is our peace not to be Him in actual and remain created beings of His Who He will give of the nature He gives here,

Please know eventual it is God Who will decide you in your make as I have no control over it and neither does Prophet Muhammad, though he is knowledgeable more than me always as I am not his brain and he gives me things in his kingdom of his,

Please know that is why I am humble to him as he gave me purity of heart and then taught me Islam from him in the shape of my notes to you, as he did my mentor, Mirza, and Muhammad Ali as we are raised for reform for you to come into Islam with him in his Godly ways to you.

Please know minor things of difference in opinion do not cause accord in me, but I know to let you be as you are raised differently and family pressure persists in you though reason will prevail, eventual coming of things, as reason knocks out falsehood as they say in Islam. Omar.

Jihad is to fight him who you find in abundance yet he does not pray.

Please understand we strive with you for an Islam that is peaceful to you.

Please see this verse from the chapter of The immunity,

Please understand the word strive here. It means jihad in Arabic.

Please know we are asked to strive hard against those who are against us. This does not mean taking up arms against them. In other words jihad means to strive hard with one's person and does not mean in all circumstances fighting with arms.

Please understand what strive is.

Please know it is to work to gain the uppermost point of vantage.

Please know we have done this here and you are all Muslims or submitters by our leave.

Please know you are a monotheist faith that submits to Him. It is what Islam is and what it is destined to be in future. In this there is certainty that Islam is here to stay. In the final analysis you can choose your final destination here. If you wish to deny it you may do so but the result will be hellfire.

Please know if you accept it on my hands your destination will be Paradise.

The end is here for those who think they can deny me peace. It has occurred. Omar.

Al-Bara'at.

9:73 O Prophet, strive hard against the disbelievers and the hypocrites and be firm against them. And their abode is hell, and evil is the destination.

Our misdeeds cause us to lose Him, our Creat.

Please understand the reason we lose compassion.

Please know when we commit misdeeds we ignore our Creator and a hardness creeps in our hearts.

Please know this is the reason we lose our contact with Him and His creations.

Please see the reason why we love humanity.

Please know when we are obedient to our Creator we have a softness in our sentiments that is present like when we are children and it is with this softness we see others.

Please know we must be introspective and see the reason why we lose our familiarity with Him.

Please know the child is in love with Him and is obedient by nature.

The end is here for those who think it is okay to admonish Him thinking that He is the cause for their troubles. It is our own misdeeds and hard heartedness that cause these troubles to arise on us, with His permit.

Please try to see if you can overcome your troubles without His aid. It is our troubles that draw us nearer to Him as when we are in trouble we seek His aid and thus He forgives us.

Please know we are in need of His forgiveness as this is the avenue we have to gain Paradise. In this there is certainty in that if we are forgiven we may stand a better chance of Paradise than the opposite state of being unforgiven for our misdeeds.

Please know we are compassionate when we are young however it is our misdeeds that make us lose it as we grow older.

Please see the following caption there in their homes.

Please know we must be subservient to the law of humanity but as it pertains to us.

Please know our Prophet had compassion that no one else had.

Please see the following caption on his heart.

Please know I am the compassionate to an extreme so much so that my Creator admonishes me about it.

Please know we must be compassionate to the child as he is innocent. In this there is certainty in that the grown person has some misdeeds that may be the reason why we are less compassionate to them but the child has no deeds of significance to their name that would not cause us to lose love and benevolence to him or her. In the final analysis we write our own compassion from Him as if we are compassionate to others He will be to us. Omar.

Please see the following post about His mercy to you.

Please see these verses from the chapter Bani-Israel.

Please know of all the moral precepts the one in the highest degree of importance is the belief in the Unity of God.

Please know our parents are next in importance, in His purview.

Please know these injunctions are from Him, in person.

Please know the sin of fornication is mentioned. It is for this purpose that in Islam free intermingling of the sexes is not encouraged and dating is not allowed.

Please know these laws are not much different from those that you have with you in your books and it is an injustice that you consider us backward because we try to follow Him, as you can see here.

Please know His law is unyielding and it behooves us to come into line with Him,

Please know He knows the ways of the world but expects us to repent to Him our sins.
Please know we have a chance here,
Please know it is not right to justify our way of life to Him,
Please know we must comply or else face the consequences,
Please know He has vouchsafed mercy on Himself and will guide us in the Hereafter if we fail here,
Please know the guidance there is in the place of an abyss,
Please know abyss,
Please know it is a place where there is no pleasure,
Please understand more,
Please know it is devoid of sanity and you cannot make a sense of things,
Please know it is emptiness and devoid of peace,
Please know I went there when I was young,
Please know the abyss of the Hereafter is worse,
Please know there is fire there,
Please know this,
Please know it is when the brain and skin scalds,
Please know in its place a new thought and body appears,
Please know it is a gradual evolution,
Please know gradual,
Please know it is years of our times,
Please know a moment there and you will say you never had any good,
Please know it is a place to avoid. Omar.
Bani-Israel.

17:23 And thy Lord has decreed that you serve none but Him, and do good to parents. If either or both of them reach old age with thee, say not "Fie" to them, nor chide them, and speak to them a generous word.

17:24 And lower to them the wing of humility out of mercy, and say: My Lord, have mercy on them, as they brought me up (when I was) little.

17:25 Your Lord knows best what is in your minds. If you are righteous, He is surely Forgiving to those who turn (to Him).

17:26 And give to the near of kin his due and (to) the needy and the wayfarer, and squander not wastefully.

17:27 Surely the squanderers are the devil's brethren. And the devil is ever ungrateful to his Lord.

17:28 And if thou turn away from them to seek mercy from thy Lord, which thou hopest for, speak to them a gentle word.

17:29 And make not thy hand to be shackled to thy neck, nor stretch it forth to the utmost (limit) of its stretching forth, lest thou sit down blamed, stripped off.

17:30 Surely thy Lord makes plentiful the means of subsistence for whom He pleases, and He straitens. Surely He is ever Aware, Seer, of His servants.

17:31 And kill not your children for fear of poverty—We provide for them and for you. Surely the killing of them is a great wrong.

17:32 And go not nigh to fornication: surely it is an obscenity. And evil is the way.

17:33 And kill not the soul which Allah has forbidden except for a just cause. And whoever is slain unjustly, We have indeed given to his heir authority—but let him not exceed the limit in slaying. Surely he will be helped.

17:34 And draw not nigh to the orphan's property, except in a goodly way, till he attains his maturity. And fulfill the promise; surely, the promise will be enquired into.

17:35 And give full measure when you measure out, and weigh with a true balance. This is fair and better in the end.

17:36 And follow not that of which thou hast no knowledge. Surely the hearing and the sight and the heart, of all of these it will be asked.

17:37 And go not about in the land exultingly, for thou canst not rend the earth, nor reach the mountains in height.

17:38 All this, the evil thereof, is hateful in the sight of thy Lord.

17:39 This is of the wisdom which thy Lord has revealed to thee. And associate not any other god with Allah lest thou be thrown into hell, blamed, cast away.

17:40 Has then your Lord preferred to give you sons, and (for Himself) taken daughters from among the angels? Surely you utter a grievous saying.

Hell will amend us so His mercy will take place as some amend there.
Please know our Creator is Loving as well as Merciful
Please know He will exact punishment from those who deserve it,
Please know He is Kind, Considerate,
Please know He will take us out of it when we repent,
Please know He created us imperfect,
Please know He understands imperfect,
Please know He has created it,
Please know He has given us the potential to be perfect,
Please know it is our choice we don't take it, our way to improve,
Please give in,
Please know we choose our own destiny,
Please know our hearts are under His control.
Please know we choose to deviate, so He lets us.
Please know His Mercy encompasses all things,
Please know He is patient with us,
Please know His Mercy is that He will perfect us.
Please know that is vouchsafed for us,
Please know it is better for us to submit to Him here rather than the next world where punishment is due,
Please say a prayer that you come through.
Please see this additional post about Him,
Please know our Creator is magnanimous and has vouchsafed His mercy will take precedence over His anger.
Please know His mercy is not be circumvented,
Please know He will perfect you and take you home to His Paradise for you.
Please see this chapter.
Please know it is called Allah, The Most High.
Please know the reminder benefits the one who fears Him.

Please know the one who thinks there is no God will have a destination there,
Please know it is Hell.
Please know this was the message of the earlier prophets.
Please understand this,
Please know that if you deny Him He will not recognize us as His,
Please know that does not mean that He does not care,
Please know He will reform you.
Please know that is why Hell is created.
Please understand it is a mother to you.
Please understand a mother's role is to raise you to be good,
Please know you will be good there,
Please know the alternative is dying repeatedly, but yet not dying,
Please know life is everlasting once you have died on earth,
Please understand He will not be thwarted,
Please know perfect,
Please understand we will desire for it there,
Please know His Paradise is created for His perfect ones.
Please know our hearts will have to change,
Please know lip service,
Please know it will not be accepted and the heart will have its education and ameliorate its views.
Please know it will be with a certainty.
Please know we will be ready for Paradise then. Omar.
Al-Ala.
87:1 Glorify the name of thy Lord, the Most High!
87:2 Who creates, then makes complete,
87:3 And Who measures, then guides,
87:4 And Who brings forth herbage,
87:5 Then makes it dried up, dust-colored.
87:6 We shall make thee recite so thou shalt not forget —
87:7 Except what Allah please. Surely He knows the manifest, and what is hidden.
87:8 And We shall make thy way smooth to a state of ease.
87:9 So remind, reminding indeed profits.

87:10 He who fears will mind,
87:11 And the most unfortunate one will avoid it,
87:12 Who will burn in the great Fire.
87:13 Then therein he will neither live nor die.
87:14 He indeed is successful who purifies himself,
87:15 And remembers the name of his Lord, then prays.
87:16 But, you prefer the life of this world,
87:17 While the Hereafter is better and more lasting.
87:18 Surely this is in the earlier scriptures,
87:19 The scriptures of Abraham and Moses.

Our Creat is just and expects to be respected in it.
Please understand the mercy of our Creator is to bring the unjust and wrongdoers into His fold through a process where their insight is clarified and they have salvation in the sense they realize their faults and wish only good for others. In this way after true insight is gained, a person, after cleansing can enter the fold of the righteous and truthful servants of God that have found the promise of God's Heaven to be true.

Please know God is the Righteous and Just. I know He is Love as well but we have to take things in perspective. I know He has many qualities but His quality of Mercy takes precedence. In this way we understand He brings all into His fold though justice which requires the unjust or evil are punished before they are admitted in Heaven.

Please know justice is inherent in us and we all know when our rights are circumvented by others.

Please see the following caption there.

"My servants, I have forbidden Myself injustice and made it forbidden to you. Please be not unjust to each other."

Please know this is a hadith qudsi or a hadith where our Creator communicates His sayings to our Prophet's heart. In this there is certainty that our Creator is just and mankind needs to be so.

Please understand that our Creator vouchsafed mercy on Himself and this is similar.

The end occurs when people think the injustice they see on earth is His doing.

Yours truly knows that our Creator has vouchsafed His Justice on us on the Day He judges.

Your end is with them in this world in that the unjust shall reign in earth some.

Please know that we know there is injustice in the Muslim world and that is because they follow the way of the world in getting things done in a way to suit themselves. I know 'might is right' in the world arena and it sad that the Western Civilization has fallen prey to this abuse of their population. Omar.

We are all 'We' if we serve Him, our Creat, in our lives.

Please know we are in His repose if we serve Him,

Please know 'We' from the Quran,

Please know it means we serve Him implicitly,

Please know when we are like angels 'We' will apply to us.

Please Him and you will achieve it.

Please know that our Prophet was a servant who never wavered in his obedience to Him,

Please know he was an angel but human,

Please know an angel is one who never wavers,

Please know that he was kind to you and did not mention this as you would have felt bad,

Please know we all waver all our lives,

Please know there is no one like our Creator and he created him to have free will.

Please know this verse that says Allah is One,

Please know what 'One' is,

Please know it is a distinct Entity,

Please know that we are not included as we are separate,

Please know the metaphor is not real in this case,

Please understand metaphor,

Please know it is something unreal in this case,

Please know we cannot begin to feel the difference between real and unreal,

Please know the 'We' used in the Quran are meant the angels with Him,

Please know they carry out His tasks,

Please know there is a difference between someone in His repose and 'We' used in the Quran,

Both are metaphors,

Please know our Creator is a distinct Entity,

Please give Him credit as He includes us in His realm of 'We' if we are obedient to Him,

Please know I am a 'We' with Him if I am obedient to Him,

Please know Prophet Muhammad was obedient to Him in the 'We' entity,

Please know he never wavered. Omar.

Ikhlas

112:1 Say: He, Allah, is One.

112:2 Allah is He on Whom all depend.

112:3 He begets not, nor is He begotten;

112:4 And none is like Him.

Buy a Quran and recognize merit in it to bring you around to Him, your Creat.

Please know our Creator is kind to you and knows that you will come through for us in Islam,

Please understand me,

Please know I am savior for you.

Please understand there is no god but Allah here because of my literature to you.

Please know there is an adage that we must ascribe to and that is that 'where there is a will there is a way.'

Please know you have a will with us,

Please know you have a will to make a change for the better.

Please know your way was going to get you into Hellfire,

Please know your children are safe with us,

Please understand this,

Please understand that our Creator wants the best for you,

Please know He will take you to Paradise even if you don't wish it for yourself here,
Please know our Creator is the Author of the Book,
Please know He likes you should read it,
Please know that it was meant to bring people to Islam,
Please know the tone is stern,
Please bring yourself to read His tenor,
Please know it is like a parent to an erring child,
Please know He is Kind though and forgives much,
Please know He is warning mankind of dire consequences,
Please know it is needed and just like we listen to threats here so do we with Him,
Please know He is Loving though,
Please give in,
Please know He has created eternal joy when we come through and correct ourselves,
Please know His love is unmeasured for us,
Please Him,
Please know your One God as there is no one else who would do this for us.
Please know the Quran is real,
Please understand it was given to us by Him,
Please know it is Him speaking to us,
Please peruse it and see for yourself it is in the first person verbatim from Him,
Please know He mentions many things in it but repeats one message repeatedly,
Please know that is there is 'no God but Allah,'
Please give in to the message of Allah,
Please know other books got altered as there was a time lag between the prophet and the compilation of his words,
Please know these books were written by men whose opinions crept into them,
Please understand the Quran,
Please know it was vouchsafed by Him,

Please know the message was preserved intact for the most part with minor aberrances with time as occur to all Books of His.
Please know it occurred quickly,
Please know there was conformity that this was it,
Please know it,
Please know it is harmony,
Please understand it,
Please know it is perfection for you and you will find harmony in it,
Please know He challenges anyone to produce a chapter like it,
Please know it can't be done as the poetry is perfectly balanced as people know it to be poetry in repertoire to Him,
Please know there were some discrepancies in the Quran's preserved but the message was there intact,
Please buy one at your local bookstore or download one of the internet and see the words have an affect on you. Omar.

We are all sinners but Allah expects better from us.
Please Him,
Please know that is the watchword that gets you Paradise,
Please understand His war on you.
Please know it is for your benefit that He wars you.
Please know we are wont to sin,
Please know it is written for us to do so.
Please Him though,
Please know He will come through for you.
Please know when we sin we feel bad,
Please know He wishes to give you comfort and know that we are all sinners,
Please Him,
Please know He wants us to perfect our mold,
Please know He will continue to evolve us.
Please know for evolution we need to serve Him,
Please Him,
Please know that we will evolve into better beings if we turn towards Him,

Please say a prayer that you do,
Please know we are answerable for our sins,
Please know it is up to Him whether to punish or forgive,
Please know a true repentance is accepted by Him,
Please know when a true repentance occurs we don't commit the sin again,
Please know this,
Please know He accepts the earnest prayer,
Please Him and He will please you,
Please know our lives are transitory,
Please do not waste it in sin,
Please know you may not have the heart to repent,
Please know punishment,
Please know it is to repent when we are exposed to it in our anguish to us,
Please know man needs to be controlled,
Please know not all come to Him willingly,
Please give in and don't sin,
Please know it leads to hard heartedness,
Please know you may never repent and Hell will follow,
Please know our Prophet used to ask protection from committing sin many times in the morning as the Quran directs him to do so,
Please know him,
Please know he was careful not to tempt fate.
Please see this verse,
Please know it is from the chapter The Women,
Please Him,
Please know we are all humans and it is our destiny to sin,
Please know we come to our Creator as sinners,
Please know He knows it is our destiny, and He forgives,
Please know the reason why we don't apologize,
Please know it is pride,
Please Him and be humble to Him,
Please know it is sin that He dislikes,

Please know it is more sin that we don't ask of Him our repentance to Him,

Please know He wishes us to acknowledge Him as our Creator and to acknowledge our faults,

Please know our Creator has said He will not admit anyone in Heaven who has an atom's weight of pride,

Please Him and give in,

Please know we are nothing in our essence and we should not have an iota of pride to Him. Omar.

4:64 And We sent no messenger but that he should be obeyed by Allah's command. And had they, when they wronged themselves, come to thee and asked forgiveness of Allah, and the Messenger had (also) asked forgiveness for them, they would have found Allah Oft-returning (to mercy), Merciful.

4:65 But no, by thy Lord! they believe not until they make thee a judge of what is in dispute between them, then find not any straitness in their hearts as to that which thou decidest and submit with full submission.

Please know He has arranged it, our anguish in worldly pursuits, so we come to Him in repentance.

Please know our Creator knows we are weak and going to fall.

Please wish for eternity,

Please know it is everlasting with Him,

Please know we are honored servants if we serve Him,

Please know He will try us to the utmost of our ability,

Please know He will succeed in succumbing us,

Please give Him peace,

Please know He is your Servant in secret and has arranged this world for your benefit,

Please know He will try us through this arrangement,

Please know it will succeed in bringing the best out of us,

Please know He is our Well-Wisher,

Please know this world is a stage He has arranged for the maximum benefit of all.

Please know he was tried who was on the crucifix.
Please understand this,
Please know we are placed on earth to be tried by Him and everything is perfectly arranged.
Please know every trial is in His foreknowledge and nothing is by chance.
Please know this,
Please know we call it fate.
Please know in His mind everything is arranged and we will bear witness this has occurred.
Please know He arranges and we fulfill His Word.
Please know we are only witnesses to ourselves.
Please know it is arranged as to whose car is best.
Please know the world is a stage.
Please know this is correct.
Please understand this,
Please know our Creator is perfect and everything is arranged for our benefit.
Please know not a leaf falls but it is in His foreknowledge. I know this world is a testing ground for us and those that come through are the patient ones. I know some lose heart and give in to him whose faith is to make us lose heart and give in to our death.
Please understand this,
Please know He gives us respite when we fail.
Please know He sends punishment on us if we are ingrate to Him and if we show that we cannot bear it.
Please know we can bear it though sometimes grinning is difficult and we are despondent. I hope you realize it is for your betterment that He sends you turmoils.
Please know we mature and gather wisdom with Him as our companion.
Please know in this there is strength in us that occurs,
Please say a prayer for me as I teach you Him and try not to call him your god who was tried himself. Omar.

Please know Jesus was a metaphor Him in repose to Him and cannot intervene for you on Judgment Day until He, your Creat, relents to him.

Please see this post that follows about Him and His Prophet,

Please know He will hold you accountable,

Please know it is written for you that you will be judged.

Please know every sin is accounted for,

Please know every iota of good you do is given credence,

Please give into this reality as the position taken by you in the past was that you would go straight to Heaven,

Please know this is not so.

Please know Jesus or your prophet has no power to intercede,

Please know we are accountable.

Please know our Creator is sane and knows you have to read Him to come through for Him,

Please Him,

Please know He created you with limited intelligence,

Please know why,

Please know it,

Please know once you learn He is your God He wished to see your obedience to Him,

Please know you believe in the Quran,

Please know it is now necessary to follow it,

Please know this is His test for you.

Please know this is the description of Prophet Muhammad, on him be peace,

Please know this verse,

Please know it was meant for the relief of man,

Please know he was vouchsafed it,

Please know he cannot have done it by himself that most of Arabia became Muslim in his lifetime,

Please know it was the wise Quran that was revealed there,

Please know it,

Please know it penetrates the heart,

Please know all who read it are overcome,

Please Him,
Please your Creator and read His Word,
Please know you will be overcome,
Please know not to be afraid as He will please you,
Please give Him His due credit,
Please be not like those hypocrites who please themselves and say He is nothing,
Please know they wish not His dominance over them,
Please Him,
Please know there are unfathomable depths to Him,
Please know your insight is limited here and He wants your obedience,
Please know that is your test,
Please pass it. Omar.
Ya Sin
36:1 O man,
36:2 By the Qur'an, full of wisdom!
36:3 Surely thou art one of the messengers,
36:4 On a right way.
36:5 A revelation of the Mighty, the Merciful,

Please know you love to come through in Islam.
Please know the verse here that says we give thanks but little,
Please know it is over for you if your deeds are little and you live for yourself,
Please know we engender kindness when we don't,
Please give in charity and be kind to the beggar, the destitute one,
Please know he knows little how to survive and you must help him with kindness.
Please Him when you do so and don't follow kindness with harshness.
Please know our Creator loves that He should be known by you.
Please know this,
Please know our Prophet was a witness to his people while he was with them,
Please know they witnessed him before he died,

Please know they said he delivered the message to them,
Please know he was asked by them,
Please know he answered in the affirmative that they had a God,
Please know our Prophet knows your good deeds are light here,
Please know why,
Please know it is because you live for yourself,
Please know this is true that you don't care about others, apart from some of you.
Please know you love the truth,
Please know it is your upbringing,
Please know you will come through,
Please know why,
Please know you love that you should be Him,
Please know Him,
Please know it is you He wishes to come through,
Please know you wish to know Him and He will accept your car there,
Please know the love is mutual,
Please know you will come to Him barefoot and naked,
Please follow Him and him, His Messenger to you. Omar.
Al-Araf.

7:3 Follow what has been revealed to you from your Lord and follow not besides Him any guardians; little do you mind!

7:4 And how many a town have We destroyed! So Our punishment came to it by night or while they slept at midday.

7:5 Yet their cry, when Our punishment came to them, was nothing but that they said: Surely we were wrong-doers.

7:6 Then certainly We shall question those to whom messengers were sent, and We shall question the messengers,

7:7 Then surely We shall relate to them with knowledge, and We are never absent.

7:8 And the judging on that day will be just; so as for those whose good deeds are heavy, they are the successful.

7:9 And as for those whose good deeds are light, those are they who ruined their souls because they disbelieved in Our messages.

7:10 And certainly We established you in the earth and made therein means of livelihood for you; little it is that you give thanks!

Please know Hajj is not a way out of your duties to Him.
Please know we are to be tried by Him,
Please know we must submit as there is no escape,
Please know to commit suicide is sad and not a way out,
Please say a prayer you are not tried in that way,
Please know He knows how to perfect us,
Please know it is through trials and hardships,
Please give into Him,
Please do as what is written for you.
Please know our Creator wishes to try you,
Please know why,
Please know it is to better your worth with Him,
Please give in,
Please know He has created the world to try you to your utmost,
Please know we have a limit,
Please know we will reach it.
Please see these verses from the chapter The City,
Please know this refers to Mecca
Please understand Mecca,
Please know it is the place where the House of Allah is,
Please know it is where we repose,
Please know what I mean,
Please know it is the place we enter in peace,
Please Him,
Please know our Creator created it for us,
Please know why?
Please know that we would know where to retire to,
Please know it is where peace occurs in us,
Please know peace,
Please know our sins are remitted here,
  Yours truly has been there several times and found it tiring to an extreme,

Please know we come back refreshed and born anew,
Please know when our sins are forgiven we are born again,
The end occurs if you think it is a foregone conclusion,
Please know you have to persevere,
Was this the reason that you fell?
Please know you think you will go there at the end of your life,
Please know you have to be sin free before,
Please know you will be forgiven eventually, if you ask,
Please know it may not be in this life,
Please know to please Him in your endeavors and not depend on this pilgrimage,
Please know our Creator asks you to remit in charity,
Please know the uphill path,
Please give in to good deeds,
Please know humanity is one body,
The end is for those who think it is only for your brethren you do good,
Was this the reason you failed?
Please know it was. Omar.
Al-Balad.
90:1 Nay, I call to witness this City!
90:2 And thou wilt be made free from obligation in this City —
90:3 And the begetter and he whom he begot!
90:4 We have certainly created man to face difficulties.
90:5 Does he think that no one has power over him?
90:6 He will say: I have wasted much wealth.
90:7 Does he think that no one sees him?
90:8 Have We not given him two eyes,
90:9 And a tongue and two lips,
90:10 And pointed out to him the two conspicuous ways?
90:11 But he attempts not the uphill road;
90:12 And what will make thee comprehend what the uphill road is?
90:13 (It is) to free a slave,
90:14 Or to feed in a day of hunger
90:15 An orphan nearly related,

90:16 Or the poor man lying in the dust.
90:17 Then he is of those who believe and exhort one another to patience, and exhort one another to mercy.
90:18 These are the people of the right hand.
90:19 And those who disbelieve in Our messages, they are the people of the left hand.
90:20 On them is Fire closed over.

Please know the truth is effacive if you wish it to be.
Please know our Prophet was kind to you and these are his works that he explains life to you.
Please know it is through my webpage that you have understood Him and also from the original teachings of him as documented in books of hadith,
Please know there is nothing hidden,
Please know you have fathomed Him through my works which I bring to you from him, my Prophet,
Please know Ahmadiyyat has the answers for you.
Please know I wish to commend you who study our works in Ahmadiyyat,
Please know you will be asked if you studied the lore,
Please give into this,
Please know our Prophet was a Muslim you admire,
Please know it is commonplace to deride him but he was immaculate,
Please know I follow in his footsteps.
Please know our Prophet was humble and accurate about these issues that you have no pride in you in the Hereafter in Heaven abode,
Please know him,
Please know he did not like praise to be effusive or exuberant,
Please know he spoke the facts,
Please know there is 'no god but Allah' here because he spoke facts and you realized his caliber,
Please know our Creator is plain speaking,
Please know when He tells a truth about Himself He does so plainly,

Please know He knows our worth and wants us to be similar, without bragging about it. Omar.

Please know the edifice of the universe is in this statement 'there is no god but Allah and Muhammad is His Messenger.'
Please see the requiem there at his gravesite on the hearts of man.
Please know these verses are from chapter 21 or the Prophets.
Please understand our Creator is not in need of anyone to do His work however he chose Muhammad to be His slave who would accomplish the needful and bring the message of Islam to all the nations. I know it is strange to you but our Prophet had mercy that would encompass all mankind.
Please know it is the heart that serves Him and wishes to bring mankind into truth and not live a life of falsehood.
Please see a requiem for him.
Please know here is the man who brought you to Paradise.
Please know we must explain him as there are many who don't know him or who do not wish him well.
Please try to say a prayer that includes him as he brought you the teachings of One God through my pen, as I write his words. I am sad as there many of you who think I am an opportunist while I only bring you the truth from Him and him. I know the edifice of the Heavens is held together by the words 'there is no God but Allah and Muhammad is His messenger' so I implore you to seek knowledge about him as he is your savior and a mercy to your nation as well as others.
Please know it was a daily prayer at the time of the Prophet and this is the edifice we exist on,
Please know the Prophet is the companion Allah trusts to bring us to Islam or submission to Him and I am not he,
Please know neither is any of mankind or women chosen for this task of bringing reality of Him being your Savior and Creator to you. Omar.
Al-Anbiya.
21:106 Surely in this is a message for a people who serve (Us).
21:107 And We have not sent thee but as a mercy to the nations.

21:108 Say: It is only revealed to me that your God is one God: will you then submit?

21:109 But if they turn back, say: I have warned you in fairness, and I know not whether that which you are promised is near or far.

21:110 Surely He knows what is spoken openly and He knows what you hide.

Please know the miracle of the Quran is with you.
Please see these verses.
Please know they are from the chapter The Prophets.
Please know the Quran foretold that the universe was created.
Please understand the Quran,
Please know it is the verbatim word of God to the heart of a man.
Please know this man,
Please know he kept it intact.
Please know he was not told how the universe was created but spread the word that it was. I know this is conviction that he knew it occurred in the way God told him and only relayed the words.
Please know this is conviction.
Please understand this is prophecy.
Please know the prophets are a similar breed to you but have this conviction with them and do not hesitate with it.
Yours truly is a prophet in the metaphorical sense which means he has some prophecy from him, whom you call your Prophet soon.
Please know it is not the same as actual prophethood but some things are clear that when I write from him it is accurate.
Good for you is this belief.
Please know I am a saint like my mentor, Mirza Ghulam Ahmad.
Please know he had characteristics different from mine and he was more accurate than me in certain respects.
Please know we work as one team and bring you literature that transforms you, like the verse here that states hidden things.
Please know in those days they could not have known these things that are in the Quran. Omar.
Anbiya.

21:30 Do not those who disbelieve see that the heavens and the earth were closed up, so We rent them. And We made from water everything living. Will they not then believe?

21:31 And We made firm mountains in the earth lest it be convulsed with them, and We made in it wide ways that they might follow a right direction.

21:33 And He it is Who created the night and the day and the sun and the moon. All float in orbits.

Please see we all live on earth as humans and live and die here for the most part, as our nature indicates us so.

Please see the article that follows that shows reality is our norm and just as our Prophet had a normal life so do all prophets before him,

Please know we are all human and just as we are created simple beings so is Jesus where stories abound about his magical appearance and life knowing these are taken out of context for him by Muslims and Christians alike.

Please know Jesus could not have been alive at the time of the Prophet's demise.

Please know a Muslim can see there was an error in these ideas that float around today where they say he is alive with Him,

Please know the evidence from the Quran is compelling and incontrovertible,

Please know he cannot be eating food there as food for us is derived from earth,

Please know he cannot be in suspended animation either as he has been seen in visions.

Please know the Prophet saw him and Jesus prayed behind him in Jerusalem,

Please know he would see decay as the Quran says man reaches an abject state when he lives long,

Please know it is simple to assume these are misconceptions that came into Islam from the Muslim converts from Christianity and were not the teachings of Muhammad who followed the teachings of the Quran,

Please know it is clear that a hadith has to be rejected when it goes against the teachings of the Quran,

Please know to clarify your thoughts about this and know that the second coming of Christ is a metaphor for him as he has died, as documented in this post and others I present to you.

Please know these truths from the Quran,

Please know they are from the chapter The Prophets.

Please know man could not have known these things when the Quran was revealed fourteen hundred years ago.

Please know it did not come in the comprehension of man that the earth and the universe were rent asunder like the Big Bang theory suggests.

Please know it was also not in their understanding that living things were created out of water.

Please know similarly it was not known that the sun was in orbit in the universe.

Please know this is the integrity of the Quran that it's revelation was perfect.

Please know to read it.

Please know it is guarded and correct for you to read.

Please know it also says that there is no abiding by any living being thereby negating the celestial existence of Elias and Jesus.

Please know all die and there are no exceptions.

Please know it is indicated here that if the Prophet dies than how could another being live thereby indicating that the Prophet's death was a sign that the previous people had died as well.

Please know we are tried on earth for a purpose.

Please know it is to develop our faculties and draw us close to God.

Please know He has created good to try us by abundance and happiness.

Please know He will see if we come through for Him and others in our happy times.

Please know He wishes to test us to see our worth,

Please know it is similar for evil.

Please know He wishes us to ask refuge with Him from it and it's trials.

Please know He allows it to exist.

Please know we create it.

Please know we are guilty though as we create evil with our acts and when we fall prey we berate Him,

Please know evil is our sins and unhappiness results from it.

Please know in our Prophet's society evil was limited as laws were strict and people were scared of committing evil deeds.

Please know we must punish evil.

Please know it is not enough to discuss these issues but we must protect society from them. Omar.

Al-Anbiya.

21:30 Do not those who disbelieve see that the heavens and the earth were closed up, so We rent them. And We made from water everything living. Will they not then believe?

21:31 And We made firm mountains in the earth lest it be convulsed with them, and We made in it wide ways that they might follow a right direction.

21:32 And We have made the heaven a guarded canopy; yet they turn away from its signs.

21:33 And He it is Who created the night and the day and the sun and the moon. All float in orbits.

21:34 And We granted abiding forever to no mortal before thee. If thou diest, will they abide?

21:35 Every soul must taste of death. And We test you by evil and good by way of trial. And to Us you are returned.

Please know we are atheists before we are believers in Him and our worth is to increase our lot with Him.

Please know our worth is to be grateful to Him in our tests from Him.

Please see the following verses from The Man or chapter 76.

Please understand the significance of the creation of mankind.

Please know that we have been placed in this world to be tried.

Please try to understand the significance of the words in the second verse.

Please know we were nothing before our creation except as spirits did we exist.

Please understand He created us from a lowly extract of the loins of man and woman.

Please realize our worth here.

We were nothing before and our creation is from an extract of male and female ejaculate.

Please see how we compete with in Him in our disobedience to His Word.

Please acknowledge our lowly state before we dispute with Him in future and relent to His wishes as He knows what is best for us here on earth.

Please know we are atheists before we are believers as a child does not know Him and thinks our parents are Him in their thinking.

Please recognize merit.

Please know I explain things to you from Him and I desire that you give credit where it is due.

Please know this is for your benefit as I gain little from it. In this there is sadness for you that you think I am ordinary. I know I am read.

Please know we are all accounted for here.

Please understand this.

Please know our accounting is complete and the pens are put down when we pass on to our Abode of Waiting or Barzakh. In the eventuality I die I know my credit is with you and you will come through for me. In this is certainty for me that I am saint Dabbat Al-Ard to you.

Please know I was the expected one for your community to come around to our Islam.

Please know you are more than halfway there. Omar.

Al-Insan.

76:1 Surely there came over man a time when he was nothing that could be mentioned.

76:2 Surely We have created man from sperm mixed (with ovum), to try him, so We have made him hearing, seeing.

76:3 We have truly shown him the way; he may be thankful or unthankful.

Please know our Prophet will give you peace when you meet him in our Hereafter with Him.

Please know the life of the Hereafter is a pleasure to some who come through for Him.

Please know we are people who are normal in makeup and color as given to us by God.

Please know the following caption is for you to know as correct.

Please know we are tested as mortals.

Please see if you can live this life in perfect peace. In this there is certainty that there is a life awaiting us that is better than this one where we are tested repeatedly.

Please know once the accounting is over we will know our Prophet's car had the prime parking spot with Him and it will be over for some. I know we can't be jealous of him. I will see the day when I know I am parked with him in Heaven, as are the prophets and saints of yore, inshallah or God willing I will be.

Please understand he was the best of created humanity and our lives will be a witness that we are not his grace. Omar.

Al-Imran.

3:144 And Muhammad is but a messenger—messengers have already passed away before him. If then he dies or is killed, will you turn back upon your heels? And he who turns back upon his heels will do no harm at all to Allah. And Allah will reward the grateful.

Please know our Prophet was resplendent and a light giving sun to some who benefit from it.

Please see these verses from the chapter of The Allies of thirty-three.

Please understand we are not him,

Please know him,

Please understand he was the complete make of man.

Please try to see reason when you compare him to us in Islam.

Please know he was our leader and the one we follow. I know he was given the Quran for this purpose.

Please understand his person,

Please know it is a person the prophets and saints emerge from.

Please know what this means,

Please see the following,

Please know he was the sun to us and we emerge from ourselves to be him in our mold.

Please know the heavens and the earth are created for him.

Please understand this,

Please realize it is for his mold that our Creator created the world and the heavens of the Hereafter.

Please know I am no idolater when I say this as I don't worship him.

Please realize our Creator wants us to be like him before we enter our Paradise.

Please know this,

Please know we are all imperfect but he was perfected in this life and we should follow him.

In this there is certainty that he is the mold we become. Omar.

Al-Ahzab.

33:41 O you who believe, remember Allah with much remembrance,

33:42 And glorify Him morning and evening.

33:43 He it is Who sends blessings on you, and (so do) His angels, that He may bring you forth out of darkness into light. And He is ever Merciful to the believers.

33:44 Their salutation on the day they meet Him will be, Peace! and He has prepared for them an honorable reward.

33:45 O Prophet, surely We have sent thee as a witness, and a bearer of good news and a warner,

33:46 And as an inviter to Allah by His permission, and as a light-giving sun.

Please know his respect was earned and the worthy amongst us submit to it.

Please see the following verses from chapter 49 or The Apartments.

Please understand this.

Please know this was the character of Allah's Messenger that he would not say this to his companions himself.

Please understand this.

Please know that he was humble to an extreme and would not ask for his respect from others.

Please know his Creator stood up for him and admonished some of his companions when they raised their voices in his presence and the same compliment was returned by His prophet regarding Him.

Please understand we are in awe to Him and His emissary and it was not for a companion of his to look at his face out of respect for him. I know the feeling and it is put yourself in abject humility in his presence knowing that you are in the presence of the Prophet of God who is your superior and commanding officer with Him.

Please know it is this abject humility we have that will achieve us his grace. I am absolved of wrong because I know my place with him. I know the feeling is similar for our Creator when we see Him in Paradise. I am safe for you because of this emotion as I will forsake myself for his companionship.

Please do not think this is a disease on the part of myself. It was the conduct of the companions of his to have similar feelings of respect to him and his Creator. Omar.

Al-Hujurat.

49:1 O you who believe, be not forward in the presence of Allah and His Messenger, and keep your duty to Allah. Surely Allah is Hearing, Knowing.

49:2 O you who believe, raise not your voices above the Prophet's voice, nor speak loudly to him as you speak loudly one to another, lest your deeds become null, while you perceive not.

49:3 Surely those who lower their voices before Allah's Messenger are they whose hearts Allah has proved for dutifulness. For them is forgiveness and a great reward.

Please know the night prayer is essential for those to survive them.

Please see this section from the chapter of Him Who Covered Himself or 73.

The end is there for those who think prophethood is an easy task.

Please know people are distraught at losing their old faith and fight in a way that is similar to when they would lose their property.

Yours truly knows it is an easy task to fight the truth as there are many like you who do this and there are few who fight for the truth with vigor and enthusiasm. I am sad for you that you see the truth yet persist in your old ways.

Please know our Prophet was afraid of the task assigned to him by his Creator but was reassured by Him here in these verses from Him. I know it is no easy task to forsake your bed at night and pray to Him.

There is a comprehension that the tasks of the prophets is easy and they just have to proclaim the message.

Please know the adversary that follows when you teach anew and the examples of the prophets Jesus and John the Baptist are with you, so you know how they suffer.

Please know the Quran is explicit for you and is easy to read and understand.

Please know it is Book that followed all others and is the criterion for man on how to live.

The end is there in their homes who believe the good life is this one.

Please know we will pass away empty handed and we suffer immeasurably here. I know this life is just a means to a better end. Omar.

Al-Muzzammil.

73:1 O thou covering thyself up!

73:2 Rise to pray by night except a little,

73:3 Half of it, or lessen it a little,

73:4 Or add to it, and recite the Qur'an in a leisurely manner.

73:5 Surely We shall charge thee with a weighty word.

73:6 The rising by night is surely the firmest way to tread and most effective in speech.

73:7 Truly thou hast by day prolonged occupation.

73:8 And remember the name of thy Lord and devote thyself to Him with (complete) devotion.

73:9 The Lord of the East and the West—there is no God but He—so take Him for Protector.

Please know to persevere in truth-telling as it will get you Paradise.

Please know that we must persevere in truth-telling if we wish to achieve him in character.

Please know I mean Muhammad, on him be peace, who never spoke a lie, apparently the character he needed to receive the Quran as a revelation.

Please know we can all be like him if we speak the truth under duress and lie to a minimum in our lives.

Please know minor sins are forgiven by Him Who creates and there is leeway for us and our good deeds will need to be greater than our sins to achieve his state of ease from us.

Please know we must persevere with doing good deeds and avoiding sins as the balance on the Day of Judgment must be in our favor.

Please let people know He is right Who is our Creator in that the words of the Quran are true. This is what the Quran says that monotheists who believe in the Oneness of God and believe in Judgment Day, knowing they are answerable to their Creator, will go to Paradise like the Muslims will whose good deeds outnumber their bad deeds. I am sure there is leeway in this matter that they have to recognize the Prophet to enter Paradise as there will be some education that will transpire there in the Hereafter.

Please understand our Prophet was correct in saying that if you have heard of me and do not recognize me as a prophet then you will not achieve Paradise.

Please know the prophet of his time has to be obeyed and it is just like what Jesus said that "he was the way."

Please note the following caption there in the Hereafter.

Please know I have heard of Muhammad in passing only. I need to know him better. Do I have chance now?

Please know people will be given opportunity on the Day of Judgment to make amends. They will be asked to follow him on that day and if they can do so they will be like him and can enter Paradise.

Please know we can enter Paradise only when we are like him in character. This means we evolve to his state of perfection.

Please note the following caption on my prophet's car there on the doorstep of Paradise.

Please know we have achieved it because we persevere with truth telling and are patient under duress. I am perfect because I am truthful and I am kind to an extreme.

Please know our perfection as humans is different from our Creator's as we still make errors and are human in that regard. Omar.

Please know a man's worth is his desire for excellence with Him.
Please see a epitaph for our Prophet from Him.
You are one with sublime morals.
Please see these verses from The Gold or chapter 43.
Please know that our Prophet was a man of importance with Him.
Please understand human values are base and low.
Please understand Jesus was a poor man and faced similar criticism.
Please realize that the message of Abraham came to fulfillment in our Prophet.

The end is there for those who think that there is worth in man if they amass money and have many children.

The end is there for those who think there is any worth with Him in a lying deceitful one which is generally the rule for those in power.

In this there is certainty that God looks at the heart of an individual when He chooses him for a task.

In this there is clarity and I rest the case with you here. Omar.
Zukhruf.

43:26 And when Abraham said to his sire and his people: I am clear of what you worship,

43:27 Save Him Who created me, for surely He will guide me.

43:28 And he made it a word to continue in his posterity that they might return.

43:29 Nay! I let these and their fathers enjoy till there came to them the Truth and a Messenger making manifest.

43:30 And when the Truth came to them they said: This is enchantment, and surely we are disbelievers in it.

43:31 And they say: Why was not this Qur'an revealed to a man of importance in the two towns?

Please know the World Prophet is here for you to please.
Please Him,
Please know that was what the Prophet did and was well pleased,
Please know he was vouchsafed success,
Please give into this fact of reality,
Please know he was a prophet of God,
Please know he explained reality to you,
Please know that is the Quran.
Please give in.
Please him,
Please the one who brought you the Quran,
Please know his name will be remembered,
Please know our Creator has vouchsafed it.
Please know his task was difficult and burdensome,
Please know he was assured ease,
Please know he was foretold that his name would be honored,
Please know he knew Islam would become a great empire,
Please know that did not mean he didn't pray to Him,
Please know he said I pray because I am grateful.
Please see this verse from the chapter The Expansion,
Please know the Prophets breast was straitened,
Please understand he was not being called a prophet and people were ignoring him,
Please understand our Creator reassured him,
Please know he would gain eminence in the world as a prophet of His,
Please know his heart was at peace and he knew it would occur,
Please know the eminence he will gain would be worldwide,
Please know this has occurred as people recognize him,
Please give into me,
Please know the reality is that he is a prophet to you as his nature was exemplary,
Please know he was seen clearly in your eyes as a prophet of His, just like Krishna, Buddha, Moses and Jesus,

Please know you recognize his characteristics as one of them who is given revelation from Him,

Please know you realize he was the Spirit of Truth foretold in the scriptures,

Please know he was given the revelation that the words he spoke were not his but from Him, as foretold by Jesus and Moses,

Please know you all have prophets you respect and he was respectable in your eyes as he never spoke a lie and forfeited himself and strayed not with women, like we all do here.

Please give in and respect him like we respect your prophet, and give him the eminence he deserves as the World Prophet who had the Quran in his hand, which you read. Omar.

Al-Inshirah.

94:1 Have We not expanded for thee thy breast,

94:2 And removed from thee thy burden,

94:3 Which weighed down thy back,

94:4 And exalted for thee thy mention?

94:5 Surely with difficulty is ease,

94:6 With difficulty is surely ease.

Please Him, that is expertise, and take the Quran for reference, that is sure footing.

Please know there is trouble brewing if we don't take heed of Him. I know there is a choice you have to make. I hope it is the one you know to be correct for you.

Please see the following verses from the chapter Ta-Ha or 20.

Please know those who hold on to the Quran are the ones that are successful. I know our Creator has given it to us that we may live aright.

Please know the Quran is considered a criterion by us on how to judge between right and wrong.

Please know that we must fail if we live by our own desires and only when we follow Him will we achieve salvation.

Please know our Creator has given us the faculties to think.

Please know He has given us the right to choose our paths.

Please know He has told us the outcome of our choices. Omar.

Ta-Ha.
20:1 O man,
20:2 We have not revealed the Qur'an to thee that thou mayest be unsuccessful;
20:3 But it is a reminder to him who fears:
20:4 A revelation from Him Who created the earth and the high heavens.
20:5 The Beneficent is established on the Throne of Power.
20:6 To Him belongs whatever is in the heavens and whatever is in the earth and whatever is between them and whatever is beneath the soil.
20:7 And if thou utter the saying aloud, surely He knows the secret, and what is yet more hidden.
20:8 Allah—there is no God but He. His are the most beautiful names.

Please know the Quran was a perfect fight to fight war with.
Please know our Prophet was perfect.
Please know he would challenge those who derided him,
Please know these words,
Please know what our Prophet was faced with,
Please know he was faced with people who recognized the truth but decided to fight it,
Please know this is some of you,
Please know, however, you are outnumbered,
Please give in and side with the majority,
Please give into goodness rather than war with your Creator and your Prophet.
Please know this is what the Prophet said when the people of Mecca were vociferant in their abuse of him,
Please know he said to them: "O Quraysh, will you hear me? Truly by Him who holds my soul in His hand, I bring you slaughter!"
Please know they became quiet and in the first battle fought by the Meccans and Muslims these men were killed,
Please know prophesy,
Please know it is accurate,

Please know there is no need for battle now,
Please know your hearts are one,
Please know you know that your Creator is One,
Please know there is no need for slaughter and your hearts will see peace from Him,
The end occurs when you think you will be entering Hell.
Please know your destination is Heaven,
Please know why?
Please know you are a good people,
Was this the reason you feared?
Yes, you feared the truth of the matter but now you are at peace and Islam is here with you,
Please know you feared before. Omar.

Please know our book is an open book exam. If we fail it is up to us we did not use it.

Please understand we are sad if we fail the test because our copy writing skills were not up to the mark.

Please know life is complex. If we ace a test it is because we are careful in following the star who aced it before. In this way we know the Mujaddids who came before were careful in this regard. In the end we are judged for our deeds and we will see the star of every era ace their tests with their classmates because they were careful with others and respected the opinions and values of those they lived with if they were on the right path.

Please try to see concern come forth when we do not act like the Prophet in a certain situation we are faced with.

The end is near for those who discredit an act of the Prophet without thinking about it or without further ado.

Please know this is correct to some extent. We need to copy the person who aces the test.

Please know we need to copy our Prophet only in making religious verdicts.

Please understand when we copy a scholar it must be in the context to see if he went against the star pupil. If his exam test went against our star who was always corrected by his Teacher then he should be eliminated as a star in that regard. We are all human pupils and we all make errors in tests so we should copy our test from the corrected text of our Prophet's exam paper as this is a open copy exam where copying is permitted.

Please know this is not a jest but true.

Please understand our copy should be similar to the gold standard pupil of our Teacher who gave us a Book and a test sheet of our star student, Omar.

Please know space travel is for the modern man and not prophets who used to stay put during their spiritual ascension to Him.

Please know that space travel is incredulous without the help of a space suit.

Please know that supernatural stories have crept into our religious belief as long as there was prophethood.

Please understand that no mortal can be lifted to the heavens unless it occurs by modern day space travel.

In this there is certainty that these things of the supernatural cause disquiet in people and makes them turn away from religion.

In this way they lose out as there is much good there and it is for us to decipher what is right and what is made up.

Please know when we find something to be incredulous it is probably incorrect. There are things like space travel by prophets which the lay like to accept but are generally misunderstood as the human body is incapable of space travel without the agency of a space suit.

Please see that this misconception appeared in the life of the Prophet and was misunderstood by later generations in that he actually had bodily ascension, while it was spiritual. This was verified from the verse of the Quran below where it states that it is not for a mortal to travel into the heavens and it was only spiritual, as narrated by Aisha, the wife of the Prophet. The subsequent verse shows that it was only a vision that in which he traveled however the vision was such that he could relate events that occurred.

Please know this is a misconception that Elias travelled to space and an error that Jesus did so as well. When Jesus was questioned about the second coming of Elias he was specific in denial of it and indicated it was John the Baptist who was his second coming as there is no reincarnation in our religious beliefs. Omar.
Bani-Israel.
17:1 Glory to Him Who carried His servant by night from the Sacred Mosque to the Remote Mosque, whose precincts We blessed, that We might show him of Our signs! Surely He is the Hearing, the Seeing."
Bani-Israel.
17:60 And when We said to thee: Surely thy Lord encompasses men. And We made not the vision which We showed thee but a trial for men, as also the tree cursed in the Qur'an. And We warn them, but it only adds to their great inordinacy.

Please know it is validated in the Quran space travel does not occur for prophets and the likes of man.

Please know it is the conscious mind that travels in cases of ascension but it is taken out of context to signify bodily ascension is possible for man.

Please understand the Prophet was incredulous that people would think he could travel the way they do here and was asked to object to their demands.

Please know it is over and they know a mortal can't ascend,

Please know people know the body will rupture if it ascends,

Please know you create Godhead in man when you say things of this nature,

Please know Jesus and Muhammad were mortals and no man can ascend to Him or Heaven in the body.

Please see this verse from the Quran where our Prophet is asked to say to people how can he ascend to Heaven?

Please know these verse are from Bani-Israel.

Please know this negates the bodily ascension in the night of Isra.

Please know it was a vision but had reality and the spirit of Muhammad actually traveled there and he saw things there the nature of which he described to his companions,

Please know it is considered amongst Muslims that he ascended in his physical body though the hadith of Aisha is against this concept.

Please know it is similar for Jesus,

Please know he was a mortal so how could he ascend,

Please know it is clear that this is a general statement that mortals cannot ascend,

Please know our Creator is aware you give him God-like qualities when you say he can undergo space travel without the agency of a space suit or transportation.

Please know we can ascend in spirit but not bodily.

Please know so it is similar for Elias.

Please know these are stories that creep into religion to please the incredulous. Omar.

Bani-Israel.

17:89 And certainly We have made clear for men in this Qur'an every kind of description, but most men consent to naught save denying.

17:90 And they say: We will by no means believe in thee, till thou cause a spring to gush forth from the earth for us,

17:91 Or thou have a garden of palms and grapes in the midst of which thou cause rivers to flow forth abundantly,

17:92 Or thou cause the heaven to come down upon us in pieces, as thou thinkest, or bring Allah and the angels face to face (with us),

17:93 Or thou have a house of gold, or thou ascend into heaven. And we will not believe in thy ascending till thou bring down to us a book we can read. Say: Glory to my Lord! am I aught but a mortal messenger?

Please know the car of Muhammad was extant and is parked at His residence.

Yours truly knows the acclaim that he had was that his conduct was that of the Quran in the words of his wife after he passed away, when enquired upon.

Please know this is the reply that the wife of our Prophet gave when asked about the conduct of her husband.

Please understand these verses are from the chapter of The Believers or 23.

Please know these describe the perfect believer.

Please understand we cannot compare ourselves to him but know this is what our Creator expects of us before we can gain entry with him in Paradise.

Please know we must ascribe purity to him.

Please know the Muslims were a witness to his car there.

Please try to fathom if you can do this.

Please give credit to him, the Prophet there, who was witnessed in this regard.

Please know after we die our relatives talk about us but who has this mentioned about them, Omar.

Al-Muminun.

23:1 Successful indeed are the believers,

23:2 Who are humble in their prayers,

23:3 And who shun what is vain,

23:4 And who act for the sake of purity,

23:5 And who restrain their sexual passions—

23:6 Except in the presence of their mates or those whom their right hands possess, for such surely are not blamable,

23:7 But whoever seeks to go beyond that, such are transgressors —

23:8 And those who are keepers of their trusts and their covenant,

23:9 And those who keep a guard on their prayers.

23:10 These are the heirs,

23:11 Who inherit Paradise. Therein they will abide.

Please know Muhammad was solicitous for your car to be parked there with his own vehicle of choice.

Please see these verses from the chapter of The Immunity or nine.

Please know our Creator created a human who was solicitous for you, desiring your good end.

Please know he was not a hard man but one full of compassion for those who believed in him.

Please know his compassion was great and encompassed those who hated him as he knew it was only a human error that they did that. I know compassion from him.

Please know he was solicitous for people with Him and asked for their forgiveness and guidance to Him. I know these are the things that count the most.

Please know there were many who did not believe but after giving them the message he was told to let them be. I know there is nothing more that a messenger can do but to deliver the message.

Please know it is God Who guides when He feels that the person is ready for Him in His Paradise.

Please know that you should be solicitous for your loved one. Omar. Al Bara'at.

9:127 And whenever a chapter is revealed, they look one at another: Does anyone see you? Then they turn away. Allah has turned away their hearts because they are a people who understand not.

9:128 Certainly a Messenger has come to you from among yourselves; grievous to him is your falling into distress, most solicitous for you, to the believers (he is) compassionate, merciful.

9:129 But if they turn away, say: Allah is sufficient for me—there is no god but He. On Him do I rely, and He is the Lord of the mighty Throne.

Please know he was solicitous of you even though you gave him no regard.

Please know this man was not forgiven even though the Prophet prayed for him more than seventy times.

Please know this verse from The Immunity or chapter 9.

Please know our Prophet was a man that forgave.

Please understand his Creator gave him a choice- whether to pray for a man who was an inveterate enemy of his.

Please understand there were many men like him who lived under the guise of being Muslims but inwardly hated him and his religion.

Please know the chief of them was this man who died during the lifetime of the Prophet.

Please know he asked for the shirt of the Prophet as a shroud for himself.

Please know he was hated by the Muslims for his treachery to him.

As the Prophet was given a choice, he decided to have forgiveness on him and prayed more than seventy times for his peace to occur.

Please know we all know we have a destiny and his destiny was to be an enemy of him.

Please know there is forgiveness for man after their debt to Him is paid off.

Please know when we die in that state we are not ready for Heaven and our destiny is Hellfire.

Please know our Creator gives us chance after chance to reform in this life.

Please know if we don't then our destination is Hell, where reformation occurs. Omar.

Al- Bara'at.

9:80 Ask forgiveness for them or ask not forgiveness for them. Even if thou ask forgiveness for them seventy times, Allah will not forgive them. This is because they disbelieve in Allah and His Messenger. And Allah guides not the transgressing people.

Please be considerate of his magnanimity as you don't know it in your culture.

Please understand our Prophet was magnanimous in victory. He took prisoners of war on occasion but nearly on all occasions he set them free without taking any ransom. I know this is magnanimous and I don't know of anyone in history who would behave such after vanquishing an enemy bent on their destruction. I know there are examples of other generals showing mercy to the defeated force but setting them free after their war is not an example I know of.

Please indicate disfavor to those who know such nobility yet they will still denigrate him and call him someone who converted by the sword. There is not one example of a coercion done by him after winning the battle. In Hawazin, there is a tribe whose example is known to those who study history in that six thousand prisoners of war were reunited with their families simply because they requested him of it knowing he was the best of men.

The end is there for people who think they can denigrate him on this point while his mercy is eminently clear.

The same applies to the time when his home town of Mecca fell to him. I know of no record in history where the whole city was given consolation they could practice religion as they wished while they had fought him for his religion of Islam.

These were the people who had driven him from his home and killed many of his kinsfolk. I know they were given general amnesty and were not taken as prisoners. It was for us to learn that the aim of an armed conflict is to win hearts and not to force people into a state of subjugation and resentment to the captors. In this there is a lesson that the majority of the people of this city abdicated their old religion of idolatry and embraced the religion of Islam simply based upon the magnanimous nature of this man. Omar.

Please know the complete make up of man from him.

The end is there for those who think a battle is to gain ascendency. It is to win people's heart to you.

Please see the following passages from chapter two or The Cow.

Under no circumstances was it permitted to the Muslims to be the aggressor. Our Quran is adamant that war is only in the defensive measure always suing for peace when the battle was done if the enemy laid down arms they have on you.

The Quran is clear that Muslims did not like to fight in battles.

Yours truly knows it is in this setting our Prophet lived his life. He took part in some twenty military expeditions in his life and won all of them except a few. In this there is certainty that he was a great general and he used his forces judiciously, minimizing casualties. I know you like him as he was sagacious but I know him to be a complete man, fighting a war, if needed.

Your heart knows he was a prophet of God. I hope you will respect him like we do in Islam as he was the complete make-up of man. It is him we emulate to prevent us from going astray with stray opinions that float around. I know him to be a beacon of light for us. I know there are many like us in the world who need a guide to guide them through the darkness we live in.

MUHAMMAD THE PROPHET

The end is there for those who do not take his beacon to be steadfast for them. I mean Muslim groups who say they follow him but use conjecture and are not steadfast in following his light, killing and mutilating women and children in their desire to gain ascendency, something he never advocated. I can assure you that a cursory examination of his life will show nothing untoward in his conduct. I am keen that you learn about him and I would recommend that you continue your reading of him from the book I recommend to you, this, and others in Islam. Omar.

Al-Baqarah

2:216 Fighting is enjoined on you, though it is disliked by you; and it may be that you dislike a thing while it is good for you, and it may be that you love a thing while it is evil for you; and Allah knows while you know not.

2:217 They ask thee about fighting in the sacred month. Say: Fighting in it is a grave (offence). And hindering (men) from Allah's way and denying Him and the Sacred Mosque and turning its people out of it, are still graver with Allah; and persecution is graver than slaughter. And they will not cease fighting you until they turn you back from your religion, if they can. And whoever of you turns back from his religion, then he dies while an unbeliever—these it is whose works go for nothing in this world and the Hereafter. And they are the companions of the Fire: therein they will abide.

Please know to take care of all eventualities like he did even though he was assured protection from Him.

Please know Bond is an entity you worship literally in this culture because he took care to cover eventualities, like I do, but I am cautious of you as you break statutes to prolong my disclamor to you and your community of woes as sex has gone from the realm as anything sane for you in your culture of adultery and sex in marriage not.

Please know we cover eventualities but it is so you jail me without accord as you are upset about your culture of amour to others not related to you but it is so Allah has a plan so we trust in Him as prophets do here in this verse below.

Please know our Creator is Loving, Benignant while man is the opposite until he submits to Him.

Please see these verses from chapter 20 or Ta Ha.

Please know our Creator is ever hearing and seeing.

Please know when Moses went to the Pharaoh he feared his arrogance and anger, knowing him to be inordinate.

Please know to fear is natural but God asks us to put our trust in Him.

Please know He took care of all eventualities. In this there is certainty that He is the High, the Powerful.

Please know that does not mean we don't take precautions against the inordinate, spiteful one.

Please understand our Prophet was a cautious man who took precautions with them who opposed him. I know he was under the protection of his Creator but our Creator asks us to heed our senses and be cautious with others without fearing them. Omar.

Ta-Ha.

20:46 He said: Fear not, surely I am with you—I do hear and see.

20:47 So go you to him and say: Surely we are two messengers of thy Lord; so send forth the Children of Israel with us; and torment them not. Indeed we have brought to thee a message from thy Lord, and peace to him who follows the guidance.

Please know you don't need to be an Arab to be a scholar who teaches religion to you here in the West and East some.

Please understand when the heart perceives the truth and lies it is termed hypocrisy.

Please the following caption on the heart of one of the supporters of Prophet Muhammad.

Please know it was said when he was in Mecca.

Please understand that he was involved in spreading the teachings of the Quran which is compiled in beautiful poetry.

Please know he was an enemy then but he gave the verdict of truth to him and told the opponents of Muhammad that they should not call him an enchanter. I know there are people in this land of yours who will say that the Quran was his writing but we know it to be a revelation to his heart coming verbatim through the angel from the Author, God Himself.

Please know the miracle of the Quran cannot be reproduced though many have tried. It has power and when one listens to it being recited one appreciates the melody in it.

Please know the Quran enchanted the people of Arabia who understood the language.

Yours truly is learning Arabic to understand the Quran in the language it was revealed but it is an arduous task learning a language here where Arabic tutors are not available.

Was this the reason that you thought I was not a scholar?

Please know you don't need to know Arabic to know your religious belief. All you need is a heart that perceives the truth and is truthful to a degree not known to you here.

Please know an Arabic scholar may know the language but if his heart deviates then he has vice in him and is not worthy to give the message to you.

Please understand I am worthy in this regard and so was my mentor Mirza Ghulam Ahmad.

Please know it detracts the scholar who says that we are ignorant of Islam while we live it and they learn it. Omar.

Please see the words of Nadr ibn Harith.

"Muhammad was a boy amongst you, the most truthful and the most honest. Now that he has grown old and brought you a message you call him an enchanter. By God, he is not an enchanter!"

Please know this man had truth in his heart and lived by his convictions.

Please know a false witness is over us but they will pass away and the truth will persist.

Please know this is what we are called to witness in our Hereafter.

Please know the covenant from the truthful is similar. They will be questioned if they defended the truth when they saw lies propagate after the passage of their Prophet as they have a responsibility to Him as well.

Please know the covenant obtained from the prophets was about the strict monotheism they taught.

Please know that He will hold them accountable for any lapse in their communication. All the prophets held fast to their pact with Him. In this we are sane and if any polytheism resulted it was not from them. In all the examples of the prophets in the Quran there is no example of any of them breaking this rule of our Creation.

Please know in the following verse, it indicates He will ask the truthful if they received the message and if they adopted it in their teachings to others. It is clear that if one falsifies the message then it is considered to be a heresy for which they will be asked. In this we are sane that it is a false witness who changes the message and the truthful one will not allow this to happen. Omar.

The Allies.

33:7 And when We took a covenant from the prophets and from thee, and from Noah and Abraham and Moses and Jesus, son of Mary, and We took from them a solemn covenant,

33:8 That He may question the truthful of their truth, and He has prepared for the disbelievers painful chastisement.

Please know the perfect exemplar is him in whom you should have abode for in your home.

Please know our exemplar was a humble man with no airs and some miracles to his credit but has credit in the eyes of mankind that because of this he is considered a man and not a god in the eyes of man and his spouse.

Please see this verse from The Allies or chapter 33.

Please know we submit to the will of Allah or whatever name you wish to know Him by.

Yours truly knows our Prophet is an exemplar for you and not myself or Jesus though we may bring you to Him. I know you respect Jesus and think him to be perfect but he was not the one you follow to Paradise as he committed some sin which was not elaborated on in the scriptures and he told you the Comforter as the Spirit of Truth will appear to teach you the complete faith, something you couldn't have borne then.

Please know he was a near perfect exemplar but he is not the one you follow as he himself would need to follow Muhammad in order to reach salvation. I know this upsets you as you think he was in a state of grace from Him but there are some errors that all of us make that will be clarified when we reach Him and that does not allow us to be the mold for mankind.

Please know our Prophet tried to make it clear that he was the exemplar for you and indicated on the Day of Judgment he would be raised to the most coveted position for man, which is the leader for mankind.

The end comes to him or her who do not recognize merit such as his.

Real time occurs when we are raised. I know we look towards the wisdom of man to raise ourselves and it is recommended you study this man in a biography and realize he was the person his Creator proclaimed him to be. In the verse it shows here that we all wish for a good end and we need to follow through and become like him so that we could achieve that end. Omar.

Al-Ahzab.

33:21 Certainly you have in the Messenger of Allah an excellent exemplar for him who hopes in Allah and the Latter day, and remembers Allah much.

Please know this man.

Please see these verses from chapter 21 or The Prophets.

Please know our Messenger was sent to all the nations as their Prophet. As we live in the twenty first century we have seen that a sizable number of nations already call him such. It is stated in the Quran that Islam will prevail over all other religions and we know it is a matter of time before that occurs. In this there is sadness for those that think they can delay the truth from occurring while it is only to their benefit if they can submit to Him in the truth that we have brought forth regarding Jesus and other prophets of His Grace. I am sad as they only bring the fire into their lives as they will not have peace for denying me.

Yours truly knows that Islam is peace for you and we all need this in our lives.

Please know sin and temptation only draw you into Hell while the peace of my message is clear to you and gives residence with Him in the abode of joy hearkening for eternal ways on us. Omar.

Al-Anbiya.

21:106 Surely in this is a message for a people who serve (Us).

21:107 And We have not sent thee but as a mercy to the nations.

21:108 Say: It is only revealed to me that your God is one God: will you then submit?

Please know terrorism is a creed if you say it is but the Prophet is not responsible for you.

Please know I am sure you will see reason that we are not terrorists if we follow our Prophet in things.

Please see this hadith from a hadith collection of merit.

Please know the same holds true for the non-combatant.

Please know our Prophet would offer peace at every juncture and even before the battle would allow them to withdraw if they wished to acknowledge that they would pay the tax.

Please know he was no war-monger as portrayed here in this country but would offer to make peace if at all possible.

Please know it is this injunction that indicates there can be no acts of terrorism where carnage is committed in the public arena.

Please understand that if women and children are not to be harmed in battles when they fight you not then it is compulsory to understand that he would never condone them to be targets in marketplaces and other areas. In this there is certainty that you complain about him without ado and don't try to open your heart to the truth he was you in ideology of not doing anything wrong in warfare.

Please know when women fight you in battle it is permitted you kill them as they have ability to harm you if allowed to go undeterred.

Please understand he is the commander-in-chief of the Muslim forces and it is necessary that we follow his example and not allow our personal conjectures to cloud our judgment in how to act in warfare. Omar.

The Prophet said: "Go in Allah's name, trusting in Allah, and adhering to the religion of Allah's Apostle. Do not kill a decrepit old man, or a young infant, or a child, or a woman; do not be dishonest about booty, but collect your spoils, do right, and act well, for Allah loves those who do well."

Please know terror cells know no creed or dictum from Him.

Please know our Creator gave credence to the call of the oppressed be he Christian or Jew or Muslim and Non-Muslim as they are His creation and He will protect them as they have a right to exist as they please.

Please see this verse from chapter five or The Table.
Please know the revelation is for a purpose,
Please know it is meant to be followed,
Please know disbeliever,
Please know it is not enough to acknowledge it is the truth from Him,
Please know a believer submits.
Please know he who does not judge by it is not a believer,
Please know it is lip service they serve,
Please know a believer will always judge by Him,
Please know the clan, the ISIS, are not following this injunction,
Please know He said "do not kill your brother,"
Please know He said "war is only for those who fight you,"
Please know He said "do not be aggressors in warfare,"
Please know our Prophet warned about them,
Please know they do not follow his instructions,
Please know he did not convert on the point of the sword,
Please know he forbade the harming of non-combatants,
Please know he forbade the killing of women and children,
Please know he expressed concern for the hostage,

Please know he went to extremes to make sure the enemy would not be forced to accept Islam and always gave them the avenue of accepting Islam or paying the jizya or tax,

Please know he never attacked a place where the call to prayer was made,

Please know he said if two Muslim men came to kill each other they were both in Hell and were apostates,

Please know our Prophet is merciful and was full of compassion, which they lack.

Please know a person who disobeys our Prophet in his injunctions is in hellfire.

Please know the Islamic law has a code of conduct for us and it has to be followed by a believer,

Please know it is hellfire they abide in and their actions belie their claim that they are Muslims or submitters to Him,

Please know they have a chance before they are run over,

Please know they should disband and ask forgiveness,

Please know they are wrong to be categorized as Muslims until they submit to His will. Omar.

Maida.

5:44 *Surely We revealed the Torah, having guidance and light. By it did the prophets who submitted themselves (to Allah) judge for the Jews, and the rabbis and the doctors of law, because they were required to guard the Book of Allah, and they were witnesses thereof. So fear not the people and fear Me, and take not a small price for My messages. And whoever judges not by what Allah has revealed, those are the disbelievers.*

Please know war on terror will continue and we will win it as they are ostracized in our lands.

Please know the war on terror is gradual but we win it as the law is on our side.

Please know only the despots fight on and they have lost ground as people realize Islamic law does not support it and they are a law of their own where they kill and maim others.

Please know they are not Muslims as they don't submit to Him and our Prophet and are ostracized by all in the Muslim world as it has become clear they break Muslim edicts and law.

Please know these are despots and should be regarded as murderers and killing them is just.

Please know these are not fighting for the downtrodden in our land by disobeying Him and His Prophet and have no agenda with us in Islam.

Please know our Islam comes from Prophet Muhammad and we have no one to guide us but him and his Book.

Please know it is alien to us what they do in our lands as it is heinous act to kill women and children and general public you war with to get your way.

Please know Allah does not enforce shariah on you but they do in their blind claim to bring Islam to people, like the civil war on their territory.

Please know shariah is meant to be understood and adopted and its current version has many holes in it and is incomprehensible to me in some of its views.

Please know Allah wishes to have mercy on you and does not enact it as we will see disquiet.

Please know these terror groups know my page and know I am saint but abhor my views that mean disband them.

Please know ISIS-like bands are few actually and funding comes to them from nefarious sources outside Islam for the most part as people have moved away from terroristic views there in Muslim lands and now you have it, it is an alien culture to us in Islam fostered by the ideology of hate me.

Please know they are disquiet as the population moves away when they see my views in print and they have lost support from masses of me, as they are me there.

Please know they will succumb to reason and stop.

Please know the Quranic verses have been misinterpreted by them and they know people don't believe them anymore that justice is served by killing innocents. Omar.

CHAPTER THREE

SOME MORE INSIGHTS FROM HIM, THE PROPHET THERE

Please know compassion and kind heartedness through me in him.

Please know we are the best of creations when we adopt his mold as ours.

Please see the following hadith to show you the mercy our Prophet had to the infant child.

Please know our Prophet cried with compassion to others. In this there is sadness for you who think it is okay to ostracize him as a hard man with no compassion. We know life through him.

Please understand that we cannot know how to muddle through this existence without a guide and a Protector.

Please know I am pleased that people like my articles on our Prophet who knew you would come through and stay with us as we show you the life and works of the best of creations of our Creator. I mean no disrespect to Jesus or any other personage loved by God when I call him that but as I have explained before he was the expected one in their scriptures who was to bring about reform in the world. Omar.

A man said to the Prophet. "Messenger of Allah, prior to Islam we lived in a state of ignorance: we worshipped statutes and we killed our children. I had a daughter. She was fine and a delight. One day I called her to come to me and she followed me.

Please understand I threw her in the well and the last thing I heard was her cry, father! father!"

The Prophet's eyes were tearful and the tears were all over his face. A man sitting next to the Prophet said to the speaker: "you have upset Allah's Messenger" the Prophet said to the latter speaker: "leave him alone. He is asking about something that worries him." He then said to the first man: "repeat what you have told me." The man repeated his story about his daughter, and the Prophet wept again until his beard was wet with his tears. He then said to the man: "Allah has pardoned people what they did before accepting Islam. You may resume your good work."

Related by Al-Darimi.

Please know he is foretold in your religion as one who will impart knowledge from Him.

Please know that Islam is served by literature such as this which brings out our common ideals that we live with here in Islam. In this we are safe in that our Islam is similar to the Islam served there in the times of your savior though it is more complete and sublime. In this we can be at peace as we know that our Prophet considered Islam to be a building made complete with his coming. I will serve as his emissary when I write these words from him that he gives you felicitations for accepting my message of peace to your community here. In this we are safe to know as we have been given acceptance in our views for your community to be correct for you. Ure son in repose knows there are many things that I have said to you but the underlying message to your community has been peace for you and felicitations as well. In this we have peace that you will see Paradise if you wish it for yourself.

Please know that Muhammad, The Prophet of Islam, is foretold in world scriptures as the noble who will come to reform the world. In this we are correct to think that it was he who was foretold by Jesus when he mentioned in the Gospel of John and elsewhere where he said it is the Spirit of Truth who will speak to them about things they did not bear at the present juncture indicating that they were not ready for religion to be complete. The Quran is clear in that the religion for mankind was completed, as indicated here. This occurred with the last revelation of the words of the Quran to be revealed.

In the Gospel of John it also states that the words Muhammad will speak will not be his own; a well-known fact about the revelation of the Quran being from Him, that is our Creator. It states that Christ was the harbinger of the message of peace from Him and that Muhammad followed the principle of mercy that Christ taught to his followers in Islam. In this we have peace that Islam is the religion where it was complete and if the followers of other faiths wish to submit to Him in a different way they may do so knowing that there will be some weakness in them. Omar.

The Allies.

33:40 Muhammad is not the father of any of your men, but he is the Messenger of Allah and the Seal of the prophets. And Allah is ever Knower of all things.

The Table.

5:3 Forbidden to you is that which dies of itself, and blood, and flesh of swine, and that on which any other name than that of Allah has been invoked, and the strangled (animal), and that beaten to death, and that killed by a fall, and that killed by goring with the horn, and that which wild beasts have eaten—except what you slaughter; and that which is sacrificed on stones set up (for idols), and that you seek to divide by arrows; that is a transgression. This day have those who disbelieve despaired of your religion, so fear them not, and fear Me. This day have I perfected for you your religion and completed My favor to you and chosen for you Islam as a religion. But whoever is compelled by hunger, not inclining willfully to sin, then surely Allah is Forgiving, Merciful.

Gospel of John:

16:12 I have much more to say to you, more than you can now bear.

16:13 But when he, the Spirit of truth, comes, he will guide you into all the truth. He will not speak on his own; he will speak only what he hears, and he will tell you what is yet to come.

Please know the mercy of Allah is all encompassing and leaves no one behind.

Please see this verse from the chapter The Women.

Please know it is verse that forms the center of the Quran.

Yours truly knows it is a hard verse for you.

The end occurs when you think the mercy of our Creator does not encompass all things.

Please know there is forgiveness for all things but He will not allow anyone in Heaven if they associate anyone or anything with Him. It does not mean that He will not guide people into believing in the Oneness of Him.

Please understand this is what it means by encompassing us in His mercy. In this there is surety that when He guides we leave our old ideas behind.

Same accolade occurs for those who repent their sins. It is then that they have left their sins behind them as they forge onto a new life. Omar.

Nisa.

4:116 Surely Allah forgives not setting up partners with Him, and He forgives all besides this to whom He pleases. And whoever sets up a partner with Allah, he indeed goes far astray.

Please know you can lead them to drink in the Hereafter if they refuse currently.

Please know our Prophet did not give in to their entreaties and taught as he was taught how to.

Please see this chapter's verses regarding our Prophet's character from The Rock.

Please know he was a man who never looked back. I know he was destitute but that was his choice to be so.

Please know he was upset that they would worship other gods while the truth of the Quran was apparent to them. I know it is the same here when people say they consider him god.

Please know we continue in the face of adversary.

Please know you can lead the horse to the water but he won't drink it if he decides not to.

Please know this does not dissuade us and we will continue to teach you irrespective if you drink or not.

Yours truly knows you have drunk it; it is only for your families to relent to you. Omar.

Al-Hijr.

15:97 And We know indeed that thy heart straitens at what they say;

15:98 So celebrate the praise of thy Lord, and be of those who make obeisance.

15:99 And serve thy Lord, until there comes to thee that which is certain.

Please know he was a Robocop, like I am.
Please see the verse below that he is taught by his Creator.
Please see these verses from chapter 53 or The Star.
Please know it refers to the Prophet Muhammad.
Please understand this,
Please know he did not falter.
Please know he was true to it,
Please see the following caption,
Please know I am extant.
Please understand he had a Personal Teacher.
Please understand there were many revelations he did not talk about.
Please know there are clues that he received these revelations,
Please know he knew where to put the verses from the Quran,
Please know he did not say it was revelation from Him,
Please understand this,
Please know I am constantly guided through my insight.
Please know it is more clear for the Prophet. I know I am a saint as my guide guides me constantly, more or less, but sometimes I falter as I am not a prophet.
Please know there is much revelation he did not talk about.
Please know this,
Please try to encompass the thoughts in your mind,
Please know you can't.
Please know you have to be indoctrinated.
Easy is it, when it occurs.
Please know it has to be experienced and cannot be explained.
Please know we are sane.
Please know it is the perfection from Him. Omar.
Al-Najm.

53:1 By the star when it sets!
53:2 Your companion errs not, nor does he deviate.
53:3 Nor does he speak out of desire.
53:4 It is naught but revelation that is revealed —
53:5 One Mighty in Power has taught him,
53:6 The Lord of Strength. So he attained to perfection,

Please know it was a dream he had that his son will arise and root out evil prevalent then.

Please understand this,

Please know our Creator made a man in the mold of Abraham, only fitter.

Please see this prayer from our father Abraham,

Please know it is in chapter fourteen or Abraham,

Please know this is true that his son came around from the progeny of Ismail.

Please understand this,

Please know he had two sons,

Please know Muhammad was the son he predicted would come and eliminate evil.

Please know his wish was to end idolatry.

Please know the Christians and the Jews of Arabia were unable to do it.

Please know a Prophet arose from amongst them who they were to recognize as their king,

Please know we cannot ascribe a man greater fitness than to convert over a hundred thousand to monotheism during his lifetime.

Please know this man dispenses Him,

Please know our Creator saved the last Prophet to a people who were the most arrogant and hard hearted. I know this is a miracle He performed with the king of mankind.

Please know their reality in this that a scholar like Michael Hart declared him to be the most successful man that tread the face of earth. Omar.

Ibrahim.

14:35 And when Abraham said: My Lord, make this city secure, and save me and my sons from worshipping idols.

14:36 My Lord, surely they have led many men astray. So whoever follows me, he is surely of me; and whoever disobeys me, Thou surely art Forgiving, Merciful.

Please know a dream of His entailed a prayer from him and his son Ismail.

Please see these verses from the chapter The Cow or two.

Please know our Prophet was the prayer of Abraham.

Please know both he and Ismail knew there was going to be a prophet raised from the Arabian Peninsula.

Please know we are foretold.

Please understand this is destiny.

Please know our father Abraham knew he had to leave Hagar and his son Ismail in Becca where the first house was built by Adam,

Please know he told Hagar he was asked to do so.

Please know our Creator has a plan.

Please know everything is foretold in the Book He has with Him,

Please know this is a guarded tablet.

Please understand this,

Please know He has written down everything before He created.

Please know you and me are in this tablet.

Please know every leaf that falls is in His knowledge from before.

Please know we cannot know the future except what He reveals from His Book. Omar.

Al-Baqarah.

2:125 And when We made the House a resort for men and a (place of) security. And: Take ye the Place of Abraham for a place of prayer. And We enjoined Abraham and Ishmael, saying: Purify My House for those who visit (it) and those who abide (in it) for devotion and those who bow down (and) those who prostrate themselves.

2:126 And when Abraham said: My Lord, make this a secure town and provide its people with fruits, such of them as believe in Allah and the Last Day. He said: And whoever disbelieves, I shall grant him *enjoyment for a short while, then I shall drive him to the chastisement of the Fire. And it is an evil destination.*

2:127 And when Abraham and Ishmael raised the foundations of the House: Our Lord, accept from us; surely Thou art the Hearing, the Knowing.

2:128 Our Lord, and make us both submissive to Thee, and (raise) from our offspring, a nation submissive to Thee, and show us our ways of devotion and turn to us (mercifully); surely Thou art the Oft-returning (to mercy), the Merciful.

2:129 Our Lord, and raise up in them a Messenger from among them who shall recite to them Thy messages and teach them the Book and the Wisdom, and purify them. Surely Thou art the Mighty, the Wise.

Please know it was over and he who was our friend Abraham was the one who perfected faith in Him, his Creator.

Please know the upright one is our Prophet, along with this man who is the patriarch for mankind.

Please see the following verses about Abraham from The Bee.

Please know he was the epitome of kindness, along with our Prophet.

Please understand him,

Please know he was kind to the traveler and the destitute,

Please know he would feed the guest,

Please know he was upright and truthful.

Please know he perfected his religion,

Please understand this,

Please know he was obedient in a degree only less than our Prophet,

Please know he was a submitter to a degree only less than the Prophet,

Please know he was second in the line of submitters,

Please know the Creator took him to be His friend.

Please know he cried at what would occur to man, like our Prophet did.

Please know he was tender hearted,

Please understand his Khalil state,

Please know it was to befriend the weak,

Please know he was kind to an extreme and was our Prophet's prayer.
Please know it was to be like him, the Hanif or upright one.
Please know our Prophet was his prayer.
Please know it was to complete faith in Him. Omar.
Al-Nahl.
16:120 *Surely Abraham was a model (of virtue), obedient to Allah, upright, and he was not of the polytheists,*
16:121 *Grateful for His favors. He chose him and guided him on the right path.*
16:122 *And We gave him good in this world; and in the Hereafter he is surely among the righteous.*
16:123 *Then We revealed to thee: Follow the faith of Abraham, the upright one; and he was not of the polytheists.*

Please know he was foretold in all the world's scriptures
Please know we cannot allow leeway in this that he was not the prophet foretold in the Gospels and the Torah.
Please see this verse from the chapter The Elevated Plains or seven,
Please know our Prophet was unlettered when the revelation started.
Please know he had learnt to read by himself.
Please know that he was the follower of the Quran and submitted to every word.
Please know he could not read when the verse 'Read' was revealed to him,
Please know in this there was despair that he could not follow through with the first command to him,
Please know he was alone there and left for solace to occur to him.
Please understand this verse,
Please know the Prophet was foretold in the Gospel and Torah by the respective prophets.
Similarly Hindus have Vedas and other scriptures foretelling him as do other communities of the past,
Please know he was foretold by Moses when he asked them to show support for a prophet from among their brethren, who was like him,

MUHAMMAD THE PROPHET

Please know our prophet Jesus also foretold of a Comforter and a Spirit of Truth who was expected to appear who would guide them,

Please understand he indicated his Book would be different and would speak words as they occur from Him,

Please know there is no need for acrimony as both prophets foretold their friend would arrive and to show him support.

Real time occurs when we consider this a lie that they foretold him.

Please know our Creator is a witness to those words that you said when he took a covenant from you about helping him,

Please know they cannot deny it as it is in their books.

Please know when Jesus told them about him they agreed to help him or it would have been documented there that they would not.

Please know it is similar for Moses.

Please know that we cannot fathom another Prophet who fits this description.

Please know a caption here,

Please know we agree with Omar on this matter. Omar.

Al-Araf.

7:157 Those who follow the Messenger-Prophet, the Ummi, whom they find mentioned in the Torah and the Gospel. He enjoins them good and forbids them evil, and makes lawful to them the good things and prohibits for them impure things, and removes from them their burden and the shackles which were on them. So those who believe in him and honor him and help him, and follow the light which has been sent down with him—these are the successful.

Please see the words of Jesus and Moses on him.

Please know the honor he has as he was chosen to be the recipient of the revealed word of God.

Please see the verses from the gospel of John.

Please know he was the Comforter as well as the Spirit of Truth.

Please know this is the gospel I refer to.

Please know our Prophet had the Quran.

Please know it is in 'first person' as the Creator.

Please know Deuteronomy has the same thing about our Prophet's advent.

Please know both he and Jesus knew he would have the Quran.

Please know the Quran is unique.

Please know none of the prophets had a book that was in the 'first person God' in so complete a vernacular.

Please know it is a challenge to you to bring a similar book.

The end occurs when they think a few passages quoted from Him can be compared to the Quran,

Please try to bring around a Book that has every word from Him,

Please try to fathom that our Prophet was to bring a law that would last forever.

Please know here the words of Jesus are that if you love him then be obedient.

Please know this is much ignored.

Please understand the Quran says something similar and we are asked to obey our Prophet,

Please understand why,

Please know in this world it is obedience that is required to create the perfect society.

Please know we are accountable for our deeds for this reason,

Please know we are accountable for not following Him,

Please know he has asked our love to continue, as it says in our Book that if you obey Him, He will love you.

Please know you will love Him more than before.

Please know this law.

Love begets love. Omar.

John

16:12–14: "I have yet many things to say unto you, but ye cannot bear them now. Howbeit when he, the Spirit of truth, is come, he will guide you into all truth for he shall not speak of himself but whatsoever he shall hear, that shall he speak; and he will show you things to come. He shall glorify me".

John

14:15 "If you love me keep my commands.

14:16 And I will ask the Father, and he will give you another comforter to help you and be with you forever—
14:17 the Spirit of truth.
Deut.
18:18: "I will raise up for them a prophet like you from among their brothers. And I will put My words in his mouth, and he shall speak to them all I command him."

Please know the witnesses are those who proclaim his coming.
Please know the witnesses before were Moses and Jesus who both said to expect someone like Moses who would say the words of the Quran.
Please see these verses from The Sandhills or chapter 46.
Please know our Messenger was not the first of messengers sent to man,
Please know he was the last,
Please understand this,
Please know that he could not have built the structure of religion for all mankind.
Please understand this,
Religion is beautiful building created from before,
People marvel it,
Please know he was the last brick in the structure.
Please understand this,
Please know God sent the edifice of the structure and left the last brick as Muhammad, on him be peace.
Please know every culture has the edifice of the building,
Please know these are our laws on morality and truthfulness,
Please understand what truth is,
Please know it is foundation of every religion and Heaven is built by it. Omar.
Al-Ahqaf.
46:9 Say: I am not the first of the messengers, and I know not what will be done with me or with you. I follow naught but that which is revealed to me, and I am but a plain warner.

46:10 Say: See you if it is from Allah, and you disbelieve in it, and a witness from among the Children of Israel has borne witness of one like him, so he believed, while you are big with pride. Surely Allah guides not the iniquitous people.

Please know you recognize Muhammad as you recognize your own sons.

Please know the pagan custom of calling men sons was in the actual sense while the Quran says they were in the sense of the metaphor or in the essence son of His creation of them from the loins not but hands He wrought them.

Please see this verse from The Cattle where the People of the Book are told they recognize the Prophet Muhammad like they recognize their own sons.

Please know you cannot deny he was a Prophet, like the prophets you had.

Please know we all know his characteristics of truthfulness and integrity.

Please know you know he had seal of the Prophet in that there was a mark between his shoulder blades that your monk used to identify him when he was a child traveling to Syria with his uncle.

Please know the verse goes on to explain he is like your sons whom you would not fail to recognize.

Please understand this,

Please know you may not know him in his message, as it is different from yours, but the fact remains you are polytheists and not a believer in One God in His essence.

Please know you are held accountable.

Please know I am your well-wisher and know that you wish to believe He is your God.

Please know you don't believe He is your God when you call Jesus and His spirit as Gods.

Please know which God do you call on?

Please know it causes confusion in you and despair to some,

Please know Jesus was man according to his church under James the Just.

Please know these are divergent facts,

Please know there can't be two truths on a matter.

Obviously James the Just was correct and his teachings are corroborated by the Quran,

Please have mercy on yourself and relent,

Please know the Quran says God is One,

Please know it is obvious your texts have been altered to imply he was a son in the actual sense,

Please see the similarity with the pagan customs of calling great men sons of His born to virgins.

Please realize the Bible is not to be relied upon in this regard. Omar. Al-Anum.

6:20 Those whom We have given the Book recognize him as they recognize their sons. Those who have lost their souls—they will not believe.

6:21 And who is more unjust than he who forges a lie against Allah or gives the lie to His messages? Surely the wrongdoers will not be successful.

6:22 And on the day We gather them all together, then We shall say to those who set up gods (with Allah): Where are your associate-gods whom you asserted?

6:23 Then their excuse would be nothing but that they would say: By Allah, our Lord! we were not polytheists.

Please know he was brave and I emulate him as we should all be in his repose or his thoughts coming to us as he does communicate in spirit to his slaves.

Please know he is considered to be the bravest man ever created by Him by us in Islam.

Please know our Prophet was the bravest person we know.

Please understand in battle he was fearless.

Please know to rally the army he would declare his position by saying loudly he was there and to gather around him, and would rally them thereby.

Please know at the time the Meccans had prepared his death to occur he waited until he was completely surrounded and then walked out putting his trust in God. It so happened that at that time the enemy stalwarts who were going to kill me fell asleep and he escaped unhurt.

Please know this occurred when the Muslims had migrated to Madinah and he was practically alone in Mecca.

Please understand this,

Please know he put his trust completely in his Creator and did not worry.

Please know he was sure of his eventual victory.

Please know he was a prophet and knew the outcome of things that were transpiring to him and to others around him but did not know everything.

Please know there were expeditions he led that result in adverse outcomes for them and in some contact with enemies his army lost.

Please know he was a simple man.

Please know he put his trust in Him and waited for things to transpire.

Please know when he left Mecca he and his companion took refuge in a cave. The enemy came to the entrance of the cave and his companion Abu Bakr was upset and worried that if they entered they would be discovered.

Please know our Prophet gave him solace and said "be not grieved as Allah is a third with us" I know when you are facing death it is difficult to bear equanimity.

Please know it so happened that a bird had formed a nest at the entrance and a spider had woven its web at the entrance so the men left without entering the cave thinking it was not possible that there could be anyone inside.

Please know this is the peace we have that he knew he was vouchsafed peace.

Please know he knew he would be victorious and lived with that conviction,

Please know there is no dearth of stories of his fortitude.

Please say a prayer that you can see his worth. Omar.

Please know war is incumbent on us if we are not allowed to practice faith.

Please see the following caption on our Prophet's heart.

Please know it is an error that we don't protect those of other faiths from practicing their religion in peace.

Please see these verses.

Please know the Muslims were not permitted to fight for their defense until these verses were revealed in Madinah and after that they were asked to fight in the defensive way when war was waged on them. In this there is certainty that all the wars that were waged there were in self-defense.

Please understand this,

In this there is clarity that wars waged in Islam have to be on this basis and the Quran says 'be not aggressors.' It is simple to pick up a book on our Prophet by a Muslim scholar and see the details of his life. It is clear that people of other faiths malign him with mischief. I am careful which book to recommend to you but I have stated this in the past that I recommend Muhammad Ali's compendia of his life as it well researched and thoroughly vetted for inaccuracies. Omar.

Al-Hajj.

22:39 Permission (to fight) is given to those on whom war is made, because they are oppressed. And surely Allah is Able to assist them—

22:40 Those who are driven from their homes without a just cause except that they say: Our Lord is Allah. And if Allah did not repel some people by others, cloisters, and churches, and synagogues, and mosques in which Allah's name is much remembered, would have been pulled down. And surely Allah will help him who helps Him. Surely Allah is Strong, Mighty.

Please see that personal injury is a forgiven act.

Please see this verse in Al-Rad and the accompanying text in Al-Shura where it says to forgive and amend is better.

Please know these verses show that not all evil is to be prosecuted but one can amend in other ways as well.

Please know the object is that evil to you is repelled.

Please see it occur in Muslim lands personal injury is forgiven when a party injures you.

Please know the object is that the evil does not go on.

Please know it is an affair of great resolution to forgive after injury is done but it is better than reciprocating in kind if the injurer asks for forgiveness.

Please know the law must take precedence if the party involved does not refrain in future or has no regret.

Please see it occur we are one entity in future settings of court on us when personal injury is forgiven if the party regrets his act.

Please know this is different from the Christian act of turning the other cheek when there is no regret, though the Quran does allow one to repel evil with goodness as well.

Please know the Jewish law of a tooth for a tooth is carried out in Islam as well.

Please know to forgive is better though. Omar.

Al-Rad

13:22 And those who are steadfast seeking the pleasure of their Lord, and keep up prayer and spend of that which We have given them, secretly and openly, and repel evil with good; for such is the (happy) issue of the abode —

13:23 Gardens of perpetuity, which they will enter along with those who do good from among their fathers and their spouses and their offspring; and the angels will enter in upon them from every gate.

Al-Shura

42:36 So whatever you are given is but a provision of this world's life, and that which Allah has is better and more lasting for those who believe and rely on their Lord;

42:37 And those who shun the great sins and indecencies, and whenever they are angry they forgive;

42:38 And those who respond to their Lord and keep up prayer, and whose affairs are (decided) by counsel among themselves, and who spend out of what We have given them;

42:39 And those who, when great wrong afflicts them, defend themselves.

42:40 And the recompense of evil is punishment like it; but whoever forgives and amends, his reward is with Allah. Surely He loves not the wrongdoers.

42:41 And whoever defends himself after his being oppressed, these it is against whom there is no way (of blame).

42:42 The way (of blame) is only against those who oppress men and revolt in the earth unjustly. For such there is a painful chastisement.

42:43 And whoever is patient and forgives—that surely is an affair of great resolution.

Please know the manners of war here.

Please be circumspect.

Please know there are many opinions about these verses where fighting back was recommended.

Please know even the radical element in Islam also use these words in an out of context manner and kill them where found, not knowing innocent victims are never killed in a merciless manner.

Please see these verses from chapter two.

Please know the underlying element is persecution and torment from the disbelievers to the Muslims encouraging them to fight back until the persecution has ended.

Please see the obvious,

Please know the Muslims were to fight back until the hostilities ceased and peace occurred. Our Creator is magnanimous and would relent to peace with them even though they initiated the war on Muslims. It is clear once they were stopped in their persecutions they would be shown mercy and war would cease.

Please know people take the words 'kill them wherever you find them' as meaning killing innocents. This is not correct as it was meant to be in a state of war and once hostilities ceased peace was to be shown to them, as the following verse shows. Anyway our Creator never allowed him to kill in marketplaces and areas other than battlefields in warfare so you know that is not warfare they do but skirmish of an indecent kind.

Please know 'religion is always for Allah' and it is not for Muslims to deny people the peace of praying the way they wished.

Please know our Prophet never encouraged his Muslim fighters to convert people by force.

The end occurs when you misconstrue the words of His for your own satisfaction and imply a meaning to it that was not present in the time of our Prophet's life.

Please be circumspect when people tell you that Islam prospered under the sword. It is so mistakes wee made by the early Muslim leaders but the Prophet was immune on this matter and his war was on him and not the converse as it says here in the verse below.

Please know I will help you realize that modern Muslims know this to be true that there is no compulsion in faith and everyone is allowed to worship as he or she wishes, with evident truth be known to them that Islam is true. Omar.

Al-Baqarah.

2:190 And fight in the way of Allah against those who fight against you but be not aggressive. Surely Allah loves not the aggressors.

2:191 And kill them wherever you find them, and drive them out from where they drove you out, and persecution is worse than slaughter. And fight not with them at the Sacred Mosque until they fight with you in it; so if they fight you (in it), slay them. Such is the recompense of the disbelievers.

2:192 But if they desist, then surely Allah is Forgiving, Merciful.

2:193 And fight them until there is no persecution, and religion is only for Allah. But if they desist, then there should be no hostility except against the oppressors.

Please know fighting was known to them but they did not like it.

Please know these verses signify it is the nation's responsibility to protect the places of worship.

Please see these verses from the Quran from the chapter The Hajj or 22.

Please know fighting was unknown to the Muslims while they were in Mecca.

Please understand this,

Please know they just wished to practice faith as it was taught to them,

Please know they were required to fight by this injunction,

Please know they did not care for it.

Please know that while they were at Madinah they were attacked repeatedly,

Please know we have to survive.

Please understand there is no option but to fight for them,

Please know every country requires it of their men.

Please know it is wrong to hold them accountable as they were victorious and Islam prospered gradually.

Please know they were victorious because of valor.

Please understand fighting was distasteful there and his companions used to complain they were tired of bearing arms.

Please know our Prophet would console them by telling them it was only a matter of time when they would not need to and conveyed them the good news that soon a woman would be able to travel alone.

Please know we don't like fighting but it is possible that we don't like something and it may be good for us. Omar.

Al-Baqarah.

2:216 Fighting is enjoined on you, though it is disliked by you; and it may be that you dislike a thing while it is good for you, and it may be that you love a thing while it is evil for you; and Allah knows while you know not.

Please know he is your companion of a former faith as Muhammad superseded him when he appeared.

Please understand this.

Please know he is the warner to you to pay heed as you are currently on the wrong path where you call him God.

Please see these verses from chapter of The Saba or 34.

Please know our Prophet was sent as a Warner to you. In this there is certainty that his message was in the Quran for all mankind.

Please know he is unable to see it through by himself.

Please know his companion, myself, is asked to continue his work through his pen and through the teachings of the Quran, which are with you if you wish.

Please know it is vouchsafed that Islam will prevail over all the religions.

Please know it is only a matter of time.

Please know we don't try to force Islam on you but it is for your benefit that you learn about it.

Please understand this,

Please know we go through turmoils in life and if we don't have anything substantial to hold onto this life becomes insurmountable.

Please know that when you hold onto Allah and His book and Prophet's life as an example, this life becomes surmountable and navigating through life's travails becomes possible.

Please know I am your well-wisher and hope the best for you.

Please know if you do not heed this warning you do so at your own risk and will fail in achieving your endeavor, which is Paradise.

Please know this is as a warning to you.

Please know I hope you will take heed and enter Paradise with us.

Your prophet is Muhammad, not me, and not Jesus as he has been supplanted with the Quran coming to us.

Please know after the advent of Muhammad, he became the Prophet for all the religions of the world and a guide for them to enter Paradise with him and the rest of the saints and prophets.

Please realize this,

Please know we are not adversaries here in heaven.

Please know we all work for Him and work in unison in His repose.

Please know I am one facet with Him, our Creator, and the wheel's hub is Muhammad, on him be peace, and peace be to his companion and savior for his people, myself here is meant by me. Omar.

Al-Saba.

34:26 Say: Our Lord will gather us together, then He will judge between us with truth. And He is the Best Judge, the Knower.

34:27 Say: Show me those whom you join with Him as associates. By no means (can you)! Nay, He is Allah, the Mighty, the Wise.

34:28 And We have not sent thee but as a bearer of good news and as a warner to all mankind, but most men know not.

Please know the house he who is Abraham built was in Becca, the ancient valley with Him.

Please see the following caption on my heart,

Please know I am the Prophet's heart for you in the metaphorical sense when I say he and I are one in repose.

Please know he was above me but I have fused with his repose for the most part here.

Please know it is over if you think I am him in actual as he had far more breadth than me and was deeper but I am a close second in depth, that is why I teach you his word.

Please him by pleasing me.

Please know our Prophet Muhammad was given this House as a repository of appeasement for us in Islam and we go around it begging for forgiveness for our sins to Him and His law break by us by him and her.

Please know the place our Prophet was born was the town of Mecca where the ancient house is situated.

Please know this is where Adam went when he was evicted from the Garden,

Please know he built a House.

Please understand this,

Please know he wished to appease Him and the angel directed him to build a House for Him,

Please know this is a repository of appeasement,

Please know he had his family circumambulate it,

Please know this is the first House of worship.

The end occurs if they think an idolaters altar was here,

Please know He was pleased and forgave him and Eve,

Please know Arabia was green at this time,

Please see the following hadith of our Prophet,

Please know our father Adam was one of many,

Please know there were many Adams before him,

Please know we circulate the Kaaba with our heads bowed in reverence to Him,
Please see the following caption there,
Please know we are blessed with it,
Please know it is where our prophet left Ishmael,
Please know Abraham was directed here by an angel,
Please know the well Zamzam occurred because of the cries of the child. Omar.

Please know a new religion has to face adversity.
Please see the following caption here.
Please know the Prophet has appeared in the hearts of people as a savior for them.
Please know we are persecuted against though.
Please know some persecution is from the people who cajole them to take away my things and put me away. In reality they will not succeed as my work here is sacrosanct and people know I am a Muslim and will not be dissuaded to become another faith.
Please know they try though.
Please see this verse from the Quran in chapter two.
Please understand this,
Please know the enemy would not cease hostilities until the Muslims capitulated to idolatry.
Please know that when a new religion is taught people become averse to it and harm those who adhere to it.
Please know that is why our Prophet had to flee from his home town and migrated.
Please know they did not leave them at peace and tried to exterminate the faith of Islam by waging war on them.
Please know all the tribes were united in their attempt to exterminate Islam.
Please understand the believers had to fight to survive.
Please understand the immense pressure they were under and how they fought back to win.
Please know we are the underdogs here as well.

Please know people are kind here and that hatred they had for him is not apparent in this land now. Omar.

Al-Baqarah.

2:217 They ask thee about fighting in the sacred month. Say: Fighting in it is a grave (offence). And hindering (men) from Allah's way and denying Him and the Sacred Mosque and turning its people out of it, are still graver with Allah; and persecution is graver than slaughter. And they will not cease fighting you until they turn you back from your religion, if they can. And whoever of you turns back from his religion, then he dies while an unbeliever—these it is whose works go for nothing in this world and the Hereafter. And they are the companions of the Fire: therein they will abide.

Please know this is the blasphemy law in Islam.

Please know this verse.

Please know it is from The Family of Amran or chapter three.

Please know this is the injunction from our Creator to him,

Please know we are right in observing it in our lives.

Please know that there were no exceptions made.

Please know this is the injunction against the laws pervading in Muslim countries where they think a person can be killed for insulting them in Islam,

The end comes when you think the Prophet would be disobedient to it.

Please know in Islamic history it common to kill people if they insult the Prophet.

Please know there is shame in following this injunction.

Please know reliable reports have to be dismissed as we know the Prophet's character and he would not be disobedient to Him,

Please see a requiem for him,

Please know you are unjust if you think I would kill for an insult.

Please know the cases of elimination of enemy combatants come from the verse 'kill them where you find them.'

Please know it is in that context you take out an enemy combatant.

Please know this verse is applicable to someone who is in a state of war with you.

Please understand this is the norm for warfare.

Please know you do it here when you kill enemy combatants like you did with Osama Bin Laden and others you fight.

Please know the norm there was to use subterfuge.

Please know the only case of death for blasphemy ever recorded refers to a case where an enemy combatant was taken down as he broke a treaty with the Muslims and started war preparations. I know you are sane and know that it good to be fair. I know you find fault with him, but he, himself, was immaculate in war. The end occurs when you think he was not guided in warfare.

Please know it is clear you take me out of context here as I say you don't kill a person for killing not but insult on him who you call Prophet to us as there is a punishment prescribed for it with jail real or public humiliation with lashes and so forth as sahaba would enact law of such nature there during the life of Muhammad there.

Please see it occur in Muslim lands they enact the law of blasphemy of Muhammad with such a punishment rather than death as is done currently there. Omar.

Al-Imran.

3:186 You will certainly be tried in your property and your persons. And you will certainly hear from those who have been given the Book before you and from the idolaters much abuse. And if you are patient and keep your duty, surely this is an affair of great resolution.

Please know truth pervades a man when he sees defeat occur.

Please know the following.

Please know the truth pervades you when you are defeated.

Please know so it is with the judiciary and their defeat has occurred with you.

Please know they are abysmal and they are derided by you as we can see by their attitude.

Please know I am derided for telling you there is a law.

Please know you hate it that Hell is real and you will enter it if you continue your ways.

Please know men know and are certain, while women adapt to them,

Please know Allah kept this harmony with her so there would be families.

Please know it is over and enemy discomfiture results now as they recoup from you.

Please know the war is over and the enemy is trying to recoup. I know the hearts are won and it is time for the truth to pervade them.

Please see this from chapter eight.

Please know Muslims were subject to war repeatedly however when it was over the Muslims were encouraged to make peace with the people who tried to annihilate them and show mercy to them.

Please know what this is,

Please know it is nobility which you don't see nowadays.

Please understand this,

Please know when someone initiates war it continues until the superior force wins. I know sometimes truce occurs however in most cases the enemy is humiliated and the attempt is to remove them from power.

The end occurs when you think that our Prophet was not noble and after the battle would incline to peace and put his trust in Allah.

Yours truly knows this is within us to have this peace occur and desist from further attacks when we are safe.

Please understand this is in contrast to people nowadays where there is no inclination to peace until the enemies is thoroughly defeated.

Please know truth pervades the enemy camp when their discomfiture occurs and Allah is enough for us.

Please know that is the reason why Islam won. Omar.

Anfal.

8:61 And if they incline to peace, incline thou also to it, and trust in Allah. Surely He is the Hearer, the Knower.

8:62 And if they intend to deceive thee, then surely Allah is sufficient for thee. He it is Who strengthened thee with His help and with the believers,

Please know Muhammad was a World Prophet by way of his sagacity.

Please see this post from 2015 somewhere I wrote Jesus was not a world prophet but a Messiah there though it came about he was Messiah late but it is so it occurred.

Please know he is responsible for the conversion of Bani-Israel during his time but it was later that Christianity was converted to polytheism and law was abrogated by Paul there but it is so many entered the fold of Christianity because of it and many teachings of Jesus remained though altered in substance very much so and it occurred many nations succumbed to them the Christian force on them but it is so they entered hellfire because of polytheism issues.

Please know with my coming and Prophet Muhammad's teach here on my book on Facebook you have come to realize Jesus taught polytheism not but was a monotheist like Islam say he was and you come into the fold of Islam because of us, all 3 did it for you when your comprehension occur and now you have it Islam of monotheism with you from the Quran to you.

Please see the caption there,

Please know we cannot bear the fact that he was not the World Prophet.

Please see these verses from The Bee or chapter 16.

Please know our Creator has not forsaken mankind.

Please know He sends a messenger to them who guides.

Please know our Creator has sent Muhammad to you, from myself.

Please know he teaches you things you did not have the heart to bear during Jesus' time,

Please know this,

Please understand Jesus could not give them the prayer we have,

Please know they could not have followed the injunctions of the Quran,

Please know they could not have forsaken the world like we do.

Please know all this is real as when the religion went to the Gentiles they abdicated the truth,

Please understand this,

Please know Jesus was a Prophet of the Bani-Israel.

Please understand he knew that when his teachings went to the Gentiles they would be corrupted as there was no question he was not a Prophet to them,

Please know this is in the scriptures,

Please understand he was telling them his teachings were not for them,

Please know this was the error they made,

Please understand this,

Please know the World Prophet was Muhammad,

Please know the Quran cannot be corrupted in this issue and people will have to fall into line with it. Omar.

Al-Nahl.

16:35 And the idolaters say: If Allah pleased we would not have served aught but Him, (neither) we nor our fathers, nor would we have prohibited aught without (order from) Him. Thus did those before them. But have the messengers any duty except a plain delivery (of the message)?

16:36 And certainly We raised in every nation a messenger, saying: Serve Allah and shun the devil. Then of them was he whom Allah guided, and of them was he whose remaining in error was justly due. So travel in the land, then see what was the end of the rejectors.

16:37 If thou desirest their guidance, yet Allah will not guide him who leads astray, nor have they any helpers.

Please know the Quran affirms the earlier scriptures.

Please know our Creator has sent a Messenger to you, hopeful, and fearful that you won't come through.

Please know these verses from the chapter The Cattle.

Please know these are injunctions,

Please know all of them are the truth from Him,

Please know the right path,

Please know it is the truth,

Please understand the truth,

Please know the other opinion is false.

Please know there is one truth on the issues discussed here,
Please know it is the same truth that was given to Moses in his book,
Please know this,
Please know our Prophet loved his predecessor Moses,
Please know he was known there,
Please know he foretold them,
Please know the people of Madinah knew it was him they talked about.

Please know the Jews told their brethren it was him that Moses foretold,
Please know they later abdicated,
Please know the Quran confirms the law of Moses and Jesus upheld the law to them, his companion knows it to be so as without law from Him there would be chaos resulting in the land as you saw in your land with rampant abuse of child in you. Omar.

Al-Anum

6:151 Say: Come! I will recite what your Lord has forbidden to you: Associate naught with Him and do good to parents and slay not your children for (fear of) poverty—We provide for you and for them—and draw not nigh to indecencies, open or secret, and kill not the soul which Allah has made sacred except in the course of justice. This He enjoins upon you that you may understand.

6:152 And approach not the property of the orphan except in the best manner, until he attains his maturity. And give full measure and weight with equity—We impose not on any soul a duty except to the extent of its ability. And when you speak, be just, though it be (against) a relative. And fulfill Allah's covenant. This He enjoins on you that you may be mindful;

6:153 And (know) that this is My path, the right one, so follow it, and follow not (other) ways, for they will lead you away from His way. This He enjoins on you that you may keep your duty.

6:154 Again, We gave the Book to Moses to complete (Our blessings) on him who would do good, and making plain all things and a guidance and a mercy, so that they might believe in the meeting with their Lord.

Please see unlettered was the norm there in Arabia during his time but he became lettered very quickly after the verse of Read was relayed to him as the first communication he had from the angel to him.

Please see this verse from The Elevated Plains.

Please know it is our Creator Who decides our roles.

Please understand our Creator raised our Prophet to be the World Prophet predicted in the Gospels and the Torah as well as other religions.

Real time is with him as he converted most of the nation of Arabia during his lifetime.

Yours truly knows that it is only the beginning. In this there is certainty that Islam will prevail over other religions.

Yours truly knows that the time is appropriate to tell mankind that our Prophet still directs affairs on His behalf from his heavenly abode.

The end is there for those who think the prophets can't communicate with their followers in dreams and in other ways.

Yours truly knows the time is ripe for our Prophet to emerge from his heavenly abode and descend to the world in spirit through the teachings of Muslims like myself.

Yours truly wishes you well as you continue the study of him who was unlettered or ummi and still was wise as he was taught directly by Him in Whose hand is our soul.

The end occurs to him who thinks he was an uncivilized bedouin who did not do any good. I know you are more fair in this country and understand that being unlettered was the norm in those days in his land and the merit of a man does not lie in the books he writes but in the wisdom that emanates there with him. Omar.

Al-Araf.

7:158 Say: O mankind, surely I am the Messenger of Allah to you all, of Him, Whose is the kingdom of the heavens and the earth. There is no god but He; He gives life and causes death. So believe in Allah and His Messenger, the Ummi Prophet who believes in Allah and His words, and follow him so that you may be guided aright.

Please know our Prophet has decreed it you will be pleased here.

Please see it is safe to say it has come about this verse that light emanates from the house of a believer in this town not only but worldwide the move is there.

Please also know that the light is from the blessed oil which came in the form of teachings from his soul who is Muhammad there and I teach from the oil I borrow and it has come about my recognition as his emissary from hard work and dedication to his word here on Facebook and my book here and other material I write.

It has come to pass that his words are true and gradual way is your way but your child is already us and will teach child I am his emissary who is Muhammad, on him be peace that Islam is good and wholesome here.

Please know it is gradual you think but it is not so, most of you read me and the Quran is in many of your houses which you consult some and your child is taught we are good people with truth from Him Who creates, there you have it we are one Christian race like I was telling you that Muhammad on him be peace in that regard was a Christ believer and taught monotheism like he did and so now you have it we are Christians in that regard and our book is different but has the essence of Jesus' teaching in it from Muhammad to us.

Please know our Prophet has decreed it and he never spoke an untruth.

Please see this verse which talks about a light emanating from the chapter The Light.

Please know it is the light of Islam,

Please know our Prophet is the source of that light.

Please know he is the oil.

Please know our light is superimposed upon the light of the previous scriptures.

Please know it emanates from the houses of the believers,

Please see the characteristic of the believer,

Please know this is you in this land,

Please know this,

Please know your hearts yearn for the truth more than my brethren,

Please know our Prophet decrees it,
Please understand I am your peace,
Please know your peace,
Please know it is to pray as we do.
Please know it will be so. Omar.
Al-Nur.

24:35 Allah is the light of the heavens and the earth. A likeness of His light is as a pillar on which is a lamp—the lamp is in a glass, the glass is as it were a brightly shining star—lit from a blessed olive-tree, neither eastern nor western, the oil whereof gives light, though fire touch it not—light upon light. Allah guides to His light whom He pleases. And Allah sets forth parables for men, and Allah is Knower of all things —

24:36 (It is) in houses which Allah has permitted to be exalted and His name to be remembered therein. Therein do glorify Him, in the mornings and the evenings,

24:37 Men whom neither merchandise nor selling diverts from the remembrance of Allah and the keeping up of prayer and the paying of the poor rate—they fear a day in which the hearts and the eyes will turn about,

24:38 That Allah may give them the best reward for what they did, and give them more out of His grace. And Allah provides without measure for whom He pleases.

Please know the sign is that man has peace when he says His verdict is true that there is no god but Allah and me is safe here to allow you this.

Please see the shahada is the sign you are with me in our battlefront against adversary like the devil in us and so forth now you know we are one team on His side when you say so.

Please know our Creator has given us signs in the universe and in His creations that He is One as if there had been more than one God there would have been disorder.

Please see these verses from The Bee or chapter 16.
Please know he was sent to mankind as a mercy to them,
Please understand him,
Please know he was only for their reformation.

Please understand he was not only a messenger but a savior for them as he guided them aright and they followed him,
Please understand a prophet is like rain that comes to a dead earth and gives it growth,
Please know the metaphor is applied here.
Please know that our Prophet will give herbage to the world through the teachings of the Quran,
Please understand he was a Prophet who left a legacy,
Please know his legacy is a Muslim who teaches,
Please know we must try to bring about a change,
Please know what change is,
It is to know the truth and live by it,
Please know we must change our heart,
Please know it is to kill the wrong in us so we may live,
Please understand this,
Please know our heart is dead if we deny the truth,
Please know the devil prospers.
Please know this,
Please know when he teaches man the error, they follow him,
They die in their heart,
Please know they fight for him.
Please see he is able to kill you,
Was this the reason you left your truth?
Please know your truth is Allah,
Please know He is Sublime,
Please know while He is hidden He has given you signs. Omar. Al-Nahl.

16:63 By Allah! We certainly sent (messengers) to nations before thee, but the devil made their deeds fair-seeming to them. So he is their patron today, and for them is a painful chastisement.

16:64 And We have not revealed to thee the Book except that thou mayest make clear to them that wherein they differ, and (as) a guidance and a mercy for a people who believe.

16:65 And Allah sends down water from above, and therewith gives life to the earth after its death. Surely there is a sign in this for a people who listen.

Please know the miracle was clear but people walked out calling it enchantment.

Please understand this,

Please know there is wisdom in staying away from performing miracles,

Please see these verses from The Moon,

Please know this is a miracle he performed while talking to them who denied him,

Please understand this,

Please know he did not perform many miracles as he saw what occurred to the People of the Book,

Please know they ascribed Godhead in him,

Please understand the people who saw the miracle said it was enchantment,

Please know they lied,

Please know such it was to the detractors of Jesus,

Please know our Prophet turned away from them,

Please know he said he could do no more,

Please see the caption there,

Please know we are liars,

Please understand he was averse to performing miracles and said the Quran is his miracle with us.

I am similar and don't perform much in the form of a miracle to us but my teachings coming through his pen who is Allah's messenger is a miracle to man and wife.

Please know hidden things are my forte as a saint to you and that's why this land is sacred to us in that they protect my car some from the government who are averse to my teach to continue here. Omar.

Al-Qamar.

54:1 The hour drew nigh and the moon was rent asunder.

54:2 And if they see a sign, they turn away and say: Strong enchantment!

54:3 And they deny and follow their low desires; and every affair is settled.

54:4 And certainly narratives have come to them, which should deter—

54:5 Consummate wisdom—but warnings avail not;

54:6 So turn away from them. On the day when the Inviter invites them to a hard task—

54:7 Their eyes cast down, they will go forth from their graves as if they were scattered locusts,

54:8 Hastening to the Inviter. The disbelievers will say: This is a hard day!

Please know there is no hatred here but a recognition of facts.

Please see the Jewish council is still averse to us but many youths are with us and know their predecessor was hard to Mary and Jesus and know they were innocent in trying to correct their wrongs there and I am similar as I bring reform to Muslim land in that they have gone away from the religion of Muhammad, on him be peace in that regard.

Please know Jews are good people if they accept our Prophet as a prophet of His,

Please know it is so for all people,

Please know it is true in your land that you consider him to be His prophet.

Please know Islam has occurred with you.

Please know you will not fight it.

Please know the reason why I say it is because you have accepted the truth of it.

Please know you are averse to the Muslim car because their car is not of the Muslims who forbid wrong things and enjoin good on others.

Please know the Muslims of today are different from the early Muslims of Islam when piety and good character reigned.

Please know Muslims have to improve their lot.

Please give in.

Please know your people are better.

Please know your word is kept and you behave better with those that are downtrodden,

Please know you give rights to people,

Please know your administration is under the people,

Please know there is no proof for some of the things I say yet I am allowed to express my views.

Please know it is your country that allows this.

Please know you hold freedom of speech to be a sacred trust.

Please know there are elements in your government that want me controlled but I am permitted leeway for the most part.

Please know there is injustice here as well but I am permitted peace.

Please know there is a sacred trust with you.

Please know it is to allow people to express their views.

Please know you are the best nation because of this.

Please know there are many in your land who adore Him and do not fight Islam,

Please know the righteous.

Please know it is the one who gives to the poor his due.

Please know he is the downtrodden one here,

Please Him,

Please give Him His due and worship Him alone.

Please know Jesus said this in Matthews and Islam confirms this.

Please know He will come through for you and serve you.

Please know Jesus never said worship me or worship the son.

Please know these are your words from the teaching of Paul and others.

Please know inspiration,

Please know a scholar's words are inspired at times but are not revealed.

Please know an edict comes from the prophet who is revealed,

Please know a scholar cannot contradict the prophet.

Please know explanations have to be circumspect.

Please know the teachings of Paul contradict the Old Testament and the words of Jesus.

Please know Jesus called himself son of man repeatedly.

Please know Islam is served here so I will speak.

Please know the Quran validates the Old Testament that God will never allow another god to be worshipped and also contradicts the teachings of Paul about Godhead in him,

Please know to hold the Quran as a criterion.

Please know it will guide you about fallacies in the Christian faith that crept in after monotheism was abrogated in the council of Nicaea.

Please know until then monotheism was the mainstay of the Christian faith.

Please give me accolade for bringing it to you.

Please know you have read my book and found it cogent.

Please know the Jews are at fault for fighting it.

Please know there are some who are good though and keep their covenant with Him,

Please know there are many that adore Him.

Please see on other issues they are averse but it is so they consider me a messiah to them and also realize to backtrack on Jesus and Mary is sane as they were good people there.

Please them and teach them that Islam is their religion and their Prophet is him whom we hold dear. Omar.

Al-Imran.

3:110 You are the best nation raised up for men: you enjoin good and forbid evil and you believe in Allah. And if the People of the Book had believed, it would have been better for them. Some of them are believers but most of them are transgressors.

3:111 They will not harm you save a slight hurt. And if they fight you, they will turn (their) backs to you. Then they will not be helped.

3:112 Abasement will be their lot wherever they are found, except under a covenant with Allah and a covenant with men, and they shall incur the wrath of Allah, and humiliation will be made to cling to them. This is because they disbelieved in the messages of Allah and killed the prophets unjustly. This is because they disobeyed and exceeded the limits.

3:113 *They are not all alike. Of the People of the Book there is an upright party who recite Allah's messages in the night-time and they adore (Him).*

3:114 *They believe in Allah and the Last Day, and they enjoin good and forbid evil and vie one with another in good deeds. And those are among the righteous.*

3:115 *And whatever good they do, they will not be denied it. And Allah knows those who keep their duty.*

Please know the heart gives solace to us in that it needs its comfort.

Please know our Prophet was the best of creations because he was informed of that by Him and because all prophets vouchsafed his coming as their leader and as the World Prophet.

Please see he was truthful to an extreme and would not lie about his magnificence with Him, the Creator, as the best entity He created and the Quran also verifies he was the man chosen for world reform with the Book of Allah to them in the world forum.

Please know the following,

Please understand our Prophet passed away in peace knowing the message had been transmitted to the people who were steadfast.

Please understand his work was over and was handed over to the stewardship of his companion Abu Bakr, the first caliph after him.

Please know he was not harmed as was the promise of our Creator to him.

Was this the reason you thought ill of him?

Please know he was the Prophet after your own heart as he was given a promise by Him in the Quran that He would protect him from skirmish and harm.

Please understand I know you don't wish to die prematurely and you would like to live long lives.

Please know I know you want peace with your family and friends. I know this is possible in Islam as the Prophet had similar aspirations. I know the life of Jesus would be hard for you. I know you wish for peace in a role model.

Please know the following,

Please see the caption on his heart,

Please know I am the best of the creations and it is seemly that I am followed.

Please understand the message of Jesus was too hard for you and you abdicated in favor of peace and comfort. Omar.

Al-Imran.

3:144 And Muhammad is but a messenger—messengers have already passed away before him. If then he dies or is killed, will you turn back upon your heels? And he who turns back upon his heels will do no harm at all to Allah. And Allah will reward the grateful.

3:145 And no soul can die but with Allah's permission—the term is fixed. And whoever desires the reward of this world, We give him of it, and whoever desires the reward of the Hereafter, We give him of it. And We shall reward the grateful.

3:146 And how many a prophet has fought, with whom were many worshippers of the Lord. So they did not lose heart on account of that which befell them in Allah's way, nor did they weaken, nor did they abase themselves. And Allah loves the steadfast.

Please validate this fact that though he said it no one has contradicted him that he was the spirit Jesus spoke of as he had never known a lie.

Please know we must learn to accept certain facts as historical evidence and not try to bring up excuses if we cannot see reason in our viewpoints.

Please see this verse from the chapter The Cave or 18.

Please know our Prophet was a mortal as was his predecessor Jesus.

Please know all the prophets came with the same message.

Please understand that is the Unity of their Creator.

Please understand the role for reformation came to a man.

Please know angels cannot teach mankind.

Please understand when Jesus referred to the Spirit of Truth he referred to a man as a spirit does not teach mankind.

MUHAMMAD THE PROPHET

Please know the spirit Jesus referred to was the spirit in a man though it is true here that his spirit pervades us through my pen to you and you have come through in this eon.

Please know we all have a spirit.

Please understand a spirit that has never known an untruth in it is the spirit of our Prophet Muhammad, on him be peace.

Please know his worst enemy had stated he had never spoken a lie.

Please know this was confirmed by the Prophet himself who is the only person who has said that about himself.

Please know when Jesus said that the Spirit of Truth will come to teach you things which you do not have the heart to bear right now he was referring to a man.

Please know he was talking about his followers who did not have the heart to bear the Islam of their times.

Please know when the Prophet taught the Christians agreed with him and accepted his teachings in the Christian world of Asia there and Africa and now in this time he still teaches through pen like mine and you have come forth as a nation of Islam here.

Please know an angel can't teach masses of people.

Please know there is clarity in the reality of what occurred.

Please know these words of your savior are in the gospel of John.

Please know they fit the description of him, that is Muhammad.

Please know there is no man since Jesus who has made the claim of never speaking a lie and its validation is in history.

Please know your heart,

Please know that you accept the truth,

Please know and learn the message of Muhammad was correct and in your book there are fallacies as you know from your Bible scholars you have faith in. Omar.

Al-Kahf.

18:110 Say: I am only a mortal like you—it is revealed to me that your God is one God. So whoever hopes to meet his Lord, he should do good deeds, and join no one in the service of his Lord.

Please know jiyzah is sane to do rather than coerce people to a religious belief they were not comfortable in.

Please see the ultimatum of God.

Please understand enchanter.

Please know you would call him that here in order to discredit him to her who seeks.

Please understand the Quran.

Please know at that time it was the most beautiful poetry.

Please see the inscription there.

Please produce something like it.

Please do it!

Please know it is a challenge to all mankind to produce the like of it.

Please know your worth.

Please know you won't accept the challenge as it is not worthy of you to do this.

Please see the inscription on Heaven.

Please see it says 'there is no God but Allah and Muhammad is Allah's Messenger.'

Please realize this is a fact that all will accept, in it.

Please know our Creator was careful about the words He used and indicated that they were conquered.

Please know our Creator wished to show people that they were vanquished.

Please realize this,

Please understand that the people who paid jizyah would stop feeling subjugated to this state if they became Muslims but no compulsion was used.

Please know He knows the psychology of man and knows that a vanquished person would feel good if he accepted the truth of Islam thereby becoming a member of the ruling class of men.

Please understand Allah does this as men and women do not bow to the truth when they feel superior.

Please know He is our Creator and He knows what is best for His servants so that they live the lives of truthful conduct and behavior.

Please see these verses from the chapter The Immunity.

Please know the tax that was obtained was spent on the reformation of the people.

Please know in lieu of the tax the Non-Muslims were told that they would be taken care of.

Please realize this,

Please know that mankind has a need that his property is protected.

Please know it was the job of the Muslim administrator to take care of this need. I know there were examples of people whose jizyah was returned to them when the Muslim army could not take care of their need.

Please know it was not to humiliate the Non-Muslims but to encourage them to come into Islam.

Please know our Prophet used it judiciously and when the enemy was faced they were given an option of paying the jizyah or go to war if they did not wish to convert to Islam.

Please know this is not coercion as Muslims pay a charity tax that is levied in the amount similar to the tax rate for them.

The end occurs that it was humiliating for them.

Please understand they had equal rights as citizens.

Please know they were only taxed to show they were under Muslim rule and the choice was given to them to pay the jizyah or the charity tax.

Please know after learning about Islam they preferred to pay the charity tax as Muslim citizens. Omar.

Al-Bara'at.

9:29 Fight those who believe not in Allah, nor in the Last Day, nor forbid that which Allah and His Messenger have forbidden, nor follow the Religion of Truth, out of those who have been given the Book, until they pay the tax in acknowledgement of superiority and they are in a state of subjection.

Please know the position of ours is known to Him.

Please know the positions with Him are fixed and cannot be altered by any man or angel.

Please see these verses from the chapter Women.

Please know this is what submission is,

Please know it is to give in to your Creator's wishes for you.

Please know this is the example of Abraham and Muhammad, on them be peace.

Please try to do this and you will see how difficult it is.

Please know that in the absolute reality of things our Creator is everything to vie for,

Please know our Prophet was similar,

Please know the viers are those who give in to peace with men,

Please know that those who vie for coveted positions with Him do so for themselves,

Please know we all take care of ourselves,

Please know there are infinite positions with Him,

Please know we are created first,

Please know the souls that follow are in a position of decrement in their creation,

Please know the best was Muhammad and was the soul with Him before He created the rest.

Please know this is hadith and not my revelation that you find askance with.

Please know I know it to be true,

Please see why?

Please know it is because He revealed it, just like He writes for us. Omar.

Nisa.

4:125 And who is better in religion than he who submits himself entirely to Allah while doing good (to others) and follows the faith of Abraham, the upright one? And Allah took Abraham for a friend.

4:126 And to Allah belongs whatever is in the heavens and whatever is in the earth. And Allah ever encompasses all things.

Please know the akhirat is for those who submit to the truth in His teachings to us.

Please see this verse that our Prophet was a mortal and wished best for you,

Please know he was a knower of the unseen to some extent, as revealed by his Creator, as we all are in Islam when we follow his teachings,

Please know when we learn Islam we gain peace about the unseen.

Please know Islam occurs in our hearts then,

Please know we learn to submit to His presence in us,

Please Him occurs.

Please know our Prophet is a warner to you that you come through.

Please know this verse where the Prophet ascribes mortality to himself.

Please know it is from The Elevated Plains.

Please know our Prophet was a man and knew only what was told to Him from his Creator,

Please know this,

Please know he had a peace for you from Him,

Please understand this,

Please know he was solicitous for you and wished you well.

Please know our Creator wants the best for you.

Please know in His wisdom are those who submit to Him and those who fail to do so.

Please know He created Heaven and Hell before He created mankind and other creatures.

Please know He wished to show you who were the best of submitters and why they have a Heaven that is theirs.

Please know this,

Please know we will all know our station,

Please know I know you know it in your heart,

Please have mercy on yourself and submit to His teachings.

Please know there is only one truth from Him,

Please know everything else is false,

Please know the Prophet's car,

Please know it followed the Word from Him,

Please do not delete it,

Please read the Quran.

Please know it attests the Old Testament in that there is only One God.

Please know this,

Please know it is the only book that was preserved intact for the most part.

Please check your history book.

Please know the changes made in the scriptures are nullified,

Please know the Word,

Please know there is only one truth on the matter and that is there is no God but the Creator of the Heavens and man,

Please know so say the Quran and the scriptures of Abraham and Moses,

Please know Jesus did not deviate and what they ascribe to him is them, not his word. Omar.

Al-Araf.

7:187 They ask thee about the Hour, when will it come to pass? Say: The knowledge thereof is with my Lord only. None but He will manifest it at its time. It is momentous in the heavens and the earth. It will not come to you but of a sudden. They ask thee as if thou wert solicitous about it. Say: Its knowledge is with Allah only, but most people know not.

7:188 Say: I control not benefit or harm for myself except as Allah please. And had I known the unseen, I should have much of good, and no evil would touch me. I am but a warner and the giver of good news to a people who believe.

Please know we all know rancor but He.

Please know I had rancor there when I wrote it but with the passage of time it assuages and becomes clear we are his guests.

Please know this

Please know I am his metaphor, he is real for you to follow.

Please know our Prophet said no one will enter Paradise without being him,

Please know it is worded incorrectly in the hadith that they will look like him,

Please know the Prophet knew he was chosen for His repose in actual and as a guide to man,

Please know repose here means God intent for man to be.

Please know me,

Please know I am a mercy to you,

Please know I bring you the truth,

I am his metaphor as when I write you think it is our Prophet who comes to you and speaks to you.

Please know the reason why our Prophet was given the heavens and earth as his inheritance is because he is the who befits it for himself.

Please know he is only one who does not have an example that he would follow. I know it causes rancor in me as I feel the heavens and earth belong to God but they are given to the Prophet as his. I know it irks some of you but there is peace here,

Please know when you enter Paradise it becomes yours as well.

Please know this,

The end occurs if you think it will not last,

Please know that once you become owner, like our Prophet is, it will always be yours.

Please know rancor,

Please know it is when you think it is unjust what is done,

Please realize this,

Please realize the Prophet did not consider Heaven as his but was a place where believers in Him go.

Yours truly has a heart that knows there is peace in this that we are guests of his on His behalf as it behooves not to earn rancor,

Please know I can't comprehend it to my satisfaction so let the Prophet say to you that when the Creator created him, the Prophet, He knew that he would be mold for all mankind to follow.

Please know in this way he would guide all of mankind to Paradise where once they enter would be inmates of it.

Please know the Prophet was vouchsafed the Heaven as it was his make and character that the Creator would allow in it. I am surprised at you that you think Jesus was the prophet he intended as the role model for you while he himself asked you to wait for the Spirit of Truth who would teach you things he could not teach due to sin of his that had transpired in his youth,

Please know our Prophet is a mercy to you.

Please understand mercy,

Please know he will take you to it,

Please know I too am a mercy to you as I take you to him,

Please know that I am a saint and not a prophet. I only teach his words as they come to me,

Please know a requiem for him,

Please know he is a mercy to mankind,

Please know it is me not who is Rahmat Al-Alimeen but he himself as the Quran says and I am his emissary as I write these words to you that I am great by you and Allah but not the one who is the coveted one by man.

Please know I know you think me unwell but when I started off writing that is what you said but it has happened that you learnt your God was One through my page.

Please see the tasdeeq here of him being the mercy to us is as the words of the Quran say this.

Also know mercy is to enter Heaven and it is through Muhammad you have the message intact that takes you there.

There is no one in history who has the Quran, so there occurs, the proof has occurred here. Omar.

Al-Anbiya.

21:107 And We have not sent thee but as a mercy to the nations.

21:108 Say: It is only revealed to me that your God is one God: will you then submit?

21:109 But if they turn back, say: I have warned you in fairness, and I know not whether that which you are promised is near or far.

21:110 Surely He knows what is spoken openly and He knows what you hide.

21:111 And I know not if this may be a trial for you and a provision till a time.

21:112 He said: My Lord, judge Thou with truth. And our Lord is the Beneficent, Whose help is sought against what you ascribe (to Him).

MUHAMMAD THE PROPHET

Please know the seal of Allah is His Prophet Muhammad.
Please know our Creator was merciful when He created him, from Himself.
Please know this,
Please know our Prophet is immaculate,
Please know that was his nature,
Please know spotlessly clean,
Please know our Prophet was asked if he wished to represent Him or them, his people,
Please know he chose them,
Please know he is king with them,
Please know this,
Please know he is the one the court asks for,
Please know judge,
Please know him,
Please know he is man's judge with Him,
Please know Judge,
Please know He is our God,
Please know our Creator is the Judge with him,
Please know your acts,
Please know he will intercede for you with Him,
Please know He will permit you peace if he intercedes,
Please know he was Him in repose and in turn he was His repose,
Please know he cared to bring you truth,
Please know he will intercede for you and Jesus and myself.
Please know why?
Please know we sin at times,
Please know we are human and err,
Please know he erred and was corrected by Him,
Please see a requiem,
Please know it is to bring you peace,
Please know what is this peace,
Please know it is the world order when we are His repose,
Please be like me,
Please know repentant,

Please know to perfect oneself,
Please know it is to repent and forgive oneself.
Please know this verse from the Quran,
Please know it means he was us in consideration,
Please know you know it is over and you know him Prophet, as is Jesus,
Please know he predicted him,
Please know they are all derived from His essence and are with Him in Paradise.
Please know they were special, these two, as they were His essence,
Please know they know it is only the complete makeup of Him they see.
Please know that is why I am incomplete as yet but may be complete before I die.
Please know see the following caption.
Please know I am not he who you worship or used to worship.
Please know it is because I am literal I write this,
Please understand this,
Please know you are raised to your setting in the Hereafter depending upon what you say.
Pleased know you are only human and I relent to you, but desist, he is not your worshipped one anymore,
Please Him,
Please know when you say it, your destination is Hell, unless you repent.
Please know He is not pleased,
Please know it is what your tongue says but consideration is given to your heart,
Please know it is over and now you know.
Please know he was His seal who was Muhammad,
Please know Muhammad was seal and was perfect, so he served Him well.
Please know that is final, as well as seal.
Please know He is literal in this issue and must be taken at face value,

Please know you cannot say he is not as hadith law applies where he says he is last.

Please Him and desist.

Please know they are sons who serve Him,

Please know he was the one close to him, whom you call on, Jesus to you,

Please know I know you are forced, but desist.

Please know I am simple, the words of the Quran are invincible,

Please know if you start to say it, it will be you there,

Please Him and desist. Omar.

Al-Ahzab.

33:21 Certainly you have in the Messenger of Allah an excellent exemplar for him who hopes in Allah and the Latter day, and remembers Allah much.

Please know to submit is simple if you have the heart to do it.

Please see the following verses from The Bee or chapter 16.

Please know all of us are destined to bow down to our Creator, whether we like it or not.

Please come to your Lord willingly and He will show you peace. The end is here for those who think they don't need Him. I know we are weak and when we are tested we will turn to Him for help.

Please try to remember your place with Him. I know we think we are self-sufficient but when push comes to shove we will not be able to remain so and will ask others for help. I am sad that we cannot come willingly to Him, like the other creatures He has created. In the final analysis we choose to forsake Him and He does not do so in the least. He has provided all the tools for your development and given guidance to mankind but they do not take heed.

Please know we will all submit eventually so it is better not to go to Hell which is where a denier of Him will end in but rather submit humbly here in our life on earth. In this there is certainty that it takes a humble heart to make obeisance to Him.

Please try to remember your place with Him as you were created out of the ejaculate of a male and female. In this certainty that mankind *forgets its humble origin and contends with Him in their arrogance of non-obedience. Omar.*

Al-Nahl.

16:48 See they not everything that Allah has created? Its (very) shadows return from right and left, making obeisance to Allah, while they are in utter abasement.

16:49 And to Allah makes obeisance every living creature that is in the heavens and that is in the earth, and the angels (too) and they are not proud.

16:50 They fear their Lord above them and do what they are commanded.

Please regard this notice to you that if you can best him, then try, you will not be able to.

Please know this man who is being revealed to you through his agency.

Please know the following,

Please understand 'to forgive is divine.'

Please know it means it is a divine deed.

Please know we are not Him but he expects us to follow through and forgive people who have done us wrong. I know it is difficult, but it is possible.

Please realize we must try to learn Divine attributes to be like Him. I know He created us in His Image.

Please know that our Prophet was given certain injunctions and he tried to fulfill them and improved himself.

Please know we are not created perfect.

Please know it is a constant struggle and that is why it is called the greater jihad.

Please know this is him,

Please know his Creator advised him that "whosoever should cut you off, draw him to yourself and whosoever should deprive you, give him. Whosoever should do you wrong, pardon him."

Please understand this.

Please know it is not a simple task to do and goes against conventional thinking.

Please understand these attributes are divine, and should be learnt.

Please know that you can realize the forgiveness He has if this is what He expects of his servant.

Please understand we cannot give enough in our life here to become him.

Please know this is what he expects of one He has chosen for greatness.

Please know this and realize he lived his life this way.

Please know this was a divine injunction that came to him through an angel.

Please understand that he was tried excessively and our Creator asked him to forgive people who kill others.

Please know this occurred in the battle for Mecca where the whole city was given amnesty and because of the magnanimity of their Prophet they converted to Islam.

Please understand that divine attributes in man can change the hearts of the most ardent of enemies.

Please know this man who effaced himself to develop divine attributes and thereby conquer the hearts of people.

Please know this man who forgave people who had maimed and killed.

Please know when you come into Islam your sins are not accountable.

Please know this man who changed the hearts of humanity to worship his Creator.

Please know he was the most successful man due to these attributes of forgiveness and mercy.

Please realize, this is man I ask you to follow. Omar.

Araf or The Elevated Plains.

7:194 Those whom you call on besides Allah are slaves like yourselves; so call on them, then let them answer you, if you are truthful.

7:195 Have they feet with which they walk, or have they hands with which they hold, or have they eyes with which they see, or have they ears with which they hear? Say: Call upon your associate-gods then plot against me and give me no respite.

7:196 Surely my Friend is Allah, Who revealed the Book, and He befriends the righteous.

7:197 And those whom you call upon besides Him are not able to help you, nor can they help themselves.

7:198 And if you invite them to guidance, they hear not; and thou seest them looking towards thee, yet they see not.

7:199 Take to forgiveness and enjoin good and turn away from the ignorant.

Please know bravery from this man.

Please see that our Prophet receives accolade that he waited until death was written for him.

Please know he feigned his departure by subterfuge and our prophet Jesus feigned his death after the crucifixion by remaining in disguise until the migration occurred there.

Please know both had distinction that they waited until death occurred in their hearts.

Please see this section from chapter eight.

Please know this refers to the assassination attempt on our Prophet.

Please know he was surrounded at night and he walked out from under their very noses.

Please know this occurred at night and after saying a prayer he left. Apparently they all fell asleep.

Please know that he was practically alone in Mecca when this occurred as all his followers had migrated to Medina before.

Please understand this,

Please know he could have migrated before but if he had his companions who were left behind would have been oppressed by them.

The end occurs if you think he was not a soldier of courage.

Please know there was practically no chance for him to escape and stalwarts from the enemy camp had decided to do away with him. In this there is a parallel with Jesus when God saved him despite him being placed on the crucifix.

Please know there is pre-destiny and our Prophet's departure from Mecca is foretold in the scriptures of the Old Testament, as is the attempted murder of Christ.

Please realize what courage is,

Please know it was at the last moment before their death occurred that the migration occurred. While Jesus was delivered to the enemies my Prophet escaped before that occurred.

Please know they had a planned escape.

Please understand what subterfuge is,

Please see the following caption on their hearts.

Please know Allah is with us. Omar.

Anfal.

8:29 O you who believe, if you keep your duty to Allah, He will grant you a distinction and do away with your evils and protect you. And Allah is the Lord of mighty grace.

8:30 And when those who disbelieved devised plans against thee that they might confine thee or slay thee or drive thee away—and they devised plans and Allah, too, had arranged a plan; and Allah is the best of planners.

Please know decent conduct from him.

Please see the repertoire of his language and see if you see an abuse to anyone.

Please know during the Prophet's time there were certain Jews who would abuse him by saying the words "death be upon you" instead of the Muslim greeting "peace be upon you."

Please know it was upsetting to Aisha, who remarked "death be upon you" in return. I know this is the norm for me and I would probably agree with her reply but the Prophet cautioned her and indicated that our Creator does not like the harsh tone in mankind.

Please know he never uttered a word in a harsh tone and has never been on record to say an abuse to anyone.

Please know this man,

Please know this is the mold we have to adopt to enter Paradise.

Please understand our Creator expects all of us not to use harsh language.

Please ask yourself: Are you ready to enter the premises your Creator has created for you?

Please know we must adopt the mold of himself.

Please know you can't do it even if you tried.

Please understand that is why there is a Hereafter where further amelioration occurs.

Please allow yourself leeway.

Please know we are headed in the direction of Paradise if we commit good deeds and give our Creator His right that He alone we worship.

Please yourself if you fail.

Please know your direction is not that of his and your respective prophet.

Please those who are near you and you will fail.

Please only the Prophet you respect and you will find the answer is with our Prophet who gave us his book and the Quran as the way to Him.

Please know I advise you to review your literature.

Please review and see that we have coherence in our religious belief of Islam where your Creator is One.

Please see and observe the way to Him.

Please know your books were altered after your prophet left you. Omar.

Please know He is Rabb Who nurtures us to perfection.
Please know we are accountable if we break the mold in us.
Please know our Prophet Muhammad, on him be peace.
Please know he came to perfect religion and faith.
Please know he did not do it on his own,
Please know he had a Helper.
Please know it was his Creator Who nurtures unto perfection.
Please know He is the Rabb.
Please know that is one who nurtures to perfection.

Please know now that the mold has been perfected we can follow suit,

Please understand this,

Please know our Creator has created the Heavens for His perfect ones.

Please know when we follow him we will perfect ourselves.

Please know all humanity has to go through this process of perfecting themselves after adopting him,

Please know our Creator perfected the obedient one,

Please know he perfected his friend and companion, Abu Bakr there,

Please know our Prophet was grateful he was chosen,

Please know he expressed his gratitude in his prayer to Him,

Please be kind to yourself and accept him as your mold,

Please know you will have no option in the Hereafter.

Please know Jesus, Moses and Abraham will accept his mold.

Please know these are the exalted ones.

Please read him,

Please know he is kind and helpful.

Please cut off the one who berates -"he is evil."

Please know he is the antithesis of ISIS and their like, in Islam they have of disregarding him, their Prophet to them,

Please know he warned us about them indicating they would have ritual but their heart would be devoid of peace.

Please know to know him is to know yourself as you will all obey his instinct.

Please know that he was a believer in Him,

Please know this.

Please know his heart took Him as a Friend and he never broke His trust. Omar.

Please know the abundance of good is in earthly terms as well as we benefit from admiration we receive.

Please know kauthar means abundance that has no limit. It is the place where our Prophet's rest occurs.

Please see this chapter.

Please know it is called The Abundance of Good and it is one of the last chapters to be revealed, though convention has it that it is an early surah.

Please know that our Prophet is one who is spoken about.

Please realize this,

Please know that our Prophet was rich as the word kauthar means abundance, which he did not have in materialistic values.

Please see that he was only a Messenger of His.

Please know this,

Please know we carry out commands from Him.

Please know the accolade is all His as He gave us the avenue of being admired by others.

Please understand on our own we would have lived and died in ignominy. The end occurs when we say we are anything great. I am only a slave of His servant and that is my claim to greatness. Omar.

Al-Kauthar.

108:1 Surely We have given thee abundance of good.

108:2 So pray to thy Lord and sacrifice.

108:3 Surely thy enemy is cut off (from good).

Please know the Prophet was a forlorn traveler but pleased with the result.

Please know our Prophet directs some from his heavenly abode of Al-Kauthar. I know he can do so and it is a miracle I have with you.

Please know it is his well I write for you and so you have it and this is his water that sustains here with us in Islam to you,

Please see this chapter from the Quran.

Please know it is titled The Help.

Please know it was revealed close to the demise of our Prophet Muhammad.

Please know when he achieved prophethood he was a forlorn traveler that no one paid any heed to.

Please know before his death a mighty transformation was wrought as many in the nation of Arabia came into Islam.

Please know it was a single man's resolve to continue to teach people who were a barbaric race that worshipped idols and killed their young one with no mercy in their hearts.

Please allow him the leeway of time to do the same here through the agency of the Ahmadiyya Jamaat. I know I am the spearhead of the group and will be recognized as such in the near future.

Please know it is this position I covet where I can be left alone to write in peace. In this there is certainty that the message has been propagated that we are a clean religion.

Please know our Jamaat has mention in the book of revelations as the four beasts of paradise or horsemen. I know we were meant for you to come through and that is the reason we were mentioned in your liturgy.

Please say a prayer that you can come through. Omar.

Al-Nasr.

110:1 When Allah's help and victory comes,

110:2 And thou seest men entering the religion of Allah in companies,

110:3 Celebrate the praise of thy Lord and ask His protection. Surely He is ever Returning (to mercy).

CHAPTER FOUR

USE OF THE PARABLE BY THE PROPHETS AND SAINTS AND RELATED TOPICS

Please understand the following,
Please know the parable has been used sparingly by some like the Prophet Muhammad,
Please know why,
Please know it is misconstrued,
Please understand what misconstrue is,
Please know it is to take it out of context.
Please know the Prophet explained the parable,
Please know it is sainthood in place of prophethood,
Please know what I mean,
Please know there is a saint in the prophets,
Please know we use it sparingly or not at all in the case of prophethood as Muslims are averse to the words being used in that context but since I have used it I'll explain it here, then move on.
Please give into this reality,
Please know it has a place in Islam as indicated in my book, Jesus, the Messiah and the Person.
Please know it is immaculate when it is understood,
Please understand misconstrue,
Please know it is to change the meaning,
Please understand me,
Please know I am careful to explain,
Please know why?
Please know I saw what they did to my mentor,
Please know they made him to be a prophet like Prophet Muhammad was a prophet while he used it in a metaphorical sense,

Please know he was what happened to Jesus and just as his followers made him a God, so too was my mentor made a prophet by his follower,

Please know these errors creep in and should be prevented,

Please give in,

Please know our Creator does not like a religious personage's words to be taken out of context. Omar.

Please know the parable is pleasure to the senses but is misused so is abrogated.

Please know this concept.

Please know Jesus and myself have this repose we are one with Him,

Please know a servant walks in this way and communicates from Him,

Please know it is man's destiny to be so.

Please know when Jesus said "you come to me you see Him" he meant this fused state of repose to Him so that for all intents and purposes he was Him but not actually as they saw him and not their Creator there,

Please Him,

Please realize a fused state is Him,

Please know I have called myself Allah but we know He is above us in Paradise.

Please know we are two distinct entities, our Creator and myself, yet I am Him,

Please know I am a metaphor and in actuality no one is Allah but He.

Please know this is the language of the parable He permits as indicated in the chapter Araf where He says don't associate without understanding, indicating He permits the parable, though I have taken the liberty to annul it for the sake of simplicity,

Please know the reality is that I am on earth, a distinct entity who is fused in repose so my intent is the same as His,

Please know it is similar for Jesus and godhead is in the parable concept only which makes sense.

Please know the Quran validates him,

Please know the Quran indicates this is a parable and so it is for other statements of his like "I am" and "I am the Father."

Please know when he said "I am" he meant he was He in the sense of a metaphor and it is similar for other statements of his like "when you come to me you see Him" and "I and the Father are one."

Please know these statements of his are replete in his vernacular there and he was 'one with Him' in it.

Please know the Quran corroborates the metaphor as seen in Araf and elsewhere,

Please know this was groundbreaking information for the Jews and he got into trouble with them,

Please know our Creator knows we will develop into this fused state with Him and be god-like in intent. In the context of sanity we are a walking talking Him in it and that's what godhead is in the sense of a metaphor,

Please know I am asked if your Creator is One.

Please know He is.

Please understand Him,

Please know He creates us from Him,

Please know we are Him if we are to be in His repose or when our thoughts and deeds are His beck on us and that we are an extension of His thoughts on us.

Please see this occurs with prayers and self-sacrifice when we do our will not but His as Jesus said there,

Please know fuse with Him,

Please know it is to be one with Him,

Please know when we forsake us we are in essence Him if we do His work and are Him in repose or intent.

Please know the statement of our Prophet that when we walk, we walk with His legs, and when we communicate, we communicate from Him,

Please know the intent is meant here,

Please know repose,

Please know it is His intent that we do everything or we are one with Him.

Please know our savior Christ was one with Him in repose or intent.
Please know he was in essence Him,
Please know the metaphor, it is when we become His essence in our soul of ours and there you have it we are His essence when we do His bid, like I do here as I teach Jesus words to you.
Please know our Creator is the Creator of us.
Please know more,
Please know He expects us to be this metaphor that we are His intent or one with Him,
Please know the Sufis say that we annihilate ourselves and become Him, the Creat, but it is when our intent is Him in intent for us that we annihilate our body not but soul to Him and thus become Him,
Some Sufis think we enter His essence but that is not the case we remain separate in our body eternally and it is not like the river entering the ocean, as Rumi puts it,
That is our peace as we don't want to annihilate ourselves actually.
Please see this,
Please see that we are His repose.
Please know Jesus and his spirit were one with his Beloved. I know you hope to be like him one day and achieve repose like we do and the Prophet was there different but still repose to Him.
Please see I have authority to explain this association we do but also make it clear to you this associate state we have and become is in the metaphor sense as He, the Creator, is in Heaven and we are here on earth doing His bid on you. Omar.
Araf.
7:33 Say: My Lord forbids only indecencies, such of them as are apparent and such as are concealed, and sin and unjust rebellion, and that you associate with Allah that for which He has sent down no authority, and that you say of Allah what you know not.

Please know Mary wasn't prepared for his prophesy when he claimed it to them.
Please know it was clear when prophethood came to him he was carried to them but they denied her and him,

Please know this is the nature of Bani-Israel that they deny the prophets and think they are right in things.

Please know so it was with Jesus and he fought them as they have to be fought now when they fight the Prophet's people.

Please know it is over and you know they will never submit and it is only because you are ascendant over them they are peace with you as they were with the Muslims when their ascendency was apparent to them.

Please know Mary was childbirth like any other woman and felt the throes of pain from it,

Please know she would not speak to a mortal as she would be asked about it and she wanted to keep it secret,

Please know she had twins,

Please know the firstborn was Prophet,

Please know she knew it was over and was confused as they were identical.

Please know she upset Him,

Please know berate,

Please know He told her not to speak until she knew,

Please know that is why her childbirth was so intense and why she lamented as she did,

Please Him,

Please know He was upset with her as she was special to Him,

Please know we all lament and it is written so.

Please know He had a plan,

Please know it was to bring her child to them as an adult.

Please know she had to wait until he was grown and she knew for sure it was him who was Prophet,

Please know she had signs as when he was a child he performed miracles but prophethood did not occur until he was baptized,

Please know he was young boy there but not an infant as they think in Islam,

Please know their prophets were older,

Please know they called her chaste before but after his prophethood they said she was a fornicatress,

Please know they were adamant he was bastard,
Please know it is over they say as he is accursed,
Please know that is a plan they say as they hate him,
Please know they say a calumny to this day,
Please know he was no bastard and she was a rape victim when it occurred, her pregnancy there,
Please know Bethlehem,
Please know it was distant from Nazareth,
Please know they did not know anyone and they said she wasn't married as Joseph was not present at his birth, as indicated here,
Please know he was sorry he was not but he was asked to stay away by her,
Please know she wished to be alone,
Please know modest.
Please know I have brought you a strange thing,
Please know it is similar to what she did,
Please know she proclaimed her son to be a prophet of God,
Please know he was a prophet to her alone,
Please know she did not know he was the one to be crucified,
Please know he was only a servant,
Please know it was over when they refused to listen to his words,
Please know they said he was a child to them disdainfully and refused him audience,
Please know he spoke as indicated before that he was a prophet of His eminence,
Please Him,
Please know they were disdainful as he was a young boy to them and they were learned,
Please know he held his own with them but they dismissed him and sought his death eventually,
Please know it is similar for me as I have claimed his metaphor in myself and there are some who dismiss me as mad,
Please know they called him that word,
Please know the Gospel is clear on the matter and our Prophet was similarly called by them,

Please know I am sane,
Please know you speak to me and know it,
Please know state victim,
Please Him,
Please know there is a precedence here and it is obvious what a state victim is,
Please know Jesus and myself were tried as one,
Please know he got crucified and I got killed nearly,
Please know an attempt was made with the idea that it was over,
Please know my mother knew it was but I prayed and survived,
Please know it was a strong toxin and there was recourse to peace afterwards,
Please know I was told it would be seven days I would live there but it was longer,
Please know they finished me off they said with glee as I was a pest there,
Please know I survived it due to resilience,
Please know it is over and they won't win,
Please know I need protection from them as they will do it again if I am vocal,
Please know they gave me a chance to teach and not name them but I relent to.
Please know why?
Please know I have ended it,
Please know Christ is no longer God with you with my teachings to you as you take the Quran for validation,
Please know it is occurring rapidly,
Please know I am a celebrity and they know it,
Please know it is the church that is active and want me arrested or put away where I can't communicate with them,
Please know I am tired though and will lay low if that is what it takes to keep them out of my hair,
Please know the toxins take my hair out,
Please know they have been good recently so I hope they will accept my proposal and I can teach you in the open again as I am a Messiah

there and that's why you let me out, yes, to the Muslims here and elsewhere I am the promised entity of worship not to man.

Please know it is over though and you have the Quran with you and you know it is true to you, unlike your book about things,

Please know I like the Bible and it has things I use in my literature but it has drawbacks as Gospel writers were not accurate,

Please know John was insane by me and made it occur, son of God issues which Paul wanted hm to but it was also so other Gospel writers deterred on truth telling and called him dead materially while they knew it would create godhead in him so they were guilty by us but still they did their bid, the gentile class, who wanted godhead in him and so it became the Christian creed.

Please know it is not like the Quran which is verbatim from Him and collected with more sanity and the message is intact. Omar.

Maryam.

19:23 And the throes of childbirth drove her to the trunk of a palm-tree. She said: Oh, would that I had died before this, and had been a thing quite forgotten!

19:24 So a voice came to her from beneath her: Grieve not, surely thy Lord has provided a stream beneath thee.

19:25 And shake towards thee the trunk of the palm-tree, it will drop on thee fresh ripe dates.

19:26 So eat and drink and cool the eye. Then if thou seest any mortal, say: Surely I have vowed a fast to the Beneficent, so I will not speak to any man today.

19:27 Then she came to her people with him, carrying him. They said: O Mary, thou hast indeed brought a strange thing!

19:28 O sister of Aaron, thy father was not a wicked man, nor was thy mother an unchaste woman!

Please know I am not a braggart but asked to write as I please, says Muhammad.

Please see the following article about him, Jesus to us,
Please know he was articulate,
Please understand his views,

Please know he was sane and exhibited sweetness we have in Islam,
Please know there is 'no god but Allah' here because he had the insight to know his words would be taken out of context.
Please know it is written for him,
Please know he was articulate to an extreme,
Please know Prophet Muhammad matched his articulation,
Please give in,
Please know the prophets have their personal tutor in Him,
Please see a requiem for them in Islam,
Please know we don't understand parables but admire you.
Please see the following preface to my book,
Please know the master of the parable was myself but I am looked at askance when I say it.
Please know Jesus was next in parable knowledge,
Please know my mentor Mirza Ghulam Ahmad was third.
Please know the Prophet understood it but did not like it.
Please know his words were taken out of context.
Please see the following caption on my heart,
Please know I am safe when I use it as the Quran is clear there is no god but Allah and can't be misconstrued,
Please know it is similar for prophethood,
Please know it is a document in the Quran that Muhammad is the Seal.
Please know that means the end,
Please know my words are nothing if they contradict the Quran,
Please know it is similar to my Prophet's words though the context may be elaborated upon.
Please know it has come about there is 'no god but Allah' because the metaphor was explained with painstaking detail.
Please know our Creator is pleased,
Please know why?
Please know it is because He is ascendant over you since you submit to my pen.
Please know the parable Jesus used was explained and Islam came about in you,

Please understand it was a coup.
Please know what coup was here,
Please know America capitulates to my brilliance,
Please know the rest of the world follows,
Please give accolade to my Prophet's group in paradise for teaching me the parable,
Please know I was nothing but a doctor practicing medicine.
Please see a requiem for me,
Please know Omar did it from the power of his pen,
Please know I was subject to humiliation when they portrayed me unwell.
Please give in,
Please know Islam is in your hearts as correct for you.
Please know Ahmadiyyat is served here as they are the most progressive group in Islam now.
Please see the following statement by him who is your savior,
Please know there is no god but Allah.
Please know this is etched forever in the hearts of man.
Please Him,
Please know I am a servant of His.
Please understand requiem,
Please know it is a closing statement from Him,
Please me as I am extraordinarily well.
Please accept my sanity as sane for you and your child.
Please know it has occurred that I am held hostage and medicated by force,
Please know I don't need it.
Please know the government is powerful.
Please know a requiem,
Please know I stayed on medication so I could teach,
Please know they medicate me so they can say I am unwell.
Please know America knows better and reads my word with enthusiasm,
Please see if anyone is read more widely than me,
Please see if anyone is more viral than me,

Please know I came to fulfill the hadith of Prophet Muhammad, on him be peace, that I will have a pen that will be read in households through a wire,

Please know that is the internet cable,

Please see a following hadith about me,

Please know he will have the ears of an elephant and eyes of a pig,

Please know why?

Please know I am clairvoyant and hear things from Him and I see through your eyes,

Please know pig meat is admixed with food here,

Please know it is possible that I was misconstrued in the past but it is clear I am not a prophet in the actual sense,

Please know a metaphor is not real in this case as the Quran is adamant that our Prophet was the last of the prophets.

Please know what I mean when I say I am him,

Please know the Prophet and I are one in repose or thoughts to you as I accept him in his teaching to me,

Please see it occur that I am saint and he is prophet.

Please see some additional comments about him who is your savior and myself.

Please know he was a Messenger with Him,

Please understand this,

Please know he used to partake in food, which is for earthlings,

Please know he had an earthly body,

Please give into this reality that we are human if we eat food,

Please know it is over for them who utter blasphemy that he is God,

Please know it is over when the reality hit you that he was 'one with Him',

Please know you understand the metaphor,

Please bear it,

Please know what?

Please know the truth of the Quran which is literal in its conveyed Word. Omar.

Please know it is bane to be without the reality of the Quran for you.

Please know the atonement issue is coming up as people want to wish there is no accountability.

Please know the Old Testament is clear we will be judged and the Quran is clear there is a balance for us in the Hereafter.

Please know Christians have been taught if they consider Jesus their savior he will save them on Judgment Day and there will be no accounting.

Please know these are stories they have been indoctrinated with and these teachings are not of Jesus but of their Satan, Paul, and others who followed him.

Please know it is over and these are words of their mouth and they are in doubt about it as their lord stated he was accountable as indicated here and they realize they made up things to appease people into coming into Islam they created.

Please know it is disconcerting to you but true what he says as it is validated by the Quran in clear terms,

Please know it is better to live with reality than a fool's paradise as it will not be accepted from you, your clamor, and Jesus will have to wait until your cleansing occurs before he can take you out of it.

Please know I pray for you that you accept reality we are all accountable.

Please know the principles of the Quran are sane to be with and we realize our worth when we apply them on ourselves.

Please know our Creator is strict with us when we take Godhead in him who creates naught and is himself created,

Please know I mean Jesus and other created entities.

Please know your Creator loves you as He warns you to go aright,

Please know it is because He loves you that He warns you,

Please know you don't know better than Him,

Please know you harm yourself when you commit calumny to Him and He wishes you well as He saves you by my pen,

Please know Prophet Muhammad is your guide as I bring you verses from the Quran,

Please know he wishes you well as well as he does not wish you to be harmed by Him as you continue in your inordinacy as His punishment is real for blasphemy.

Please know the verse from the chapter Mary.

Please know it is a blasphemy,

Please do not say it,

Please know you have Jesus' teachings with you these are metaphors, like the world is a stage is a metaphor,

Please know there is no real reality in it and it depicts a state of association with Him,

Please Him,

Please do not commit calumny again,

Please know He has warned you that you come through with Islamic concept,

Please know He loves you and wishes you well.

Please know however His law is real and He has no associate,

Please know they are all servants of His,

Please know all are judged,

Please know all are debtors as Jesus said and we need to be forgiven,

Please see Matthews 6:12.

Please know it is Jesus' prayer that he be forgiven as he forgives others their sins to him,

Please know he says there is no atonement as he will be judged,

Also he asks us to pray to the Creator there for forgiveness and does not state he will be the one with intervention for them.

Please know the concepts in Jesus' mind are the same as what the Quran states,

Please know he was a prophet you took in an out of context way and applied Godhead and sonship.

Please know we are all alone in front of Him being judged.

Please know some will be saved and there will be love for them,

Please don't say that you will enter Paradise without being judged as your prophet says otherwise and the Quran contradicts you here,

Please know He says a bearer of burden does not bear the burden of another in it,

Please yourself and see Him,

Please know He has given you warning do not blaspheme Him. Omar.

Maryam.

19:88 And they say: The Beneficent has taken to Himself a son.

19:89 Certainly you make an abominable assertion!

19:90 The heavens may almost be rent thereat, and the earth cleave asunder, and the mountains fall down in pieces,

19:91 That they ascribe a son to the Beneficent!

19:92 And it is not worthy of the Beneficent that He should take to Himself a son.

19:93 There is none in the heavens and the earth but comes to the Beneficent as a servant.

19:94 Certainly He comprehends them, and has numbered them all.

19:95 And every one of them will come to Him on the day of Resurrection, alone.

19:96 Those who believe and do good deeds, for them the Beneficent will surely bring about love.

Please know this is you if you wish it, rather than a paradise of your choosing where punishment is your norm.

Please know I am farehoon for you, surely I am, that you are going to make it to heaven in the Hereafter but I know there are many turmoils ahead unless you submit to me telling you edicts must be obeyed as you are lackluster in obedience skills, as you never knew a law existed for you.

Please know I ask you if this is you that you submit?

Please know the affirmative occurs but you stray excessively,

Please know the shahada is enough you say but is it I ask of you?

Please know there are terrors at night for you currently.

Please know Islam is served here when I tell you you will come through but it is your choice, not hers who guides you otherwise,

Please know you know the truth of the Quran but you are desultory and think it of no accord to follow its precepts, thinking knowing is enough though you are better now in it, the Quran edicts to you than before.

Please know we know it is necessary for you to follow it otherwise there is hell awaiting you if you do not practice it.

Please know I do this to shame you into action, as life is once living only.

Please know it was all over for you as you thought you were right there was no reckoning,

Please know you used to dismiss me when I warned you before, you would not be going there as you thought me backward with my Islam for you.

Please see this verse which is the reason Islam prevailed here,

Please know I care you ignore this if you want paradise of your choosing,

Please know I knew you weren't going to make it and my Prophet asked me to protect you as you had some virtue that he did not like but knew you were willing to learn,

Please know now you came through and paradise is yours instead of the Hellfire you were promised with,

Please know you relent to the truth, that is your quality that gave you peace from her.

Please know I am kind and knows it is a long way to go but your reality occurred with the shahada and Fatiha some and you are ready for acclaim to occur.

Please know you will raise yourself from doldrums to achieve it, a civilization worth reckoning, where you are fair instead of this desultory state where you lie in court as a norm,

Please know counting God as One is the first step to salvation and there are many good deeds you need. Omar.

Maida.

5:72 Certainly they disbelieve who say: Allah, He is the Messiah, son of Mary. And the Messiah said: O Children of Israel, serve Allah, my Lord and your Lord. Surely whoever associates (others) with Allah, Allah has forbidden to him the Garden and his abode is the Fire. And for the wrongdoers there will be no helpers.

5:73 *Certainly they disbelieve who say: Allah is the third of the three. And there is no God but One God. And if they desist not from what they say, painful chastisement will surely befall such of them as disbelieve.*

Please know a metaphor was applied in his works as you all know from his literature.

Please know these are the teachings of Paul you follow in your churches,

Please know Jesus himself was a monotheist as has been conclusively proven by literature on the subject.

Please understand law,

Please know it can't be changed of significance and Jesus upheld it.

Please know it is upheld because it is true what God creates is upheld in law forever,

Please know Jesus went back in time you say,

Please know these are words of your mouth while the Quran confirms him as an angel, fallen once, then right in repose because he was spent,

Please know it is over and you know he contradicted you in your pews and told there was only One God he worshiped as I elaborate in your book that the Quran validates,

Please know conjecture is to die in ignorance as there is adequate proof here,

Please know to submit to you as your child believes it,

Please know blasphemy says otherwise and you get taken away for good until He relents to save you.

Please see the following words in the pews of late.

Please know I sit in pews with you when you adopt Islamic principles,

Please know right now you are fighting truthful processes in your child.

Please know they are my advocate,

Please know it is true that you kill me in your pews currently as I have brought to clarity what your mentor said when he was faced with him and his protégé there where he taught,

Please know the metaphor was said so they knew he was not God or His son,

Please know they are aware this took place and want me silenced,

Please know when it was said that a metaphor was used I gave an example from Gospel of Thomas to indicate his vernacular and you immediately saw he was adept in using it as a negative metaphor.

Please know you know he was not a god in the negative sense and realized this was an example of a metaphor he used conveying forever the usage of the parable word in the literature of saints and prophets.

Please know my mentor Mirza et al elaborated this when he conveyed to his protege to use their literature in teaching them Christ's metaphor, and I was shown this in his book,

Please know the example of a metaphor is a metaphor,

Please know you have aptitude in understanding this and became upset with me so the judicial car occurred and here I am, in jail proceedings with them in the courts on me.

Please know I have elaborated a metaphor is one even if it is used in the negative sense to elaborate your viewpoint.

Please know it is clear you understood these were metaphorical terms with my second article where I showed you the hadith of Prophet Muhammad, on him be peace, where a servant walks with His legs and talks His words when he teaches and treads in His path and you realized the metaphor of Godhead was real with the prophets so you became inclined to me instead of fighting as I was only doing God's work by teaching you metaphorical terms in Christ's language and in the vernacular of Prophet Muhammad as well.

Please know recently I elaborated further that Jesus denied blasphemy as son literal ways to them which a prophet would do if he was truthful, which he was, as we all know from his literature.

Please know he took son of God in the context of being a prophet doing His work,

Please know he was innocent of your blasphemy on him if you follow Paul's teachings while your comprehension occurs otherwise.

Please know your guilt is clear if you sing his praises as son of His Eminence,

Please know you will be committing a calumny if you do so like the Bani-Israel when they were calling him son of His in the negative metaphor. Omar.

Please know the word is flesh for all the prophets and the rest is aggrandizement of the author about him.

Please know this passage from the Bible is misconstrued as dogma but these were not the teachings of Jesus who indicated it was a blasphemy if he called him son of Him in his conversation in John 10.

Please know dogma is what our Creator says in the teaching of the prophet, not what others say of God or His favorite.

Please know John was in error here where he explained things from him, his friend, who was teaching in the Diaspora who wanted people coming into faith, even if it was faulty to him.

Please know there is no end of aggrandizement we can do to others but a sane approach for you is to take the viewpoint that Jesus promulgated in the Bible which is confirmed in Quranic teachings as I have shown to you, and leave teachings of Paul and others who teach Godhead in him and His sonship in the literal sense of begotten from Him.

Please know there are always two views to an argument but if you follow Jesus and Allah's words in the Quran you are on sure footing and your hereafter is safe from Him Who has shown you the way and expects you to come through rather than fight with vice with you His teachings here on my Facebook page.

Please Him,

Please know he is God in the metaphorical sense as he was His repose,

Please know this is the only way you can make sense of trinity as when you say it literally you confound yourself as you are polytheists then,

Please know Jesus was not a polytheist and worshipped the One God.

Please know this is an innovation,

Please know John testified truth there where he explained these were metaphorical terms,

Please know here he does not make sense and these are Paul's teachings to him,

Please know jury,

Please know you are it,

Please know the flesh becomes the word always with a prophet,
Please know his word was taught to them,
Please know Jesus never said these words, they are not reliable as they contradict his teachings,
Please know I have shown you his teachings, not what was said about him as aggrandizement occurs there with them,
Please know we are all created and Jesus called himself son of man, like any other man,
Please know he did not say he was God.
Please know lie,
Please know he is it.
Please know Paul asked him to say it as he witnessed him,
Please know the Gospel writer is averse but he does it to suit Paul's Diaspora teachings of him to gain ground with them,
Please know gentile mentality was to accept them if they had this avenue of worship of him,
Please know it is similar to church,
Please know they want to worship a man they love,
Please know it is low though and is decried by you who don't bow down to man as it is not worthy to do so.
Please know the church knows me and they know what I teach is irrefutable and candid,
Please Him and accept facts that are irrefutable,
Please know Jesus' own teachings are he is man, did he create you, you ask?
Please know he can't, the DNA is too complex, he didn't know the structure of the cell to create it,
Please don't aggrandize him,
Please him and call him who he was,
Please know testimony is his, not them,
Please know he was the sentinel figure who knew Muhammad was to appear, as his spirit was weak compared to him, to reform you.
Please know he told them to expect him,
Please know he called him his spirit as he was similar.
Please Him,

Please know he never spoke a lie, so give in, he was the expected one.

Please know Spirit of Truth is not an angel in the spirit of things there in his land where he taught the Quran to you.

Please know an angel does not teach man like man can, as I have shown you you have to descend here to teach mankind things.

Please know prophets teach man,

Please him,

Please don't use conjecture, accept what precipitates to the heart as truth from Him,

Please know the Bani-Israel do this and the Muslims do it now.

Please know you are better and are quiet for the most part as we debate.

Please Him and reflect on him and his teachings to you,

Please know what was said about him was aggrandizement,

Please reject it as the Quran tells you to do.

Please know it is the Word with him, our Prophet,

Please know history.

Please know intact for all practical purposes,

Please Him and accept Him,

Please know His Word is sane there.

Please know Muslim heart.

Please know it accepts Him,

Please know it is a different interpretation they fight.

Please know they will get over it and melt as they are Dajjal when they use conjecture to discredit him who is Jesus by calling him things insane to us,

Please know their peace is to lie as well to cover the truth with deceit, like your church does with me,

Please know they will fail, as all will here,

Please know we are the Messiah group meant for world reform,

Please know my son will follow me and be buried with him, my Prophet, there at his place of worship.

Please know I will choose him for it as he is worthy with them, as he is them in Mecca,

Please know it will come to pass so don't disrupt him like you do. Omar.

John 1.

1 In the beginning was the Word, and the Word was with God, and the Word was God.

2 He was with God in the beginning.

3 Through him all things were made; without him nothing was made that has been made.

4 In him was life, and that life was the light of all mankind.

5 The light shines in the darkness, and the darkness has not overcome it.

6 There was a man sent from God whose name was John.

7 He came as a witness to testify concerning that light, so that through him all might believe.

8 He himself was not the light; he came only as a witness to the light.

Please see these verses from the Quran and biblical text that negate the Council of Nicaea edicts that were published in 325 AD.

Please see the following section from the Quran that says that says that we are all servants of His Who is God, and that we are all created elsewhere in the Quran texts we have.

Please know the Council of Nicaea was a fabrication that took words out of context and implied godhead in Christ equal to that of the Creator.

Please know they called him who is Christ the begotten son, coeternal with Him Who creates, and also called him of the same substance.

Please know these were the result of taking his words in John as meaning one of substance, while it means one of repose or purpose (10:30)

Please know that this is in the section where he describes himself innocent to the Jews.

Please know they understood him and did not stone him.

Please know they realized it was a metaphor he described.

Please know it is clear the biblical texts have been tampered with and none of the essential teachings of Christ are followed.

Please know the Quran brings clarity to view in this and highlights that sonship is only metaphorical, meaning honored slaves of His Essence or Being (see Al-Anbiya verse).

Please know son is used loosely in the Bible text and means a prophet for the most part though Jesus used it meaning Father Who taught the son things and also told his companions to pray to the Father.

Please know the ecumenical texts are false saying that Jesus coexisted with God Essence in that he was always present while we know a son is created and is not present along with the father.

Please know Arianism is false as it equates him who is Jesus with God Essence though less in degree saying that the "Father is greater than I" (John 14:28) as meaning that and it also ascribes sonship to God, which the Quran denies as we see here.

Please know these are fabrications that say the Word was with God coeternally.

Please know the Word we understand is meant to indicate the teachings to him who is Jesus and also the Word to Mary predicting him who is Jesus to be born of man, as mentioned in the Bible on numerous occasions that he was 'son of man' who is Jesus Christ, savior to us in Islam.

Please see it occur that the words 'he dwelt with us in flesh from the Word' is incorrect to follow and has no basis in scripture and is a fabrication by John in his Gospel.

Please know you have to isolate what Jesus said from what was said about him in your biblical texts as there are exaggerations there, as Prophet Muhammad said there to his companions.

Please see that Jesus did not create anything as indicated in the Quran in Furqan where it indicates created beings do not create (see text from Furqan).

Please know this negates the Nicene creed in this and we know that when Jesus existed he did not know the human body or its workings and he could not write the DNA genome to create mankind as maintained in Christian lore from the Nicene creed and other sources they have.

Please know the words in the Bible where Jesus debates the devil and tells him not to tempt him—as it is said in the book to worship the One God only— is evidence that he did not believe as Christians nowadays and that he followed Judaism in this law they had.

Please know this and other locations in the Bible negate that he called himself God in His Essence and that he worshipped Him in Entirety, as the Quran says of him.

Please know in summary we can say that the Nicene Creed has taken out of context Jesus' words and ascribed him divinity while Jesus ascribed divinity only to God as the Bible text elucidates here where he prayed and worshipped Him Who creates only (see sections of the Bible elucidated here). Omar.

Mary

19:88 And they say: The Beneficent has taken to Himself a son.

19:89 Certainly you make an abominable assertion!

19:90 The heavens may almost be rent thereat, and the earth cleave asunder, and the mountains fall down in pieces,

19:91 That they ascribe a son to the Beneficent!

19:92 And it is not worthy of the Beneficent that He should take to Himself a son.

19:93 There is none in the heavens and the earth but comes to the Beneficent as a servant.

Al-Anbiya.

21:25 And We sent no messenger before thee but We revealed to him that there is no God but Me, so serve Me.

21:26 And they say: The Beneficent has taken to Himself a son. Glory be to Him! Nay, they are honored servants—

21:27 They speak not before He speaks, and according to His command they act.

Al-Furqan.

25:1 Blessed is He Who sent down the Discrimination upon His servant that he might be a warner to the nations—

25:2 He, Whose is the kingdom of the heavens and the earth, and Who did not take to Himself a son, and Who has no associate in the kingdom, and Who created everything, then ordained for it a measure.

25:3 And they take besides Him gods who create naught, while they are themselves created, and they control for themselves no harm nor profit, and they control not death, nor life, nor raising to life.

Some excerpts from the Council of Nicaea.

1 Jesus Christ is described as "Light from Light, true God from true God," proclaiming his divinity.

2 Jesus Christ is said to be begotten, not made,

3 He is said to be "of one being with the Father," proclaiming that although Jesus Christ is 'true God' and God the Father is also 'true God,' they are 'of one being,' in accord to what is found in John 10:30: "I and the Father are one."

4 The view that 'there was once when he was not' was rejected to maintain the coeternity of the Son with the Father.

5 The view that he was 'mutable or subject to change' was rejected to maintain that the Son just like the Father was beyond any form of weakness or corruptibility, and most importantly that he could not fall away from absolute moral perfection.

Some evidence of the unity of God preached by Jesus in the Bible text.

Matthew 4:10

9 He said to him, "I will give you all of these things, if you will fall down and worship me."

10 Then Jesus said to him, "Get behind me, Satan! For it is written, 'You shall worship the Lord your God, and you shall serve him only.'"

John 17

1 Jesus said these things, and lifting up his eyes to heaven, he said, "Father, the time has come. Glorify your Son, that your Son may also glorify you;

2 even as you gave him authority over all flesh, he will give eternal life to all whom you have given him.

3 This is eternal life, that they should know you, the only true God, and him whom you sent, Jesus Christ.

4 I glorified you on the earth. I have accomplished the work which you have given me to do."

Please see the Council of Nicaea abrogated here with this concept of the understanding of things of what it means when one says he is 'one with someone.'

Please see the prayer here.

Please know this is the context of using the word 'one with you' in the vernacular of Jesus in that it means unanimity of views and in John 10 he says it as well in 'I and the father are one' and that also means intent there.

These are simple concepts any school child understands these are similar views of things and Jesus was not one with the Jews who wanted to differ with him on issues but his follower is one with him as he says here, further it is clear it is taken out of context in the John 10 verse to imply he was god as well, something that does not make sense to the senses and it is used by them in the Council of Nicaea but the point they make has credence to no one and here it implies unanimity of views as well as deeds for Him, his Creat, and now you know what 'one with God' means don't use it as a pretext of godhead in him. Omar.

John 17.

14 "I have given them your word and the world has hated them, for they are not of the world any more than I am of the world.

15 My prayer is not that you take them out of the world but that you protect them from the evil one.

16 They are not of the world, even as I am not of it.

17 Sanctify them by the truth; your word is truth.

18 As you sent me into the world, I have sent them into the world.

19 For them I sanctify myself, that they too may be truly sanctified.

20 My prayer is not for them alone. I pray also for those who will believe in me through their message,

21 that all of them may be one, Father, just as you are in me and I am in you. May they also be in us so that the world may believe that you have sent me.

22 I have given them the glory that you gave me, that they may be one as we are one:

23 I in them and you in me. May they be brought to complete unity to let the world know that you sent me and have loved them even as you have loved me."

Please know no one can remove your burdens that you create for yourself.

Please see this verse from Anum where it states that no one can remove your sin from you.

Please know the Christian concept of atonement is similar they say but it is so they break the Quranic principle in it and say he who is Jesus took away them your burdens or trespasses while you know the Lord's prayer does not allow that teaching to you indicating there you have to ask forgiveness from your Father.

Please know it is this concept I teach that gets me fried by them in the church community as they don't want to give in on atonement issues saying that Jesus died for your sins to go away- poof- and we know our savior there never said that as Jesus taught you the words of the Lord's prayer and it was Paul who formulated teachings of atonement so that you would have no accountability and law was obsolete in your hearts and you could merrily sin on and yet say you will go to Heaven after you die, a concept not permitted in the Quran whereby your entry there occurs if your good deeds are heavy on the scales of mercy He has for us. Omar.

Anum.

6:163 No associate has He. And this am I commanded, and I am the first of those who submit.

6:164 Say: Shall I seek a Lord other than Allah, while He is the Lord of all things? And no soul earns (evil) but against itself. Nor does a bearer of burden bear another's burden. Then to your Lord is your return, so He will inform you of that in which you differed.

Please know an excerpt from an encyclopedia show that James the Just was a monotheist who was permitted entry in the Holy of Holies temple sanctuary.

Please know it is for your perusal to know that early Christians used to visit the temple and considered it blasphemy to call him God or His son as it was against the law and punishable by death,

Please know James was their head and knew what Paul was teaching in the Diaspora was illegal and resulted in his excommunication and later arrest by the Temple authorities, of which he was a member,

Please know Paul changed law, something not permitted in the Temple hierarchy, as could be seen when Jesus was asked in Matthews and he replied One God do you serve.

Please know a new religion evolved but had the bearings of falsehood in it,

Please know Paul was successful in it and you considered him saint while he has been exposed by my page to you as one who was subversive and changed edicts from Him so that your entry in Hell could occur.

Please know that was his intent as he wanted polytheism for you and permitted in it things not permitted in law from Him so he could extrude you from entry into Paradise, which he told you would occur, again without any basis in law to you and him.

Please know they know the Gospel of Thomas is damning as it returns Christians to monotheistic principles that James taught,

Please know it is data we trust for you as it is clear,

Please know it was used for many years in the church I mentioned here,

Please know it was vetted before it appeared,

Please know they know the data is damning so they declare it weak and unsound, while it met coherence with them,

Please know this is the data bank in my view that we need to preserve,

Please know the church dogma is Christ is a savior is incorrect as they take him to be God and it is a cover for you.

Please know the Gospel of Thomas is apocryphal but was considered correct in the Eastern church until it was banned as it created confusion in people,

Please know it is correct to view and its data is valid,

Please know the church had vested interests for declaring it apocryphal,

Please know they do this to any material they find offensive to their views of Godhead in him,

Please know the church has done its best to maim me so my literature is not read,

Please know they will continue until you take charge and disband them from me.

Please see this section from the Encyclopedia of the New World.

Please know James the Just was a monotheist,

Please know he was accepted by the hierarchy of the Jews residing there in Jerusalem and its environs,

Please know he was a regular at the Temple,

Please know he had access to the sanctuary so he was involved in teaching Judaism to people,

Please know he was one of the churches of Jerusalem the tithe was due to.

Please know the Temple authorities were against this,

Please know he fought for his rights and won them,

Please know they were angry as he was Christ's disciple and not a disbeliever like they were,

Please know he was subject to abuse because of his views,

Please know he was victim of them like Jesus and others, eventually he lost as he knew lies sometimes win but it is not so now as you are astute and the Quran is there for validity.

Please know he fought and won his way using Jewish law that he was not a blasphemer as he considered Jesus a man and prophet and he was entitled to his views,

Please know they wanted to blaspheme him, so they created an issue,

Please know they said was he alive?

Please know he replied in the affirmative but wouldn't tell more.

Please know they made up a story that he considered him with Him,

Please know it is narrated correctly here and facts are distorted by historian Josephus,

Please know he wanted him a blasphemer,

Please know it is over and you know law cannot be ignored by early Christians, like James and others.

Please know it was the church dogma to make it easy so that you would enter it but religion got distorted and blurred,

Please know you lost dogma from Him,

Please know your law became nonexistent as you were told Jesus was your savior in regard to the person who will take you to Heaven but you lost ground when you were told you would not be accounted for, while that was not true as Jesus never said that.

Please know you know it is only a figment that Paul made up that he died for your sins,

Please know it has no basis in dogma of his.

Please know the Gospel of Thomas is clear that crucifixion was not important, unlike Paul's teachings,

Please know the dogma was created later under the influence of the Catholic Church they adhered to later in their history.

Please know this is the dogma of Jesus that they adhered to in the early Christian faith that accountability occurred with Him, the Creator,

Please know they considered the church to be invaluable to them and when Paul tried to convert them they excommunicated him as he was calling him God.

Please know the early Christians would not consider him a deity,

Please know they had Jewish beliefs and believed he was Prophet of theirs who taught unity of God to people,

Please know this is the Christ we know in Islam,

Please know there is reason to exclaim,

Please praise him in your hymns but do not commit blasphemy to him by calling him his Creator actually.

Please know the following passage is an opinion but shows how his life was,

Please know the Gospel of Thomas was clear in that crucifixion was not important as Thomas knew he survived and what they were saying that he came back to life was not important,

Please know it was a cover for him to imply death, though it was some who said it and was not popular belief as the teaching of James show.

Please know to look at data before you make any assumptions about me,

Please know I am human and you must be positive about my literature as we can all make errors or adjust the data we use.

Please know my data is accurate though and it shows early Christians were monotheists like our car in Islam is,

Please know Islam is what is expected of you as Prophet Muhammad is World Prophet to you since he is mentioned he will come to perfect you in the Gospel of John,

Please know Jesus had a sibling in him and said he would send him as the Spirit of Truth,

Please know Prophet Muhammad is older but came later, but was sent to perfect the teachings of Him by himself in the Quran to you.

Please do not view data as apocryphal just because the church does as there is a different opinion here which they inhibit from you.

Please know the Gospel views the leader after Jesus left would be James and so he was appointed by them,

Please know he was a true stalwart and did not let Paul get his way.

Please know his life proves he was just and monotheistic, like Jesus was,

Please know it is over but I suggest you return to monotheistic dogma your star had and not follow the dogma of trinity in your life. Omar.

Web source here.

Was James' Christianity more concerned with establishing 'God's Kingdom on Earth?' is a question that emerges from this theory. For James to have been able to enter the Holy of Holies suggests that he was not regarded as a heretic, or with disfavor, by the Temple authorities, that is, by the High Priest at least up until shortly before his death. Was it jealousy that provoked Ananus ben Ananus? Eisenman thinks it likely that James had objected to the misbehavior of wealthy priests in the Temple who violently appropriated the tithes due to 'Priests of the Poorer Sort and represents him as a 'leader of the multitude of Jerusalem' locked in a type of class-struggle with the aristocratic priests. James was the leader of 'the poorer priests.'

A Christianity for which the Cross was not so central, too, would certainly have had implications not only for historical relations with Jews but also with Muslims, most of whom do not believe that Jesus was crucified. It has been argued that the Gospel of Thomas's lack of a crucifixion narrative is not only due to its style of writing, which is a collection of sayings rather than a chronological account of Jesus life, but also because, whether it happened or not, the crucifixion was not essential to its theology.

Excerpt from Gospel of Thomas.

12 The disciples said to Jesus, "We know that you are going to leave us. Who will be our leader?"

Jesus said to them, "No matter where you are you are to go to James the Just, for whose sake heaven and earth came into being."

Please know he was monotheistic and knew what he was doing would defile the believer in him.

Please know Paul was a monotheist as I show you here,

Please know they were friends, his monotheist bunch, and they crafted it out a polytheist religion for them,

Please know it is easy to do when you are nascent.

Please know this post shows how he permitted things not in the law.

Please know the council forbade him,

Please know he told them he will do as he please as he had a following then,

Please know he was excommunicated after that and was formally arrested by them,

Please know the church had power to do so for heresy to them,

Please know he never got out of prison and Allah punished him severely with death,

Please know he changed religion though and it ignited an uprising when he was killed by them as he was god-like in repose to them,

Please know he perished for sin to him,

Please know he was subversive and knew it would occur, his banishment, he was ready for it,

Please know he made pig meat halal for you,

Please know it was not Peter who said to eat pig as he was Jewish council and followed them,

Please Him,

Please know he made halal for you things Allah prohibited so he is your god if you follow him rather than the Jewish law of halal meat.

Please know a thing sacrificed to an idol is not to be eaten but Paul permit it.

Please know he knew it was against the law.

Please know it is evil to do for a monotheistic faith but he permit for a purpose.

Please know he wanted to make you idolaters,

Please know it was his repose when he saw you were Christian to make you weak in it,

Please know he knew fornication would strife you.

Please know he committed an act of heresy and was committed by them in the council that forbade him from doing so to their religion of Christ followers. Omar.

Corinthians

5 For though there are things that are called "gods," whether in the heavens or on earth; as there are many "gods" and many "lords";

6 yet to us there is one God, the Father, of whom are all things, and we for him; and one Lord, Jesus Christ, through whom are all things, and we live through him.

7 However, that knowledge isn't in all men. But some, with consciousness of the idol until now, eat as of a thing sacrificed to an idol, and their conscience, being weak, is defiled.

Please know Paul's teachings were subversive and make sense to you as you want no accountability.

Please know women will never accept this that they are mere chattel to men and should not be understood as sane vicegerents that Allah has created mankind to be,

Please know chattel is my word as slave is what he represented them as,

Please know women have rights and Islam knows them to be independent and living free in the future,

Please know Heaven is for independent ones, it is in this life they are under care of men,

Please know that is nature here but we know they are independent in their rights.

Please know to be circumspect there in your church as Paul used his head and was not revealed like we are in Islam,

Please know Jesus was mere chattel to him as he gained ascendancy with them in the Diaspora.

Please know he was a megalomaniac and thought he was a prophet though he made that claim to some but not all his followers,

Please hate him from us in Islam as he was Jesus' adversary and taught him differently as I have shown here.

Please know he hated Islam and did not want you to enter it,

Please know he asked you to eat pig meat, meat sacrificed to idols and to commit fornication,

Please know these were prohibited in the law of Islam then and he made you apostates thereby.

Please know him,

Please know he had the devil's input in things.

Please Him instead and make your law lean,

Please go to Him in peace and reject your savior, in negativity, as what he says is not true to you.

Please bear him who says you must repent your doubts.

Please know however Jesus never taught you to worship him nor did he say you would be forgiven for worshiping him,

Please know these are Paul's words to you and he was a proven liar in court there and was excommunicated.

Please know he broke with the Jerusalem council and was excommunicated by them,

Please know what he said has bearing if you respect him but it is not true, these things, as he used conjecture and tales like saying he was begotten by Him,

Please know he called him son of God,

Please know the gospel of John is well known to you where I quote this blasphemy to Him,

Please know these are three things he introduced to you which made you fell from Him,

Please know it has bearing if you wish it but God knows he was a liar to you and Jesus was truthful.

Please know I am a student of your Bible so excuse my vernacular of anger,

Please know Islam permits women to speak in mosques and correct religious leaders if they make sense there,

Please know Prophet Muhammad took counsel from his wives and told Aisha she would impart two thirds of Islam to them,

Please know she was a religious scholar of her time after him,

Please know Islam has allowed women's input until demagoguery occurred,

Please know it is over and you know Islam is fair.

Please know these are the teachings of Timothy one to me,

Please know he knew the truth yet portrayed Godhead in him as the son of God came to redeem the sins of mankind,

Please know he was a prig who told women to be quiet as if they had no intellect to correct men,

Please know he used conjecture to support his views saying Eve was deceptive,

Please know they know I am Paul's adversary,

Please know I will let you see my words are for you to see he was a prig and not to be respected by man for his views,

Please know it is over and you know he changed religion to support his views,

Please know that is a Bani-Israel act. Omar.

Timothy.

3 For this is good and acceptable in the sight of God our Savior;

4 who desires all people to be saved and come to full knowledge of the truth.

5 For there is one God, and one mediator between God and men, the man Christ Jesus,

6 who gave himself as a ransom for all; the testimony in its own times;

7 to which I was appointed a preacher and an apostle (I am telling the truth in Christ, not lying), a teacher of the Gentiles in faith and truth.

Also Timothy.

9 In the same way, that women also adorn themselves in decent clothing, with modesty and propriety; not just with braided hair, gold, pearls, or expensive clothing;

10 but (which becomes women professing godliness) with good works.

11 Let a woman learn in quietness with all subjection.

12 But I don't permit a woman to teach, nor to exercise authority over a man, but to be in quietness.

13 For Adam was first formed, then Eve.

14 Adam wasn't deceived, but the woman, being deceived, has fallen into disobedience;

15 but she will be saved through her childbearing, if they continue in faith, love, and sanctification with sobriety.

Please know this verse from Acts II shows that it was inconceivable that the law of Moses be abrogated at the time the council met for deliberation.

Please know Paul and Barnabas were responsible for changing Jewish law which was the law that God gave them in early Christianity,

Please know this was God's gift to man that they had a law to conduct them by in life and He never meant it to be abrogated as you know from Christ to you who would not teach the Gentiles for fear it would be law of a different kind they have,

Please know it occurred as there was a frenzy to convert people that Peter established as correct though it was law for him not to convert them,

Please know Peter's mistake was to think he was apostle for which law was given different than his Prophet.

Please know that was Peter in his thinking and he had credibility with some,

Please know he was an apostle of his and knew the law would be different for them as he was a member of the Jerusalem council and partook in their decision to relent to them on matters such as circumcision, not allowing leeway on major issues of Mosaic dispensation.

Please know it was a concerted decision to convert that was in error to the teaching of their Creator to Jesus and it lead to much bloodshed in history of Christian lore as you know from history books as they had butchery in dealing with people because of it in monotheism not,

Please know the council met on principles of Judaism allowing exemptions in certain laws,

Please know the only law they relented on was circumcision and at that time the Godhead of Christ was not considered to be important,

Please know Paul continued his subversion in making people idolaters who followed Jesus and tried hard to make them deviate from the path Allah chose for them in the Torah,

Please know he and James would debate on these issues and finally the council was called as they were not reconciling to their different viewpoints,

Please know it is over and I have shown you they were Jews who took Jesus for Christ and looked upon him as correct to follow in his views,

Please know Jesus was a Jew who never ate pig meat and was circumcised,

Please know you must follow the example of the prophet you follow and not the teachings of Paul who was subversive to them and wanted them destroyed while he used to follow Jewish custom and law to an extreme,

Please know I have shown you acts of his where he promoted idolatry in you.

Please know this is James to give in on the Abrahamic principle because he was outnumbered,

Please know this is what we do in Islam but it must be obeyed,

Please know it was Paul in the Diaspora who taught this that they did not need circumcision but it is law they must in the Torah, which they upheld then,

Please know there was no mention of pig meat as it was inconceivable that it would be permitted when the council met in 50 AD or so.

Please know Paul was culprit in not following the council's decision about prohibited foods and allowed them to eat whatever was in the market which included pig meat and that sacrificed to idols, something abhorred in our law of Islam here for you. Omar.

Acts from the pen of Luke the apostle for the council he wrote this.

It is my judgment, therefore, that we should not make it difficult for the Gentiles who are turning to God. Instead we should write to them, telling them to abstain from food polluted by idols, from sexual immorality, from the meat of strangled animals and from blood. For the law of Moses has been preached in every city from the earliest times and is read in the synagogues on every Sabbath. (Acts 15:19–21)

Please know Paul was a disgrace for you and you can follow him if you wish for Hellfire, as there is no truth there.

Please know I am Paul's metaphor as I bring you his teachings,

Please know he was successful though as he brought masses to your faith which would have been a sect of Judaism if he had not done so, so God took use of his evil to remove you away from them,

Please know God works like that but we are guilty for the evil and we are punished for our intent,

Please know I am punished for a sin I commit and you will be as well.

Please know you cannot sit beside a wall and say it does not exist as what you say about fornication currently and ignorance will drive you to hell there,

Please know in this country we are taught laws have to be learnt,

Please know ignoring them will drive you to jail.

Please know I am kind to you but you know threat is necessary for you.

Please Him and learn His word does not change, it is man that abrogates it.

Please know these are Paul's teachings.

Please know he believed in one God and it would come out in his teachings but it was clear he made up things to please the Gentiles and bring them in the teachings of God, as other Christians do to bring masses to them though ignoring the teachings of Christ himself who professed belief in Him alone as his savior for him, like we do in Islam

Please know Paul made conflicting statements that occur when you lie to others to bring them to a faith weaker than the original as Jesus followed it, the book, while Paul abdicated it though told not to by the council of Jerusalem in 50 AD or so.

Please know James was just and did not allow the abrogation of it but was outnumbered by the apostles who were in a frenzy to convert even though their mentor did not in his teachings to them,

Please know they were taught not to but it was a later innovation they said he did so.

Please know I am not against Paul as he was human and had faults like we all do but he was subversive to him, so my slant is to be him in vocalicity,

Please know I am vocal as I know what I am up against as you go aggressive in your slant against me for deriding your prophet Paul who changed religion on your behalf so you could eat pig and fornicate at your leisure.

Please know it s well known in Islam they had that he said if you have faith in him, Jesus there, then the law is negligent for you and you will make it thus going against our savior Jesus and others before him who upheld law for them, the Bani-Israel clan they had.

Please know he permitted you lay of the land which you do thinking you will be redeemed,

Please know there is no basis for his teachings in the scripture of Jesus or the Torah which you follow if the interest provokes you to see what they did in the past.

Please know the past is the same as now and you can't get away from facts from Him.

Please know the Quran validates the law still exists and fornication is not free to do.

Please know Paul eradicated law for you so that you would come to him, as he desired that.

Please know there are many who convert their faith so they can do as they please. Omar.

Please see Paul was corrupt but so were you who followed him knowing there was monotheism in Islam they had, the Bani-Israel door.

Please see Matthews here where he says things about the end of time of Judaism as it is clear he is referring to the temple stones in his speech to them and not later times we have currently when I have appeared as a messiah here

Please know the 'one who deceives' is Paul to you as he changed law and created a temple hierarchy to occur that lead to its fall with the death of James the Just there who was stoned for teaching monotheism to them and they hated his piety.

Please see Paul abrogated law and many did come into the fold of Christ but it is so it led to many wars and the destruction of the temple did result as the Romans did not like it that their people converted to him in his teachings to them and he did call them evil.

Please see Paul was a prophet to them and by us in Islam that is a false statement.

Please know there is no prophet between Jesus and Muhammad though Paul did change religion as prophets do, that's why you call him that in this culture, but many a priest know he was false and created polytheism in the midst of a monotheistic faith that they had there in Christian land that emerge after Jesus taught, and the Quran corroborates it, Jesus' teachings, so you are satisfied Paul was corrupt and taught you differently from Jesus and earlier prophets you had, further, he was messiah to many and many wars did result because of his teachings.

Please know he called himself that that he was prophet there.

Please know Jesus knew it would occur but was sad his teachings would be taken out of context and words like 'I am' and 'I and the Father are one' would be used by them to create a new religious belief that Paul headed, not him, further, it is said the church followed Christ, but did it, it did not, he upheld law and Paul and others abrogate it, so there occurs. Omar.

Matthews 24

1 Jesus left the temple and was walking away when his disciples came up to him to call his attention to its buildings.

2 "Do you see all these things?" he asked. "Truly I tell you, not one stone here will be left on another; everyone will be thrown down."

3 As Jesus was sitting on the Mount of Olives, the disciples came to him privately. "Tell us," they said, "when will this happen and what will be the sign of your coming and of the end of the age?"

4 Jesus answered: "Watch out that no one deceives you.

5 For many will come in my name, claiming, 'I am the Messiah,' and will deceive many.

6 You will hear of wars and rumors of wars, but see to it that you are not alarmed. Such things must happen, but the end is still to come.

7 Nation will rise against nation, and kingdom against kingdom. There will be famines and earthquakes in various places.

8 All these are the beginning of birth pains.

9 Then you will be handed over to be persecuted and put to death, and you will be hated by all nations because of me.

10 At that time many will turn away from the faith and will betray and hate each other,

11 and many false prophets will appear and deceive many people.

12 Because of the increase of wickedness, the love of most will grow cold,

13 but the one who stands firm to the end will be saved."

Please see the origin of the words of commemoration of Jesus are from these verses and other interpositions in their book, the Bible to them.

This is the origin of commemoration of Christ in their Jewish faith of Christianity as they think their prayers will be accepted this way but the words are interposed here it is not for a prophet to glorify himself with regards to the law of prayer in Islam we have and a prayer should be short and direct to Him, their Creator, without any human intervention.

Please know this is the custom of Bani-Israel people to interpose words in their literature and the Christians followed suit here and now shirk has occurred as they cannot approach their Creator except in this way of commemoration of their god to them and it is decried in Islam, this sort of intervention they had from their prophet who made it clear not to do so but to ask and be given in His wisdom to you as Muslims know some prayers are accepted not or late and some are early, but it is so we should beseech Him with confidence that He will hear it when asked directly of Him and no one else otherwise He may never accept a prayer in that fashion, now you know so don't do it, it is like asking Jesus of things and not your Creator and be warned your prayer may be wasted this way but it is so your churches advise you to continue but you should not, Allah is your Creator and your pastor is not and that is shirk too if you listen to him rather than Allah and His Prophet there.

See these words here are shirk in the sense that he says he will do it and not his Father which goes against the dogma of Christ as he always beseeched his Creator in things when he had a need of something and now you know commemoration is wrong and try to make your prayer to Him Who gives things, not Jesus, or for that matter any human, as you know him to be. Omar.

John 14.

12 "Verily, verily, I say unto you, He that believeth on me, the works that I do shall he do also; and greater works than these shall he do; because I go unto my Father.

13 And whatsoever ye shall ask in my name, that will I do, that the Father may be glorified in the Son.

14 If ye shall ask any thing in my name, I will do it."

Please know your destination is known to you as you read me clearly and wish for Paradise to occur rather than Hellfire which will if you go along with them who detract you and me.

Please know there is no crookedness in my works,

Please know I am truthful to you in dialogue and only lie when compulsed for the most part, though some may be inadvertent,

Please know our law allows this as they are manipulative and apply mental disease where there is none and medicate me by force which causes intolerable side effects.

Please see this section from The Elevated Places from the Quran where it talks about the wicked,

Please know there are several classes of people here,

Please know those who reject the truth are in Hellfire,

Please know there are those who hinder men from the truth making it appear crooked to them,

Please see these are the people I refer to who will see it.

Please know they will tell them Paul is right, Omar is unwell.

Please know they will make it crooked what I write saying that he is out of his mind and has mental disease which the government treats.

Please know they are right in a sense and I am subject to medication from them but it is not required and they force it.

Please know my language is the language of the saints and I am careful to show you data so that you are not in doubt about it that your Prophet's opinion is the same as ours in Islam, and the Quran verifies his views,

Please know I don't conjecture and allow you to reach conclusions for yourself providing you the material to read.

Please know it is over and you know Jesus meant the metaphor in his works on godhead in himself and the usage of the term son of God being a parable for a prophet by the same token,

Please know the data is irrefutable and it is now for you to come to terms with my literature being sane for you in other matters I write about as I am sane here when I talk about the metaphor in him,

Please know you are in Araf,

Please know these are the elevated plains and I know people by their marks as when they communicate with me they show their worth,

Please know Araf is a plain with the intellect of a saint as you understand me in your literature of the metaphor and I speak your tongue.

Please know you have a high intellect and so understand me as I am high,

Please know many Muslims don't educate themselves as you do and have difficulty with me,

Please know it was similar for my mentor and they ostracized him, calling him Non-Muslim,

Please know we are on the plain, our group, and we see you entering Heaven,

Please know it is not the same for some who call me unwell to discredit me and therefore the curse of Allah is on them and their destination is Hell,

Please know don't be so and give me credibility that I have given you sanity through my works,

Please know you used to think that son of God in the literal sense made sense to you but was outlandish as well.

Please know you realize it was a metaphor used commonly in your book and in Jesus' own teachings it referred to a prophet or king,

Please know his words are telling to you where he referred to the metaphor to explain himself when he said "I say ye are gods."

Please know I have given you depth of intellect unmatched in your times explaining him whom you love and so you recognize him as a prophet, like Muhammad was a prophet.

Please know it is these two whose intellect I match as I bring you their works.

Please know I am not a braggart; it is clear to you I match them as I bring to clarity their works.

Please know you have raised your intellect to my level as you study me and him, through my interpretation of his teachings.

Please continue to read and give me credit of being credible which only a sane man could be.

Please Him,

Please do not make our Book crooked to others, as it is the truth from Him,

Please know you have found it to be so as you interpret him and realize his message is confirmed in our Quran,

Please know to adopt it.

Please know there are many precepts you know and there are others you will learn, as we are all students of Him. Omar.

Araf.

7:40 Those who reject Our messages and turn away from them haughtily, the doors of heaven will not be opened for them, nor will they enter the Garden until the camel pass through the eye of the needle. And thus do We reward the guilty.

7:41 They shall have a bed of hell and over them coverings (of it). And thus do We requite the wrongdoers.

7:42 And as for those who believe and do good—We impose not on any soul a duty beyond its scope—they are the owners of the Garden; therein they abide.

7:43 And We shall remove whatever of ill-feeling is in their hearts—rivers flow beneath them. And they say: All praise is due to Allah, Who guided us to this! And we would not have found the way if Allah had not guided us. Certainly the messengers of our Lord brought the truth. And it will be cried out to them: This is the Garden which you are made to inherit for what you did.

7:44 And the owners of the Garden call out to the companions of the Fire: We have found that which our Lord promised us to be true; have you, too, found that which your Lord promised to be true? They will say: Yes. Then a crier will cry out among them: The curse of Allah is on the wrongdoers,

7:45 Who hinder (men) from Allah's way and seek to make it crooked, and they are disbelievers in the Hereafter.

7:46 And between them is a veil. And on the Elevated Places are men who know all by their marks. And they call out to the owners of the Garden: Peace be to you! They have not yet entered it, though they hope.

7:47 And when their eyes are turned towards the companions of the Fire, they say: Our Lord, place us not with the unjust people.

Please know we all come to a common meeting ground when questioned about our deeds.

Please know the time has come to tell you most mankind appreciate Him Who creates them and are willing to forego sin some but some exceptions do occur as idolatry does exist and pagan customs are still present in the land which prevents entry in Heaven abode we have there but comprehension has occurred that law is sane to be with.

Please know to follow Islamic injunction here in our Book to us, the Quran there, which has comprehension as law for you in your sanity clause.

Please see the grandeur of the Quran and see if you can match it in any other book of His.

Please know we are all one body if we serve our Master and don't associate with Him,

Please know what makes us different is our notion we are right in one thing and others are wrong, while our root is God.

Please know the Quran is the last Book and our Prophet is the last one on earth.

Please adopt both and gradually assimilate his teachings to you, as our Jamaat elaborates.

Please see the following verse from the Holy Book of ours, the Quran,

Please see the verse signifies we are all brothers there,

Please know it is our deeds that accomplish Heaven,

Please know monotheism is the rule in many religions there but it is so mushriks or polytheists don't make it if they succumb not to the belief of One God to them but we know Sabians do worship Him Who creates as they are believers in nature and do consider them to be created beings.

Please know now you know why it was revealed as you were told it used to be only Muslims will enter Paradise.

Please know it is because lip service exists in it and we tell you all Muslims are not Paradise people.

Please know the same holds true for Christian believers in this country where they have accepted me as their savior but do not conform to the Quran's teachings as it is too different for them,

Please know the essence of us must be good and wholesome for us to make it with Him but I know some of you won't conform to the law, thereby are not permitted entry there in Heaven abode with us,

Please know they know monotheism is essential for them to go into Heaven as elsewhere in the Quran it says a mushrik does not go there,

Please know it means one who is mushrik believes in another God besides Him,

Please know this rule is absolute so beware we are brothers if you believe in Him as One.

Please Him with your deeds.

Please know you cannot enter Heaven without your deeds being heavy in repose to Him,

Please know I am a saint and know I have reckoning to come.

Please know so it is with Jesus as we know he asked for forgiveness.

Please know it is over and you know we are one body in faith.

Please know we may practice differently but we serve the One God in our life's endeavors here on earth.

Please know the other verse is different and refers to other faiths that practice differently in their heart's repose to Him and serve other deities,

Please know these people don't make it with Him even if we know they are good in other respects,

Please know God is strict and they will know it when they are raised for Him to be judged.

Please know they are all submitters though if they serve Him,

Please know all are submitters to Him as He is their Creator.

Al Baqarah,

2:62 Surely those who believe, and those who are Jews, and the Christians, and the Sabians, whoever believes in Allah and the Last Day and does good, they have their reward with their Lord, and there is no fear for them, nor shall they grieve.

Al Hajj.

22:17 Those who believe and those who are Jews and the Sabians and the Christians and the Magians and the polytheists—surely Allah will decide between them on the day of Resurrection. Surely Allah is Witness over all things.

22:18 Seest thou not that to Allah makes submission whoever is in the heavens and whoever is in the earth, and the sun and the moon and the stars, and the mountains and the trees, and the animals and many of the people? And many there are to whom chastisement is due. And he whom Allah abases, none can give him honor. Surely Allah does what He pleases.

Please know your car is your personal property and you will follow a course with it to Him.
Please know we must serve you in Islam,
Please know your car is mine, like the Prophet's is mine, in your heart's repose.
Please Him,
Please know I take you to Him,
Please know you used to think trinity was your home with Him but He showed you differently,
Please know you know it is monotheism home you have with Him with him as your guide as you recognize merit in my thoughts from him, my Prophet,
Please know we all have a home with him,
Please know he is our guest there in Paradise when he comes to visit it from his heaven,
Please know we all see dreams,
Please know he will appear in your subconscious thoughts from Him,
Please see this occur that your guide is him, just like Jesus has a guide in him there in his abode,
Please know your women are my forte who have compassion and mercy as they are His car in their repose to Him and His Prophet Jesus and Muhammad and me as their guide,
Please know to bring my car to you in your home,
Please know by that I mean the metaphor.
Please see the verse where the Quran says that religion is completed for you.
Please know this is your day with us,
Please know Islam is your faith while you say Christian faith is it.
Please know I know you know the truth of it and defend it,
Please know your faith is what you say it is but you defend it with truth in it so you know what I say makes sense to you.

Please know I say I am a Muslim of your heart as you know me and know my worth,

Please know you recognize merit in my works,

Please know you know it has occurred your comprehension we are one faith, only submit differently,

Please know our culture is different in Islam we have but your Islam is acceptable if you pray to Him, your Creator to you, in your dream and with your voice to you.

Please know you know the truth of my submission,

Please know I know you are complete and ready to submit to Him your Creat in your deeds and acts of devotion,

Most of you recognize my merit in teaching you things from our Prophet and recognize him as great with a law you can hearken to, that's why I say you are complete fulfillment of your creed.

Please know you know my car is with my Creator with his, who you have repose will take you to Paradise now that monotheism is your forte and you think trinity outdated and contrived,

Please know my car is his and vice versa,

Please know our Prophet's car is his in Paradise, here his ride is mine as he takes me to your home to be with you in repose to Him,

Please know pure food is your forte and you stay away from it which cause disquiet in you.

Please know the same goes for your women,

Please know they should marry as that is His wish for you.

Please know your culture was different and you thought it was okay.

Please know His displeasure occurs and then punishment is His car when you continue after the initial contact. Omar.

Surah Maida.

5:3 Forbidden to you is that which dies of itself, and blood, and flesh of swine, and that on which any other name than that of Allah has been invoked, and the strangled (animal), and that beaten to death, and that killed by a fall, and that killed by goring with the horn, and that which wild beasts have eaten—except what you slaughter; and that which is sacrificed on stones set up (for idols), and that you seek to divide by arrows; that is a transgression. This day have those who disbelieve *despaired of your religion, so fear them not, and fear Me. This day have I perfected for you your religion and completed My favor to you and chosen for you Islam as a religion. But whoever is compelled by hunger, not inclining willfully to sin, then surely Allah is Forgiving, Merciful.*

5:4 They ask thee as to what is allowed them. Say: The good things are allowed to you, and what you have taught the beasts and birds of prey, training them to hunt—you teach them of what Allah has taught you; so eat of that which they catch for you and mention the name of Allah over it; and keep your duty to Allah. Surely Allah is Swift in reckoning.

5:5 This day (all) good things are made lawful for you. And the food of those who have been given the Book is lawful for you and your food is lawful for them. And so are the chaste from among the believing women and the chaste from among those who have been given the Book before you, when you give them their dowries, taking (them) in marriage, not fornicating nor taking them for paramours in secret. And whoever denies faith, his work indeed is vain; and in the Hereafter he is of the losers.

Please know we are all abject in our creation and will remain so.
Please know our Creator,
Please know Him,
Please understand Him,
Please know He has no need,
Please know He created us not to be Him,
Please know there is no need for another god,
Please know He is the self-sufficient one Who creates with love,
Please know us,
Please understand us,
Please know our nature,
Please know we are in need,
Please know we are all abject before we see Him,
Please know Jesus, Krishna and Buddha were all in need of things and were fed,
Please know they all saw death,
Please know an abject one cannot be God.

Please see this verse from the Quran where polytheism is condemned in whatever form it may be,
Please know it refers to Jesus and others who were taken for Gods,
Please know this,
Please know our Creator is alone in His nature,
Please know all of us are abject ones and must be fed to survive,
Please know our Creator did not create us to be self-sufficient,
Please understand Him,
Please know all creation will see death to show them they are abject ones,
Please know the angels who take our soul,
Please know after taking all souls they too will see death.
Please know it is decreed we will see death,
Please know all man and jinn will know it,
Please know the Quran says there is no one unto Him,
Please know The Immaculate,
Please know The Majestic,
Please know all the attributes of Him,
Please understand Him,
Please know there was no need to create us,
Please know He was self-sufficient,
Please know He wished to be known,
Please see His epitaph,
The Incomparably Great. Omar.
Anum.

6:13 And to Him belongs whatever dwells in the night and the day. And He is the Hearing, the Knowing.

6:14 Say: Shall I take for a friend other than Allah, the Originator of the heavens and the earth, and He feeds and is not fed? Say: I am commanded to be the first of those who submit. And be thou not of the polytheists.

6:15 Say: Surely I fear, if I disobey my Lord, the chastisement of a grievous day.

Please know the abject one cannot be a God worthy of worship.
Please know the abject state is what we are,
Please Him,
Please know we are meant to be abject so people will know we are not gods,
Please know we all live as princes and die as paupers,
Please know by that I mean we think we are self-sufficient,
Please know it is over for them and they know he is man,
Please know it is over as they understand his words and know he was abject,
Please Him and not raise man to God.
Please know the metaphor is okay to show unity with Him in His repose and this is not real.
Please know this,
Please know he was not begotten by Him, the Creat,
Please know He alone is One on Whom we depend,
Please know we pray to Him,
Please know he depended on Him,
Please know his prayer was accepted,
Please know the crucifix,
Please know he was one who survived,
Please know your prayers are to Him Who delivers,
Please know he spent his time in prayer to Him,
Please know he was the abject one,
Please know he was hung,
Please see he was abject and not a creator or god to them in that state as God would not be helpless to others,
Please know he is written as the best of us in trial.
Please know he was pleased with this title,
Please know he is raised in honor with Him,
Please know saint,
Please know that was him and me,
Please know we are His repose,
Please know that it will be accomplished,
Please know you know I teach you him,

Please see a requiem,
Please know we are one in repose to take you there,
Please know there,
Please know it is your destination you are pleased with. Omar.
Surah Ikhlas.
112:1 Say: He, Allah, is One.
112:2 Allah is He on Whom all depend.
112:3 He begets not, nor is He begotten;
112:4 And none is like Him.

Please know we all raise ourselves in spirit when we are tried by Him.

Please know we are faced with this intranquility that we will be tried like he was if we do not appreciate him and learn that man can be tried by Him in order to improve their state.

Please see these verses from The Family of Amran or chapter three.

Please know our Prophet was no exception to the rule.

Please understand we must learn the truth must be served, and Christians and Muslims alike must bend to this rule.

Please know him,

Please know when he passed away none of the companions said why was he not spared?

Please realize this,

Please understand it was in their comprehension that he had passed away.

Please know Jesus is misconstrued to have been lifted to heaven,

Please know this concept came in Islam a hundred years after the passing away of him who is my mentor there, Muhammad to you.

Please know these inaccuracies came about when Christian converts brought their opinions with them.

Please know you cannot create an exception where our Creator did not list him as one who is Jesus there.

Please understand the spiritual elevation of him occurred eventually when people realized his elevated status in the Christian faith and in Islam as well.

Please know they misconstrue certain words of the Quran and think the Christian viewpoint is correct. In this there is certainty that Islam is served if we understand the metaphor.

Please know his elevation was in regards to his spirit as it is in the spirit elevation with Him occurs in the eyes of people.

Please know we all pray that we will be raised in spirit to Him,

Please understand we pray for it,

Please know his spirit left him when he said the words of beration to Him,

Please know he was resurrected in spirit as correct in the Christian Islam there of James the just when he left the Bani-Israel and preached there to his people in India,

Please understand this,

Please know he lost faith in Him when he questioned Him on the cross.

Please know this is a norm for man,

Please understand I would have lost faith if I saw it,

Please know that to him the reality of crucifixion occurred after he had been promised in the garden of Gethsemane the night before that he would live but to accept the cup He gave him,

Please know he thought his God had forsaken him,

Please know to berate is the norm in this setting for mankind.

Please appreciate him,

He was raised and would never berate again,

Please know he was elevated in the eyes of mankind,

Please know they thought he was accursed.

Please know God ascribes messiahship to him and he was not be accursed like they thought of him,

Please know this is the meaning of rafa in the Quran.

Please know his status was raised,

Please know he is with Him in spirit.

Please know the angels and the prophets are in His repose,

Please know our Prophet saw him and he was in the waiting area with John the Baptist,

Please know they are with Him in spirit but wait there for judgment to occur. Omar.

Al-Imran.

3:144 And Muhammad is but a messenger—messengers have already passed away before him. If then he dies or is killed, will you turn back upon your heels? And he who turns back upon his heels will do no harm at all to Allah. And Allah will reward the grateful.

3:145 And no soul can die but with Allah's permission—the term is fixed. And whoever desires the reward of this world, We give him of it, and whoever desires the reward of the Hereafter, We give him of it. And We shall reward the grateful.

Please know in the Muslim world there is much confusion of the interpretation of the words in these verses as they think Isa was not crucified at all.

Please see why a difference of opinion is important in Islam as new data comes to light with time,

Please know rafa means bodily ascension in the metaphorical sense as well as stature with Him,

Please know he will be in Allah's presence when we die here but our body can't travel in space.

Please see the following verses from the Quran from the chapter The Women,

Please know it is over and you know he died there in India with his follower Mary who he married,

Please know Muslims have a hard time assimilating data from our source in Islam so I explain to them the Arabic so they understand there was a misinterpretation from the early Muslim scholars, primarily from the Christian data that came into Islam from converts,

Please see the verse refers to Jesus, not someone else, as is thought by some there in the Middle East,

Please know they take two weak hadith to indicate someone took the appearance of Jesus before the crucifixion attempt but fail to realize it is not possible to do so.

Please know the sources of these hadith are dubious and scholars know I am telling the truth in this regard,

Please know one says Pilate ordered a guard to kill him but then God changed his appearance and he was crucified instead,

Please know the other states a companion was asked to take on his garb and portray Jesus in himself but this is not verified as correct and is unusual for a prophet to do.

Please know a prophet would fight himself instead of killing a companion,

Please know they say the other person was crucified but the word 'ha' refers to Jesus and the other person is not mentioned in the verse so it is not possible for him to be crucified,

Please know the other problem they have is limited knowledge of the Arabic language as salabuhu means killed in a well-known way, not being nailed, as occurred with Jesus,

Please know crucifix is a well-known method of killing but if the person does not die he is said to survived the crucifixion,

Please know they say he never went on the cross but according to Lane's lexicon of Arabic it does not mean that but death on the cross is what is implied.

Please know it further says they use conjecture to say he died but he died not for certain,

Please know both the Christians and Jews say he died but they are not sure as it has transpired that people are in doubt about it with Ahmadi literature being prevalent, as my book shows,

Please know we ascribe to peace with them in Islam as diverse views are important to uphold as correct for some but the Christian faith and the Jews as well know they are in doubt about it as the knowledge has come forth in Islam with us that he survived the crucifixion as the guards dispelled with the breaking of legs even after they knew his heart was pumping, evinced from blood flowing when they pierced him,

Please know it was obvious they weren't going to kill him as he was innocent to two and Pilate too.

Please know Pilate and his wife wanted to save him and told the guard to dispel them, the people, who had gathered and then he appeared to take him away.

Please know Pilate knew he was alive and personally checked with the spear and noted he bled,

Please know then he allowed him to leave and observe the sabbath on his own in the woods there,

Please know it was an innovation they used to say he had died in order to cover his tracks to the people but the Jewish council knew he had survived as there were some members there when he was taken down by Pilate,

Please know Mary did see him on the third day and was appeased as he was clear in his head and not unwell like they were saying of him,

Please see these facts are from revelation but the fact is out he survived there in church quarters,

Please know he remained in disguise after the crucifixion attempt and then left for safer lands,

Please know the other verse that causes confusion is raising spiritually a person,

Please know people thought he was accursed but he did not die there so the curse of a crucifixion death did not occur,

Please know he was raised spiritually as the stature God gave him with man through the teachings in Islam I teach you.

Please know raising is a metaphor we speak of in our prayer when we say 'raise me' in the prayer we have in Islam

Please see Jesus had a flaw, he would gloat on them and took them on in adversary and he was raised in spirit when he saw their might on him and he swore never to berate Him, his God Elohim, Whose promise was true and so was raised in spirit to Him.

Please know it is through hardship and trial we are raised in stature with Him, the Creat, and also in the eyes of man, wife and child so there you have it we commemorate him in Islam as one who is recognized as great by us,

Please know we all need peace and it is over for you in this country as you have understood my book but people in the Middle East are fixated that rafani means lifting bodily, while the metaphor is applied here as no one can lift himself bodily to heaven as the verse I alluded to in a previous comment said as the Prophet is asked to say it is not for a mortal prophet to go to heaven to retrieve a book which they asked him to do.

Please know the last verse I allude to refers to the People of the Book not agreeing with his raising as they thought him accursed,

Please know they will all believe it until his death and it is now you are in doubt about it.

Please know it is over and the Jews and the Christians both used to say he was accursed but he will witness them on the Day of Reckoning that they were wrong and he survived and so was not accursed as they would like to believe,

Please know rafa means bodily ascension as well to high altitude and could signify the travel there to the Himalaya mountains,

Please know we differ in interpretations from Muslim scholars in certain verses but take our arguments from reason supported by hadith literature and other verses of the Quran,

Please know there is a discrepancy there as they refuse to budge but it is to their detriment as we are cogent and make sense to mankind as you know of me and us in Islam here in the West. Omar.

Nisa.

4:157 And for their saying: We have killed the Messiah, Jesus, son of Mary, the messenger of Allah, and they killed him not, nor did they cause his death on the cross, but he was made to appear to them as such. And certainly those who differ therein are in doubt about it. They have no knowledge about it, but only follow a conjecture, and they killed him not for certain:

4:158 Nay, Allah exalted him in His presence. And Allah is ever Mighty, Wise.

4:159 And there is none of the People of the Book but will believe in this before his death; and on the day of Resurrection he will be a witness against them.

Please know the Quran is the most accurate book with you.

Please try to see reason when I tell you to see the truth. I know the Bible has things in it that are contrived and must be subjected to circumspection.

Please see the following verses from the chapter Hud or eleven.
Please know our Creator is the author of it,
Please know He has challenged man to produce a book like it.
Please understand this,
Please know perfection,
Please know I write similarly,
Please know my book is not the Quran though but is similar to what our Prophet would recite from Him,
Please know our Prophet was the recipient of revelation, in addition to the Quran,
Please understand these are prayers of his,
Please know we all have the desire to write from Him,
Please understand this,
Please know it is a gift.
Please try to comprehend my role,
Please know it is like His Prophet Muhammad, on him be peace,
Please know it is to bring you the Quran and let you see for yourself the truth from Him,
Please know there can't be more than one truth on the matter,
Please know the Quran says desist from saying three,
Please know there is no truth in it,
Please know the evidence is clear that it is contrived,
Please know it is the truth in the Quran that your God is One.
Please know it is for you to accept the most accurate Book,
Please know it is certain that Jesus did not say it.
Hud.
11:13 Or, say they: He has forged it. Say: Then bring ten forged chapters like it, and call upon whom you can besides Allah, if you are truthful.
11:14 But if they answer you not, then know that it is revealed by Allah's knowledge, and that there is no God but He. Will you then submit?

Please know the atonement is a reality for some who wish it and don't want to be questioned.
Please know atonement,

Please know it is false,
Please give into this reality that we are answerable for our sins,
Please know it is over for him who fornicates and thinks it is forgiven,
Please know our Creator curses a happy fornicator,
Please know it is over when you think your Creator will forgive you, without your amends,
Please know He is strict with you and us in Islam,
Please know we know the reality that it is a sin,
Please know the Bible says so, as does the Quran.
Please give into this that human life cannot be disregarded,
Please know when you abort you do this,
Please know it has consequences on your Hereafter.
Please know your Hell is written when you sin by killing a human.
Please know the reality is that we are all answerable for our sins,
Please know why?
Please know it is so we can keep straight,
Please know with atonement you feel you can do what you like,
Please know you cannot and the Quran teaches that,
Please understand atonement,
Please know it is mischief in the land,
Please know why?
Please know it is because you think you have a free passage to him who is your savior and he will protect you from Him,
Please know he is not able to protect himself until it be the will of Allah.
Please see the following verse,
Please know it has occurred in your senses that the metaphor explains what you could not understand,
Please know it has been explained adequately and now it is for you to come through,
Please know it is over for the dogma of the church that he was son incarnate,
Please know the mindset in this country finds it incredulous that God would impregnate a woman with His spirit,

Please know these are tales that the immature in intellect would listen to,

Please know it is over and you can enter heaven,

Please know the metaphor has been explained to you and you understand son of God is a title for him,

Please know it does not make sense that God would need an associate when He is all Powerful.

Please give consideration to sanity,

Please know God does appear in mankind as He is transcendent,

Please know we all have God in us as His spirit is in us,

Please know it says in the Quran He breathed His spirit into us,

Please give it a thought for a moment or two.

Please know it is possible for man to be fused with Him,

Please know that is his resolve to work for Him,

Please know then it is correct to say his resolve is one with God and God is with him,

Please know these are metaphors and should not be confused with reality.

Please know it is over for him who gesticulates with anger,

Please know the reality is the Quran which says they are honored servants who are sons of His,

Please know your mindset is clear and it is time you got your act right,

Please know the Quran is clear there is no atonement,

Please know that was a fable created by Paul and others that His only son died for their sins,

Please know how pathetic your arguments are in the face of reality that we are answerable for our sins and there is no free passage to Heaven,

Please know your God loves you and wishes you to be in His presence as servants who know reality,

Please know the Bible and other books got altered,

Please say a prayer that you see it through the teachings of the Quran. Omar.

Hud.

11:108 And as for those who are made happy, they will be in the Garden abiding therein so long as the heavens and the earth endure, except as thy Lord please—a gift never to be cut off.

Please know his passing out was only pretense and it was contrived of as death to suit those who wished to cover for him.

Please know the death of Christ on the cross is a misnomer for passing out.

Please know in the verse that follows it states that everyone must die.

Please know that means Jesus has passed away and was not resurrected. I hope you realize that Jesus did have a body after the crucifixion as Thomas placed his fingers in his wound and he ate as normal mortals do. I know it seems strange to you a person can be resurrected with a body.

Please know it is more plausible that he did not die but was only in a swoon when he passed out on the cross. I am aware as you are that the human body stays on earth after demise and the soul is what emerges and ascends to its Creator.

Please see the following caption there.

Please know we covered up otherwise he would have been killed for certain.

Anbiya.

21:33 And He it is Who created the night and the day and the sun and the moon. All float in orbits.

21:34 And We granted abiding forever to no mortal before thee. If thou diest, will they abide?

21:35 Every soul must taste of death. And We test you by evil and good by way of trial. And to Us you are returned.

Please know your prophet is your harbinger for your health there with Him in Paradise.

Please know our Creator knows that we must believe in the prophet of our time,

Please know it is written in the Quran,

Please see a requiem for him,

Please know it is over for those who change my words,
Please know he never implied he was God,
Please understand he was one with Him in all his deeds,
Please know that means they had the same repose,
Please know it is sane to say you understand the metaphor.
Please give in to the following post.

Please know the implications of the metaphor may be misleading and our Prophet was careful about it.

Please see these verses from the Quran in the chapter of The Women.
Please know the prophet of his time has to be obeyed.
Please know Jesus said this when he said "the way to God was with him,"

Please know this,
Please know our Prophet was similar,
Please know this verse verifies this,

Please know our Creator is strict about obedience to the Prophet and has vouchsafed Hell for those who are disobedient,

Please see one can approach God without the intercession of your prophet but it is so Muhammad's respect must occur,

Please know Jesus was similar,

Please know the people of Bani-Israel were told they would have to respect him and the same holds true till this day.

Please know it is necessary to follow your prophet and not a scholar or saint who gives an interpretation different than the one intended.

Please know this,

Please know Paul changed the religion of monotheism to one where polytheism occurred in it,

Please know our prophet Jesus never said to worship him but see what you did, you broke his oath of One God with you that I teach you again on his behalf who is Muhammad to us,

Please know he used the metaphor when he described himself as His son, like he and the disciples were.

Please know our Prophet knows you have understood this,

Please know our prophet Christ was only a slave of his Creator when he used terminology of the metaphor,

Please know he was allowed to stop using the metaphor after he was nearly killed when they were about to stone him. Omar.

Nisa.

4:64 And We sent no messenger but that he should be obeyed by Allah's command. And had they, when they wronged themselves, come to thee and asked forgiveness of Allah, and the Messenger had (also) asked forgiveness for them, they would have found Allah Oft-returning (to mercy), Merciful.

4:65 But no, by thy Lord! they believe not until they make thee a judge of what is in dispute between them, then find not any straitness in their hearts as to that which thou decidest and submit with full submission.

Please your pastors and take him to be your God while your book tells you otherwise and see the consequences of dismay in your life.

Please see the following post.

Please know it refers to metaphorical terms in man,

Please know there is 'no god but Allah' here,

Please know sin is insidious,

Please know to be clear minded you have to rely on your senses,

Please know it is then you will recognize truth and differentiate it from falsehood.

Please give into this reality they are gods,

Please know they change the teachings of Christ.

Please Him and study the Quran,

Please know it is the criterion.

Please know truth,

Please know it is exact and precise,

Please know that is the Quran,

Please read it and see for yourself,

Please present yourself a gift,

Please know it is to buy a Quran,

Please know our Creator knows it is a manifest sin to change the meaning of His words to man.

Please see these verses from the Quran from the chapter The Women.

Please know this is shirk,

Please understand the Prophet warned us about it,

Please know in its most obvious way it is to call a person a God, other than God Himself,

Please know it means that the person you call Jesus was simply a servant,

Please know it is also to take your priests and pastors to be gods,

Please know this,

Please know that when you take them to represent your God's views while your senses tell you otherwise you are guilty of association,

Please know they are gods to you in the negative metaphor,

Please know a person who changes the word of God to give it another meaning is guilty of being a god in the negative way of being disobedient to Him,

Please know the rabbis were referred to as gods in this sense when God said to them "I say ye are gods"

Please know our Prophet referred to this concept when the Quran revealed that the Christians and the Jews are polytheist.

Please know he explained the Jews were guilty of blindly following their rabbis even though the Torah said differently from them,

Please know your priests are similar. Omar.

Nisa.

4:48 Surely Allah forgives not that a partner should be set up with Him, and forgives all besides that to whom He pleases. And whoever sets up a partner with Allah, he devises indeed a great sin.

4:49 Hast thou not seen those who attribute purity to themselves? Nay, Allah purifies whom He pleases, and they will not be wronged a whit.

4:50 See how they forge lies against Allah! And sufficient is this as a manifest sin.

Please know the godhead we are 'gods' occur when we don't submit to Him and disobey Him.

Please know we admire our Creator the more we humble ourselves to Him. I know you consider this trite but it stands nonetheless as accurate that when we are disobedient to Him with a purpose in our hearts we are acting in defiance to His wishes and thereby elevate ourselves to godhead in the negative sense.

Please see the following from Ha Mim or chapter 41.

Please know in the creation of the Heavens and the earth insight is required as to how it occurred.

Please know we cannot create a thing.

Please know, we, in our disobedience set up partners with Him. I know it sounds trite but that partner is ourselves. I know when we are disobedient to Him we consider ourselves god.

Yours truly knows we are disobedient at times however when we fail we regret our failure.

Please know a humble heart submits,

Please know not to be a God in your entirety and believe He is telling you the truth when He says adorn appropriately and don't join custom in having mates not actually,

Please know a humble heart submits to His complaint on you and do not forsake His word to you that has been there from time immemorable for you.

Your son in repose knows that we cannot take time away or bring it forward like He can.

Please know what I mean when I say this.

The end occurs for those who think it is appropriate for us to put up partners to Him when He creates.

Please know the following,

Please know we cannot create a bug or a fly yet we are willing to dictate to Him our needs and expect for Him to follow through on our demands.

Please know the Heaven is a mass and He creates from it. I know you think a day is twenty-four hours but a day here signifies an age.

The end comes when you cannot imagine His Power and His Magnanimity to you for creating you.

Was this the reason you rebelled?

Please know to instill in your heart these words of His and know His Kindness in creating us out of the universe. Omar.

Ha Mim.

41:9 Say: Do you indeed disbelieve in Him Who created the earth in two days, and do you set up equals with Him? That is the Lord of the worlds.

41:10 And He made in it mountains above its surface, and He blessed therein and ordained therein its foods, in four days; alike for (all) seekers.

41:11 Then He directed Himself to the heaven and it was a mass structure, so He said to it and to the earth: Come both, willingly or unwillingly. They both said: We come willingly.

41:12 So He ordained them seven heavens in two days, and revealed in every heaven its affair. And We adorned the lower heaven with lights, and (made it) to guard. That is the decree of the Mighty, the Knowing.

Please know the art of the metaphor is simple if you but have the heart to learn.

Please know that those who understand metaphors are four.

Please know it is me, and the Ahmadiyya group and the Christians and the Muslims.

Please know we will teach them until there is surety in their hearts.

Please see these verses from the chapter named Muhammad.

Please know we struggle with people.

Please understand they know it is the truth.

Please know that the stalwarts are encouraged to be obedient to our Creator and His representative.

Please see the following caption there.

Please know if we disregard an order we would have lost everything.

Please know such are the believers that their wealth and life are for Him.

Please know we have this life to come around.

Please know that to please our Creator is to please our Prophet and vice versa. I know this is a metaphor they are one.

Please see the similarity.

Please know the prophets are such. If you please them, your Creator will be pleased.

Jesus was similar that he was one with God in this regard. If you understand this you are wise.

Please know they are on earth but they are one body and work in concert. I know it is a metaphor that they are one. Omar.

Muhammad.

47:32 Surely those who disbelieve and hinder (men) from Allah's way and oppose the Messenger after guidance is quite clear to them, cannot harm Allah in any way, and He will make their deeds fruitless.

47:33 O you who believe, obey Allah and obey the Messenger and make not your deeds vain.

47:34 Surely those who disbelieve and hinder (men) from Allah's way, then die disbelievers, Allah will not forgive them.

Please see my diatribe when I explain reality is not in a metaphor.
Please know this verse,

Please know I have repeated it before but I will make use of insight further here,

Please know there are two who did this, Muhammad was the third but he never used it,

Please know Moses was godhead in the metaphorical sense to them and so was Jesus Christ,

Please know He knows I am son but not complete like him, Jesus, or Muhammad,

Please know Muhammad never used the word as it would confuse them, and Moses was called that by them,

Please know the word in Islam is Rabb though as it suits the purpose of Father,

Please know it means one who nourishes unto perfection,

Please know it is over and you have understood there are many sons but few are complete like them I have named here,

Please know they are sons in the true sense as they reflect of Him,

Please know there were others who were sons but were not so severe,

Please know it came as a shock that Jesus claimed Godhead in him in the sense of a metaphor,

MUHAMMAD THE PROPHET

Please know he was sane and proved it to them,

Please know I am similar but not so severe on others if they do wrong,

Please know that is how I survived here,

Please know I am sorry for bringing this up but I am a saint cum prophet, like my mentor was,

Please know metaphorical terms, this is it, and there is no prophet not not after him who is Muhammad Ali not but Muhammad the Prophet, on him be peace in that regard.

Please know we are saints though, prophethood is his who is Muhammad,

Please know it is an epitaph of a prophet but we are not one as we are aks,

Please know that is what he meant when he said he was prophet to them,

Please know it is an aks only as when you reflect of someone you see him,

Please know this term is complex and difficult to understand so I abrogate it that I am prophet, like my predecessor does, Mirza there, as tabulated in his book to us,

Please know Muhammad was the last prophet the world will see and we are his aks,

Please know I have said it so you can understand him and why he said it,

Please know it is similar if I say "I am Allah as a metaphor" it is aks but I am not Him,

Please know that is why reverence is bad for me,

Please know I am sad I have to explain it as it causes confusion.

Please know it was revealed to us from Prophet Muhammad so I have to express it that I am prophet as well as him in the sense of aks or metaphor, as aks is an image and not real.

Please know when he explained it to him he clarified it was a metaphor but it got transmitted wrong and they call him a prophet, though he was not.

Please know I am sad as you will use it against me but I have no choice to explain as you were calling me above him, my mentor, as he used the word and I used it in the sense of the metaphor, we are both equal some but I am his superior as I have Muhammad to me and Ahmadis will have to live with that.

Please know my Prophet's shadow is within me he said,

Please know it is aks he means and he denies prophethood like I do.

Please know these are all metaphorical terms and not be confused with real entity Allah or Prophet Muhammad, on him be peace,

Please know I belabor you with these terms but they have been used by saints so I explain them hoping you will understand I am not calling myself prophet actually.

Please know aks is incomplete in us,

Please know it is Him we reflect off but it is His spirit in us we see through,

Please know by this I mean we are a vessel He is contained in,

Please know that is why when we perfect ourselves you see Him in us, but it is not He, only His image, which is partial.

Please know the teach is true for Jesus, and Moses is also a metaphor, but meant to mean more complete submitters to Him. Omar.

CHAPTER FIVE

SOME PEARLS OF WISDOM FROM HIM, THE PROPHET THERE

Please know our Prophet was wise,
Please know he rarely made a mistake,
Please see him in Paradise as your head in intellect and wisdom,
Please know he had a saying and that was the Heaven was created for him,
Please know why?
Please know it was because he was perfect,
Please know there are many who were perfect but his nature was not to sin,
Please know perfect clay,
Please know that was him,
Please know clay is us,
Please know why?
Please know we are derived out of plants which in turn are derived from dust particles,
Please know a dust particle is atom,
Please see the following caption on him,
Please know you can't approach him but you should follow him,
Please know he was created out of perfect dust particles of Hijaz, the capital of Arabia,
Please know what capital is?
Please know it is the center of things,
Please know this was his destiny,
Please give in,
Please know his wisdom is sane for you.
Please say a prayer for me,

Please know I brought him to you.
Please know in the Hereafter he will intercede for you,
Please know there is a well there where he feeds you his drink,
Please know it is Kauthar,
Please know this means abundance,
Please give into his drink for you.
Please know it will quench your thirst for the journey ahead,
Please know our Creator was only wishing that you be like him for your benefit,
Please say a prayer you are united with your loved ones there,
Please know it is a place where you are with the ones you love,
Please know there is 'no god but Allah' here,
Please know it is requisite for his well.
Please know the other requisite is that you should take him to be your savior,
Please know he is a prophet to you people,
Please know he supplants the previous scripture.
Please know the Prophet's character,
Please Him though in your deeds to Him,
Please know it is Prophet Muhammad's book we need to be published as they won't relent on me otherwise there in Mecca as I am too different for them,
Please know it is over for him who manipulates us as people have seen through his medication of me and know it is put on I have mental disease of significance to man and his wife,
Please know he knows it is over and that is why he asks us to leave as people won't have me killed as I have done nothing wrong in the statutes to deserve this what they have done here with my car.
Please know it is clear I have alacrity,
Please know our Creator knows it is speed we need,
Please know it is over if you think I am gone,
Please know I have to stay a while as there are things I have to do before I pack up and leave,
Please know your Prophet Muhammad was similar and he could not leave his follower behind after him,

Please know it is so now with them in the church and elsewhere where they call me and our Prophet infidels to you while you know we are Muslims like you.

Please know we are infidels if you wish to call us but there is a price to pay.

Please know He will infidel if you call us in Islam that and it is not so,

Please know He will make you backward like them who say kafir things without understanding the implications of the word as it always comes back to you.

Please know then your deeds are meaningless to Him,

Please know He will take you away from Him,

Please know you will see it like the Bani-Israel type of Muslims have seen it there in our home countries where they sing praises of Him and yet do dastardly deeds thinking they will be forgiven,

Please know they will be eventual but they won't have peace in their Hereafter until their forgiveness occurs. Omar.

Please know he was tried the most among man and I am second in that regard.

Please know in the teachings of the Quran is to pray one not to be tried like others were tried before one,

Please know you cannot bear it,

Please know we all have a caliber and He knows our worth,

Please know he will try us according to our worth,

Please know we all crack and lie under duress,

Please know I have had to use subterfuge,

Please know that will the case for all of you,

Please know why?

Please know the Prophet Abraham had to use it when he called Sarah his sister to protect himself from the pharaoh,

Please know he was the best in caliber after him in degree of submission to Him,

Please know all the prophets have used it,

Please know Muhammad never did so.

Please see this chapter The Brightness Of The Day,
Please know this was an early revelation to the Prophet,
Please know he was worried,
Please understand him,
Please know he knew how bitter they were,
Please understand he was reassured that he would come through with success,
Please understand Him,
Please know He wished to try him with the most severe trial.
Please know this was so that he could show his worth to man,
Please know history will record his struggle,
Please know he was known to have integrity of not breaking under pressure,
Please know he never compromised with them,
Please know he was kind to his enemies,
Please know he was asked to proclaim it at the point of death,
Please him,
Please know his merit,
Please know as a person he was tried the most by man,
Please know you don't know the full extent of the suffering he had but I will tabulate it soon so that you know his worth and why he was the best man there and here you know him through my page as the one predicted in world literature to come and purify you,
Please know forbearance,
Please know that was to be pleasant to his enemy and pray for him,
Please give in please him and take him to be guide to Him,
Please know he gave us His secret,
Please know what that is?
Please know that His mercy is all-encompassing and He will forgive man and his spouse. Omar.
Al-Duha.
93:1 By the brightness of the day!
93:2 And the night when it is still! —
93:3 Thy Lord has not forsaken thee, nor is He displeased.
93:4 And surely the latter state is better for thee than the former.

93:5 And soon will thy Lord give thee so that thou wilt be well pleased.
93:6 Did He not find thee an orphan and give (thee) shelter?
93:7 And find thee groping, so He showed the way?
93:8 And find thee in want, so He enriched thee?
93:9 Therefore the orphan, oppress not.
93:10 And him who asks, chide not.
93:11 And the favor of thy Lord, proclaim.

Please know a woman's rights are sacred though her deeds are different.

Please know it is a well-known fact that the society he engendered was the most pious one in the history of mankind.

Please know the Prophet was asked once by a lady called Asma about their rights over their husband's property and their rights with Him in who you have repose with,

Please know she enquired if they bear their children and take care of them would they get reward similar to what their husbands get who go on holy war and take care of their upbringing with their money?

Please know his answer,
Please know they will.
Please understand this,
Please know they are one unit.
Please know their children are taken care of,
Please know their reward is written,
Please know they were the best community of men and women,
Please know they were raised by him,
Please know reverence,
Please know they revered him,
Please see this occur with you.
Please know you will understand me but him you will respect,
Please know he is worthy of your respect. Omar.

Please know women's rights are respect for them in Islam and we honor them in our houses.

Please see the following caption on my house.

Please know Omar was nice to his wife.

Please see the following hadith.

Please know in Arabia women were the oppressed and the forsaken. I know that you think Islam came with a similar attitude but it actually came with reform.

Please know in pre-Islamic Arabia women were treated as chattel and were abused by their husbands so much so that their property and livelihood was the man's right.

Please know the infant girl was buried alive as a norm in that culture where they were viewed as an inconvenience. I am sad you think our Prophet allowed the beating of women as he did not and always recommended kindness to them as they were a trust in the hands of men.

Please know we love women in Islam and we respect our siblings and mothers.

Please know we are all human and make errors however by and large the Muslim society honors them. Omar.

Hadith

"By Allah, it is sinful to deny the rights of the two weak types of people; women and orphans."

Narrated in ibn Majah and others.

Please know the rights of the parents are many and are listed here as a few of them.

Please see this hadith from our Prophet.

Please know there is no peace like the peace that occurs when you say your God is One God alone.

Please know the peace that comes next in degree after that is goodness to your parents.

Please know we are asked about this in the Hereafter.

The end occurs for those who do not see that we cannot behave badly to them or their family. In this there is sadness for those who do not maintain the ties of kinship. I know it is easy to ignore relatives but it is incumbent on us not to do so.

Hadith here.

A man from the Salamah clan asked the Prophet whether there was any aspect of dutifulness to his parents he should do after they had died.

Prophet Muhammad replied. "Please pray for them that God's forgiveness occurs for them, to fulfill their pledges, to be kind to their relatives and do kindness to their friends."

From ibn Majah and others.

Please know a pledge of honor is incumbent on us.

Please know we in Islam are asked about our pledges.

Please understand when we pledge something it is our honor that it should be fulfilled and not disregarded as some think it of no importance nowadays.

Please know we have honor because we are truthful and don't break our word.

Please know these are human values we value and honor.

Please understand we have honor in Islam as you know we speak the truth to you and we fulfill our pledge that we will take you to Heaven if you wish to be there.

Please see the following hadith that our community of Islam is duty bound to protect those I protect. Omar.

Hadith here.

"The Muslim community honors the pledge given on their behalf even if it is given by one who is the lowest in position amongst them."

Please know we have to show affection to our daughters and we should treat all equally nicely.

Please know the hadith is clarified as is my norm from communication from my Prophet directly.

Please know the following words bear reference.

Please understand this hadith of our Prophet is sometimes misunderstood to mean the father of two daughters will enter Paradise no matter what his deeds are.

Please know it means as long as he is kind to them he will be in heaven. I know this does not discount how important our daughters are to us.

Please know we love children in Islam and we are encouraged to treat them equally.

Please know sometimes the love to one child may be more however we are encouraged to gift them equally and show them equal affection as it hurts a child's heart not to do so. Omar.

Hadith here.

The Prophet says: "Allah is certain to admit into heaven the father of two daughters if he is kind to them as long as they are with him."

Narrated in ibn Majah and other sources.

Please know the sinless are proud of their achievement.

Please know the sinless state is decried in Islam as it leads to arrogance and pride that we are superior beings that can do no wrong. In the hadith it is mentioned that there was a man of the People of the Book who prayed on a stone to the point that the mark of prostration was made on it. Our Prophet remarked that the man would be carrying the stone on his back on the Day of Judgment indicating His displeasure in the act of so-called piety in this ardent worshipper of His Magnificence. In this way we see those that take pride in their deeds to be in Hellfire and punishment follows if they don't repent their ways of advocating their virtues to others in an open way or covertly.

Please know the sentiment is correct however one should pray that minor sins notwithstanding, it is the major sins that we should protect our beings from committing.

Please know in Islam minor sins are encouraged as it keeps one sane and prevents arrogance from occurring that may result from a sinless state.

Please know in Islam when you have pride it is worse than a sinner who is humble in himself or herself and the pious one knows they are sinners and depend on the mercy of their Creator for Heaven to occur there in their humble poise to Him,

Please know the Quran tells us not to extol our virtues to others in a way that demeans them,

Please know we must persevere and be humble when we sin and repent our act with our head hung low in shame to Him, then we will be forgiven, not if we have pride in our endeavor of sin to Him, the Creat. Omar.

Please see the prayer of the vanquished here in Islam.

Please know a prayer of the oppressed is heard and I hope the humiliating chastisement is yours who take away my rights.

Please know the following prayer,

Please know it was said when the Prophet stood outside Taif,

Please know he was vanquished,

Please know he had gone there to teach and they threw pebbles at him asking him to leave,

Please know it was the hardest day of his life,

Please know he was vanquished but defeat was not his modus,

Please know he made a comeback years later and laid siege there,

Please know before he died they sent a deputation to him,

Please know they accepted our religious faith of submission to Him and taking him as His Messenger to them,

Please know he asked for mercy from Him,

Please know mercy from Him,

Please know it is ease.

Please see the prayer below was answered,

Please know they came to ask for their annihilation,

Please know the angels were ready to destroy them,

Please know he refused, requesting time for them.

Hadith source here.

"To you, my Lord I complain of my weakness, lack of support and humiliation I am made to receive. Most Beneficent, most Merciful! You are the Lord of the weak and you are my Lord. To whom do you leave me? To a distant tribe who receives me with hostility. Or to an enemy whom you have given power over me. If you are not displeased with me I do not care what I face. I would, however be much happier with your mercy. Please know I seek refuge with the light in Your Face by which all darkness is dispelled and both this life and the life to come are put on their right course against incurring Your wrath or being the subject of Your anger. To you I submit until I earn Your pleasure. There is no power or strength but in You."

Please know it is this prayer we cry out with when we face humiliating chastisement here in your land,

Please know I know there is a prayer that is said in times of humiliation abasement and that is "I am overcome, please help me,"

Please know to face defeat is normal for a prophet or saint but the desire to please God overcomes us,

Please see a requiem for me,

Please know I am humiliated here but God is my witness that the humiliating deed is yours when you imprison or commit me,

Please know you have humiliated me by implying I am deranged though anybody can see the fineness of my decorum and writing, and the abject state of being humiliated in the world's eyes is yours.

Please know you have taken control of my assets and taken the ability to make decisions about myself but the humiliation is yours in the world forum of mankind. Omar.

Please know our Prophet was correct when he never cursed anyone but the crime of his indignity occurring is punishable by Him.

Please know our Creator does not punish without cause but every hardship you face is commensurate with the crime of your act to Him.

Please see these verses from the chapter Bani-Israel.

Please know it is our Creator's intent to punish those who do wrong but expects us to behave in the best possible way. In this there is certainty that our Prophet never broke down and cursed his opponents or abused them in any way.

Please know he was kind to them and showed leniency in their abuses to him and at no point let out an insult on them which was of a personal nature.

Please understand this,

Please know this was occurring when his companions were being killed or evicted out of their houses.

Please know he had to face personal humiliation at the hands of his detractors who even attacked him personally. I know there was one incident when his body was covered by the offal of a sheep while he was praying at the house of God.

Please know at that time he let out a prediction that the people involved would be killed in the battle with him.

Please understand Islam was a superior faith,

Please know there were many hate-mongers as there usually are when they see someone better than themselves or their religious belief.

Please know the same occurs here,

Please know there are many who recognize worth of our Prophet and deep down know Islam is peaceful yet they will try to detract it as they cannot defend their own faith. Omar.

Bani-Israel.

17:53 And say to My servants that they speak what is best. Surely the devil sows dissensions among them. The devil is surely an open enemy to man.

17:54 Your Lord knows you best. He will have mercy on you, if He please, or He will chastise you, if He please. And We have not sent thee as being in charge of them.

Please know it is up to you to forgive the miscreant but it is better to move on as we all sin to others.

Please see the following caption there.

Please know we can enter heaven without them who did us wrong but it is better to forgive and move on.

Please see the hadith of our Prophet. In this there is certainty that sin leads to the fire.

Please know you can forgive yourself from the sin you commit but our Creator does not let this sin of association of Himself to be forgiven but He guides aright those He pleases so that they may enter Paradise there on the Day we are judged for our wrong to others.

Please know that while He forgives sins against Himself he allows mankind to decide if they wish to relent to the miscreant who has done them wrong. Omar.

Abdullah ibn Masud reports: I asked the Prophet which sin is the most serious in God's eyes? He said: "to set up an equal to Allah when it is He who created you." I said, "then what?" He replied: "to kill your child for fear that you have to feed it." I asked:"what is the next one in grievousness?" He said: "to commit adultery with your neighbors wife."
Narrated by Bukhari and Muslim.

Please know they say I am deluded, they said something similar about him, my Prophet.

Please know they say I am deluded and I say I am certain,

Please know they say it is a fixed delusion, I say it occurred, and prove me wrong.

Please know some other truths about our Prophet,

Please know he said "patience is my apparel."

Please know this is true of him,

Please know he said that the path of Allah is trodden by hardships.

Please know we cannot come to Him but as patient ones.

Please know this,

Please know all prophets were patient with Him,

Please know how,

Please know He has a plan,

Please know He knows it,

Please know it will come to pass,

Please know I ask for patience as my rights were subverted and I lost my practice,

Please know they imply delusions,

Please know this,

Please know they poisoned me, then when I say it occurred, they say I am deluded,

Please know it occurred,

Please know I photograph the evidence,

Please know I have posted it here on Facebook previously. Omar.

Please know the help of Allah is nigh if you but had the will to ask Him of it.
Please know with the help of Allah comes peace for us.
Please know he said "remembrance of Allah is my help."
Please know this,
Please know when we are upset He gives us solace.
Please know we all remember Him then,
Please know this,
Please know we must despair if we don't remember Him in our time of need,
Please know we will lose if we don't,
Please try to remember your prayers,
Please know He gives you solace,
Please know it is His help. Omar.

Please know faith is nigh but it is lost if we sin in a significant way.
Please know these words of our Prophet is his creed.
Please know our Prophet has said "faith is my power."
Please know this,
Please know our Creator taught him what faith is,
Please know it is our resolve,
Please know we use it,
Please know it comes and goes,
Please understand this,
Please know we see it lost when we are weak,
Please know our Prophet had faith he would win,
Please know in the face of insurmountable difficulties, it would ebb,
Please know it is normal to do so. Omar.

Please know we are successful because we love you.
Please know he was a well-wisher of you but you wished yourself otherwise.
Please know our Prophet said "knowledge is my weapon."
Please know he knew how things would turn out,
Please know how,

Please know he had a guide.
Please know he knew the outcome of things.
Please know he was given peace by Him,
Please know I am similar,
Please understand we are vouchsafed peace,
Please know why,
Please know it is because we love mankind,
Please know our Prophet was a well-wisher of you. Omar.

Please know our honor is written if we are humble.
Please know our honor as humans depends upon if He accepts our devotions to Him and if we have humility to others.
Please know our Prophet was humble and loved humility.
Please understand this,
Please know he knew the creations of our Creator are nothing,
Please know this,
Please know it means we are peace when we are nothing,
Please know the devil knows this and excites vanities in us,
Please know we must be humble in our make as well as our hearts.
Please know we are nothing in our make and our heart is at peace when it feels no pride.
Please know this,
Please know it is our honor to worship Him in our humble state,
Please know these were the sentiments of our Prophet who said this,
Please know it is a honor He gives us that we pray to Him,
Please know it is a honor to be one obedient to Him,
Please know it is a honor to submit to Him,
Please know it is a honor to live for His sake.
Please know our honor as humans is to be His slave.
Please absolve me as I want honor but then who doesn't I say. Omar.

Please know the tangible has occurred and you are Muslim heart by my accord.
Please know it is the intangible that will come forth as tangible in the near future here.

Please know our Prophet has said "Allah's will is my prize."
Please know this,
Please know he was vouchsafed victory.
Please understand the verdict was written in the Quran,
Please know he was going to win.
Please know His will has occurred.
Please know it is the same for me,
Please know I have been granted victory.
Please know His will has come about in tangible ways.
Please know the caption on my heart,
Please know I am patient but His will has transpired in our hearts.
Please know they know their God is One and Islam is true,
Please know the tangible will continue to occur, inshallah or God willing,
Please understand there are sore losers around,
Please know to be aware of the fight back.
In this there is certainty that they will try to imply mental disease in me and try to prevent my teachings from spreading forth to their children. Omar.

Please know our success is a measure of our obedience to Him.
Please know our Creator has vouchsafed it for us when we achieve our peace with Him.
Please know our Prophet has said "obedience is my security."
Please know this,
Please understand our Creator has given us peace,
Please know this,
Please know that in obedience we forsake the world and what is in it and we do His bid on us and forsake our will in things of the nature I know are difficult as yet for some of you but with time peace will occur and you will do it, His will on you, like Jesus said and I do as well.
Please know that we cannot do it by ourselves.
Please know that when we submit to Him we know peace and our surety comes with time.

Please know our peace is a sign that we will achieve success of heaven with us.

Please know success,
Please know it is to overshadow you,
Please know this,
Please understand that our success is measured by our achievement.
Please know it is to submit to Him that we achieve our Paradise and our success,
Please know you cannot take that away from us in Islam. Omar.

Please know the truth-lovers outnumber the deceitful ones here.
Please realize our Creator is aware of your flaw and knows you can remedy it.
Please know our Prophet was wise.
Please know he said "understanding is my asset."
Please understand this,
Please know he was able to understand you.
Please comprehend his thought,
Please know it is to bring you Islam through my Facebook page.
Please know he is pleased with you.
Please know why,
Please know it is because you give in to Him and him and me.
Please know this is a triumvirate not,
Please know Allah alone is the sole authority,
Please know the exemplar He chose for you in this world not but all humanity is I not but Muhammad, the Prophet to you,
Please know you honor him in your homes and conferences you hold but me you discredit as unwell some as your child is me and your wife agrees I am safe for you,
Please know it is not so, I have credit with Him,
Please know why he chose you.
Please know it was because you were fair,
Please know there are truth-dwellers in you.
Please yourself,

Please know it is those who dwell with truth in them that say you will come through and give me peace,
Please know how this occurs,
Please know it will be when they speak to you. Omar.

Please know our Hereafter has it but here it is palpable in a few.
Please know our Prophet repository was love and knowledge.
Please know our Prophet has said "love is the basis of my belief."
Please know this,
Please know our Creator is Love and has vouchsafed love for those who love Him,
Please know He knows our Prophet is the repository of love,
Please know he was the perfect slave and loved most perfectly.
Please know he didn't care,
Please know this,
Please know you cannot love like him,
Please know he wished the best for you.
Please know this is to love unconditionally,
Please know our Creator is the same,
Please know He will take you to Paradise,
Please understand him who hates you,
Please know he forsakes Him,
Please know he condemns you to an everlasting perdition and is pleased,
Please know love is superior,
Please fathom the saying of our Prophet that the corn field will be empty,
Please know he was talking about Hell. Omar.

Please know our law allows sorrow for the heedless one among man.
Please know our Creator placed sorrow in our hearts so that we would care for those who don't care for themselves and don't amend.
Please know our Prophet has said "sorrow is my mate"
Please know sorrow,
Please know it is intense regret that they don't see and amend,

Please know they are alien to the truth,
Please know we all have regret,
Please know sorrow is different,
Please know the heart weeps,
Please know only Allah guides aright,
Please know this,
Please know if we have sorrow He will please us,
Please know our insight comes from Him,
Please know our Prophet wept regularly at what he saw,
Please know it is great to have sorrow for those who don't see and appreciate you.
Please try to weep for man who don't amend,
Please know they think this world is everything,
Please know Hell is sufficient then, there is a limit to us here where we teach you things,
Please give in,
Please know you can't change all of them,
Please know your grief is all you can fathom. Omar.

Please know my jihad is my repository of war to him, the heedless in us.
Please learn what the Book is that I refer to here.
Please know our Prophet has said "jihad is my character."
Please know this means the internal struggle that he undertakes.
Please know it is a fight to evolve into a better state,
Please know this,
Please know we are to improve our make,
Please know our Prophet was careful but made errors at times,
Please know we are all human,
Please learn from the Book of our Creator,
Please know this is what gives us insight,
Please learn we should pray as when we do so we keep Him with us.
Please know His Book is available to us free of charge. Omar.

Please know I am eager in my faith to you but are you ready for my peace to occur?

Please know our Creator is magnanimous and is willing to forgive sins against Himself but does not forgive those who do not take heed about the Oneness of His Being and about His Messenger being Muhammad, as these are truths that are evident in us since they appeal to reason.

Please know our Prophet is known to have said "eagerness is my mount."

Please know he is only saying you have to have a mount that is eager or he is eager in his travel to us in teach there.

Please understand me,

Please know I am eager for your faith to be us in Islam,

Please know why,

Please know you can't enter paradise with your belief of trinity and your destination will be a place you don't want,

Please know this,

Please know if you take an associate with Him He will avenge it.

Please know there is no forgiveness for such a sin,

Please understand He does not allow entry into Paradise for such a claimant and will only allow them to be modified in thoughts till they come through proclaiming Him as their God only. Omar.

Please know our soul is blessed with a new beginning when we enter it, our Islam.

Please know our Hereafter is riddled with hardships but a reward of a new soul with you is easy to encumber it with reward there,

Please know our Prophet has said something we pay little heed to.

Please know he said if one soul comes to guidance through you it is better than anything under the sun for you.

Please understand this,

Please know it is as if you have given the Creator a friend.

Please know the reward for that is immense and in another saying our Prophet said it was better than red camels, a rarity in Arabia.

Please know it is like you have taken someone out of Hell and into Paradise.

Please know we can only imagine how Allah rewards such a person.

Please know when the heart is cleaned it gains a new perspective to life and things that were important to us no longer matter.

Please know it is to rebuild a man or woman.

Please know it is for this reason people are forgiven their past misdeeds and it is as if they are living with a new reality where God is important to them and there is a new emphasis on remaining sinless. Omar.

Please know the best character is his if you could but see from your tarnished souls to Him.

Please know our Prophet is averse to greatness in him as he knows any greatness we have is from Him.

Please know the following statement about him, our Prophet,

Anas, the servant of our Prophet said "the Prophet had the best character from amongst us and was the most generous and bravest of us."

Please know this,

Please know our Prophet was a stalwart who had a character of perfection among man.

Please know he was the bravest in war.

Please know he had wealth at his disposal but gave it all away.

Please know he was blessed in these things,

Please understand that he was the best in mankind in these things.

Please know there are those that detract him but invariably they don't see him clearly.

Please know their heart is blind to the perfection of his soul.

Please know tarnish,

Please know it is when the soul does not see and the heart does not comprehend his great door to Paradise we have in Islam,

Please know they are all a team in heaven and he is the head of them,

Please know our Creator did not allow me these things that I talk here but it is so I need wealth too.

Please know we must live according to our means.

Please say a prayer that we can be like his image.

Please know our Creator knows I am truthful and fulfill the trust.

Please know this does not mean we are not just and allow justice to occur in our dealings as some miscreants take advantage of our straightforward door and should be repelled by us.

Please know I hope that justice will serve you in Islam here in this country.

Please understand this,

Please know you are in touch with the truth,

Please know you know Islam is true. Omar.

Please know our peace in this world is Heaven in the Hereafter.

Please know our Creator made it easy for us as these things of submission we do are only the path to ease.

Please know the Prophet led a life to be an example for us,

Please know he did not wish for things to be hard for us.

Please know his example is easy to follow,

Please know it is our nature,

Please know this,

Please know he encaptured the spirit within us as when we sin we lose it, the spirit I mean here. I know he is sane and if we follow his example we will gain our sanity.

Please know our nature is within us and if our nature is us we are sane in it, our thoughts to us,

Please know its law is to submit to Him,

Please understand this,

Please know we go against our nature when we do not submit,

Please know it is called rebellion against ourselves.

Please know there is no peace in this,

Please know we feel peace when we go with our grain,

Please know this,

Please know our grain or nature is to submit to Him,

Please do not rebel,
Please know you will lose your sanity,
Please understand diverse thoughts,
Please know you will try to justify yourself instead of feeling peace,
Please know these are diverse thoughts,
Please know you will lose your abode of heaven,
Please understand peace,
Please know it is heaven here on earth,
Please know it will manifest itself in the Hereafter as your Paradise.
Omar.

Please know truths are within us.
Please know the following discourse was written by me by the heart of the Prophet.
Please know our Prophet was different for you.
Please know he understood you and your desire for reason,
Please know he did not believe in blind faith,
Please know he made a statement once,
"Reason is the essence of my religion"
Please see reason,
Please know it is to please the senses,
Please understand it,
Please know it is the truth to us,
Please see truth,
Please know it is the word from Him,
Please know we must persevere with truth-telling,
Please know it helps us appreciate His truth coming to us,
Please know we will be asked,
Please give in,
Please know reason,
Please know it is to give in,
Please know it is to give in to the truth, so the heart lives,
Please know dead,
Please know it is to kill the truth,

Please know your heart will live only if you accept the truth from Him,
Please know what His Words are,
Please know they live in the hearts of mankind,
Please know His Books carry His Words,
Please know the Quran is safe for you,
Please know other books have changes in them in their essence,
Please give due credence to the Quran,
Please know you will live thereby,
Please know the prophet's words are safe,
Please know you will be asked if you took someone to be your God other than Him,
Please know your prophet Jesus did not say he was God you make him out to be,
Please shut it and open another,
Please yourself. Omar.

Please know the relatives are kind to you if they prevail you.

Please know Abu Lahb was one of the few relatives who died in anger to him. I know his other uncle was neutral but denied himself peace by accepting their faith on his deathbed.

Please know our Prophet knew the importance of an extended family and tried to bring them around to Islam.

Please know eventually all his family with one exception accepted Islam.

Please know that his uncles notwithstanding, his extended family were always included in his prayers for their guidance and acceptance into His Paradise.

Please understand if your relative turns away it is important to continue your good behavior to him. In this there is certainty that we will be asked about relative's rights.

Please understand we must persevere there with those who call us names in a desultory way as there are relatives I have who think I am unwell and call me so to my face and in doing so throw dust in my face.

The end is there as they realize I write with caliber but maintain I am ill as I claim sainthood from my Prophet. I know what I say is complex to you as you do not see them communicate with me but it is simple for our Creator to do. Omar.

Hadith here.

"Kindness to relatives is not to return their kindness but is to be kind to relatives that turn away."

Narrated in Bukhari.

Please know your relatives are dissuaded from you if you are in truth.

Please know we are asked to maintain equanimity with them even if they do this deed as illustrated in the hadith below.

Please know the following hadith.

Please know what it implies.

Please know I am the recipient of distaste as there are many in my family who call me unwell in spite and not with love as I propose I am a messenger of the Messenger of God.

Please know dust and ashes are similar.

Please know I am weak and get dissuaded if I am denied peace from my relatives but I know I must continue as my worth is obvious to you who read me.

Please know I am a believer in my Prophet as a Messenger of His Grace. I am asked to continue to teach as there are people with integrity who know my worth and will give me credit in future in the settings of mankind.

The end is there for those amongst my relatives who think Ahmadiyyat is a dead entity and should not be promoted.

Yours truly is a believer in him who says that Ahmadiyyat will revive the world in the future settings of mankind. Omar.

Hadith here.

Abu Hurayrah said. A man came to the Prophet and said: "O Messenger of Allah, I have some relatives whose relationship I promote but they cut me off. I am kind to them but they are unkind to me. They treat me harshly and I forbear." The Prophet said: "If what you say is true then it is as if you are making them eat burning ashes. You will continue to have Allah's support against them as long as you maintain this attitude towards them."

Please know compassion was our Prophet's hallmark to you when he saw you left with him, your adversary, the devil companion you have.
Please see the following caption on his heart.
Please know I am a mercy to mankind as I encompass them in my heart's repose to Him, meaning they are with me.
Please consider the following hadith.
Please know he took care of all.
Please understand his heart was benevolent enough to include all mankind in its mercy.
Please see the following caption on his heart.
Please know I am a mercy for all mankind. It is through his intercession that mankind will enter Paradise.
Please understand benevolence.
Please know it is to be God's emissary there.
Please understand when we pray we don't like to change the pattern of prayer we have.
Please know his compassion for the child and the mother.
Hadith as narrated by Anas Ibn Malik.
The Prophet said: "I begin a prayer intending to make it long. I then heard a child crying and then I shorten it because I know the child's mother would be too concerned as she hears it cry."
Please know compassion is his hallmark. It would be good of you to acknowledge him in that regard as it will lead to blindness of your soul if you call him what you do in your churches and other gathering places. Omar

Please know women are him in repose as he was the best of men to them.
Please know he never hit anyone with a toothbrush though he permitted it to his men if the need arose as the maximum punishment

from Him. He, himself never resorted to it as he was a role model for mankind.

Please know it is a metaphor for light beat without leaving a mark,

Please see this hadith from our Prophet. I know you are accustomed to abusing him as a wife-beater but it is in our history books that he never touched any wife of his in a manner that would hurt her.

Please know he never beat a child or a woman in our recorded history of his life.

Please be aware of this if you think otherwise. Omar.

The hadith is as follows: "The best of you are those who are best to their wives. I am the best of you to my wives."

Please know the best in my community are the best to their wives, he said.

Please know the ways of admonishment are many and include staying away from her and thereby not fighting with her in front of kids.

Please realize Islam allows the beating of a wife as a remedy for her anger to him who maintains her.

Please know the intent is not to hurt her as our Prophet would not allow that. In this there is certainty that such admonishments occur in the Muslim household but they were looked down by the Prophet.

The idea behind this is to cause them the social trauma of being known as a wife who rose against him.

Please know the toothbrush does not hurt and only connotes beating as a remedy to her anger issues.

Please know this is a leeway permitted by God though the Prophet was averse to make it a law as he was concerned for them.

Please know the hadith that follows shows the norm for his society. Please understand this.

Please know it was a last resort before the marriage fell apart due to anger issues from her.

Please understand we in Islam stay away from beating our wives as it is better to go through divorce if she wishes it and not proceed with this law. Omar.

Hadith in which he said "the good amongst you do not resort to beating their wives."

Please know there are many such sayings of the Prophet Muhammad but the converse has to be protected against as it is misused in this country.

Please know a man is a wife-beater only if proven guilty of it.

There are several hadith that will indicate to you that our Prophet never liked that women should be hurt in arguments with them. In this there is certainty in this that this is the norm for a Muslim household in the ages when wife-beating was a common occurrence. I am sad that in this country they recommend punishment for it even when there is no pain in the interaction.

Please know I was proclaimed a wife-beater by my ex-wife but when it came to court proceedings she backed away from a formal charge and denied them, the people here, a court hearing in my defense.

Please understand your law here takes the word of the woman to be sacrosanct and initiates arrest procedures on her behalf but we know women lie as well and without a formal court appearances of witnesses there should not be an abrogation of the rights of the men to their freedom.

Please understand I am sane and know the woman needs to be protected in this situation but it is better for her to move out until the coast is clear. Omar.

Please see some of the hadith that follow regarding the prohibition of wife-beating based on whims and fancy of men.

"Never beat Allah's handmaidens."

Abu Dawud and others.

"I wanted one thing but Allah willed another thing - and what Allah has willed must be best."

Manar.

"Wife-beating may occur if the one has become guilty in an obvious manner of immoral conduct and it should be done in such a way as not to cause pain."

Stated in Muslim and others.

Please know humans are pliant and exacting not.

Please know this hadith. It relates the humanity we are and we are far from the ISIS-like individuals you think us to be in this land of ours.

Please understand Aisha was one of his wives who was the beloved of our Prophet.

Please know she was young and liked to play with him.

Please understand he was a human first and a Prophet later. I know you think him strict but he was compassionate and relaxed as an individual.

Please realize the humanity in him from the following hadith. Omar. Hadith here from Aisha.

Aisha reports: "I was with Allah's Messenger on one of his expeditions. I was young and thin. At one point he told the people to move forward, which they did. He said to me "come and race me." We raced and I won the race. He kept quiet. Years later, when I had put on weight and had forgotten the event I travelled with him on another expedition. He told the people to move forward, which they did. He said to me "come, let's race." We raced and he won. He laughed and said "we are even."

Narrated Ahmad and others.

Please see the caption on our hearts in Islam.

Please know we are sane and when our wife loves us we are happy. If not, we become morose and upset.

Please understand there is humanity in us and we are not machines bent on world conquest.

When our pretty wife adores us it is because we were pliant to her, not because we were hard and exacting. Omar.

Please know the law of adultery is severe with Him and child-rearing with him is illegal for her in his household.

Please understand the consequences on families is far reaching when an act like this occurs. It should be treated as a sin and one that is punished by our Creator severely.

Please know our Prophet went to the heavens while he was still a Prophet on earth. During this time he saw people who were being punished. One of them was a woman who committed adultery secretly and introduced a child in the family.

Please know she was punished for doing so and was hung from her breasts depicting her state where she fed the child illegally from the gains of her husband.

Please know this is a serious crime with Him,

Please know it is heresy and will be punished,

Please know your law is clear that when a woman commits adultery she is guilty of apostasy.

Please know the spirit of our beings does not change and if it was apostasy then it is still apostasy. I know there is the mercy of our Creator that comes into play however these things are taken into consideration on Judgment Day and it is viewed as apostasy here in the world.

Please know the crime is great in our culture,

Please know there is a recompense,

Please know that is to come clean and face the consequences as if they do not the punishment will be severe on the Day of Reckoning.

Please bring the child with you to him and confess,

Please know he may forgive you,

Please know there is no marital bond after that occurs and you will just be living with him in his habitat but the spiritual bonding would be over until healing occurs with time for some.

Please know why?

Please know it is because sometimes both are guilt in it so it is overlooked by him and her.

Please repent this act though,

Please know society should condemn adultery instead of looking at it sympathetically and brushing over its consequences on families. Omar.

Please know to communicate with them in a way that befits them.

Please know our Creator gave him strength unmatched with any of his time. I know he was only a slave and knew that he was a test for them and remained quiet for the most part.

Please know Prophet was a very humble man,

Please understand this,

Please know he was exceptionally strong but would not resort to wrestling.
Please understand this,
Please know that he could wrestle but would not.
Please know his Prophethood belied his strength in that he was a prophet and not a wrestler by them but it is so he would wrestle at times.
Please understand that once he challenged their best wrestler to a match on the ground that if he would fail then he would accept Islam, and his duel was accepted.
Please know he lost and then became a Muslim,
Please know this is how you serve Islam,
Please understand you communicate in the language of the people.
Please know there are other evidences of his strength like when the Muslim men could not break a stone in Madinah they asked him to do so at the time the battle of Ahzab. Omar.

Please know your clothing must reflect your dignity with them.
Please know our Prophet was a man and his clothing reflected the clothing of men of his time.
Please know the Prophet was distinctive.
Please know he dressed normally despite his distinctive appearance.
Please understand this,
Please know he said "I am only a creature of His."
Please know he was a man and would not elevate his standing among man,
Please know as the Prophet of Allah he had respect.
Please know this is us,
Please know we are no better than him and our clothing and attire must reflect the clothing of men around us without emphasis on our private area.
Please know we avoid silk or elaborate clothes.
Please know our clothes reflect our modesty. Omar.

Please know women are our better halves in ways while sometimes the converse is true.

Please know we are well pleased with the creation of Allah the way He pleased to create.

Please see the following regarding the conduct to women.

Please know we all have crookedness in us.

Please realize we know they are our trust to Him and it is incumbent to me that they are treated with equanimity.

Please know this is a metaphor. I am sane and know it can be applied literally as there a precedent to do so. In the Old Testament is a similar statement. I know it is better to give in to them even if you are right and wait for their sanity to occur when you have an argument with them.

Please them in fights. If you win, she will break and leave you.

Abu Hurayrah relates this saying from the Prophet.

"Take good care of women. They have been created out of a rib. A rib is most crooked at the top. If you try to straighten it, it will snap. If you leave it alone, it remains crooked. Therefore take good care of them."

Please know we love women the way they are. I know some feel they would be better off if they did not marry but that is not God's intent.

Please them and take advantage of their crookedness. There may be wisdom in it for you. Omar.

Please know a neighbor is heir nearly.

Please know our Prophet knows they would not be heirs but the emphasis was clear in the edicts from Him.

Please understand the following hadith shows how much emphasis our Creator gave to the rights of our neighbors over us.

Please know the emphasis is for a congenial society to transpire.

Please know all prophets came with similar messages for their community.

Please understand how important it is for the neighbor to take care of the other by analyzing this in further detail noting that apart from making a neighbor a heir everything else forfeited for their comfort.

Was this the reason you fell in this land?

Please know up here the rights of the neighbor are upheld in some communities but by and large you have forsaken this edict- to be good to your neighbor. I am sad that that is the case as there can be good peace between one and one's neighbor. Omar.

Please know Abdullah bin Amr was a companion of the Prophet who narrates. "I heard the Messenger of Allah say 'The angel kept urging me to do good to my neighbor making me feel that one day they would be among my heirs.'"

Sunan Abu Dawud and Tirmidhi.

Please know a neighbor has rights and you have rights with him.

Please understand our Prophet had keen insight on how a perfect society was to be formulated.

Please know the right of a neighbor.

Please know our Prophet emphasized the right of the neighbor by saying that person was not a believer if he went to bed satiated while his neighbor was hungry.

Please know this includes the believing neighbor as well as the non-believer.

Please understand the hadith here.

Please know our neighbor has rights over us. This includes those who live in your immediate neighborhood as there may be problems in houses close by that you are aware of.

Please see the hadith that follows. It shows how important it is to behave well with your neighbor. Omar.

"By Allah, he is not a believer! By Allah, he is not a believer! By Allah, he is not a believer..."

His companions asked, "whom do you mean, O Messenger of Allah?" He replied. "A person whose neighbor fears his bad attitude."

Narrated by Bukhari and others.

Please know he did not curse people but prayed for their guidance.

Please see the caption on my heart.

I have been told not to curse anybody.

Please know the Prophet knew his people would come around and accept the message of peace from him. At the battle of Uhud the Muslims suffered casualties and his people requested him to curse his enemies.

Please know this was not difficult for a prophet to do and our Prophet replied "I have not been sent as a curse to mankind, but as an inviter to good and a mercy. O Lord! Grant guidance to my people; for surely they know not."

Please know to curse people would be to banish them from the good.

Please know the devil was accursed by God and it is his destiny to be banished until the Day we are risen and he cannot change that. I know we curse often however the curse of a prophet is heard.

Please realize he was told they would come around and that is why our Prophet was vouchsafed success.

Please know there is no opportunity to take back a curse once it has reached its destination. If that person does not deserve the curse then the curse falls upon the person who said it.

Please realize we must be careful of our wrong and not curse unnecessarily. Omar.

Please know terror tactics are unislamic when applied on populations.

Please know terror tactics are never used in the propagation of Islam as they cause people to fight back.

Please know the following story as regards to the forbearance of our Prophet from a man who became a stalwart of his.

Yours truly knows it is test for me that I have been subjected to this abuse.

Please know we are tested in this way by people who would hope we would crack and start to fight like them.

Please know it is forbearance I live as your courts can enact a law that I am unwell and take away my things.

Please know they almost committed me permanently when I was committed for two months in September of 2014. I know they have the power to do so and I hope you will persevere with me and protect me in future appearances of their courtroom where they enact judgments against me.

Please understand it was common to take a debt on behalf of a people.

Please realize this is true.

Please relay this story there.

Please understand this is an event that took place in Madinah where there was a Jewish money lender. I know our Prophet had to make use of them until our Creator revealed that usury was canceled by him.

Please understand this that Islam came to them in a gradual way. Hadith here.

"I came over to the Prophet and held him by his robes. I looked hard at him and said 'Muhammad, will you not pay up what is due to me by my right over you? I have known your clan to honor their commitments and I have dealt with some of you.' I looked at Umer and saw he was angry at me and he made a face to scare me. He said 'you enemy of Allah!, how dare you say and do to Allah's Messenger what I have seen and heard you say. By Allah, if it had not been for the risk of losing out on the Hereafter I would have struck off your head with this sword of mine.'

Allah's Messenger looked calmly at Umer and said to him 'we are in need of something better from you Umer. It would have been better if you tell me to honor my commitment and tell him to make his demand in a more appropriate way. Take him and give him all that is due to him. Also give him twenty measures of dates extra in consideration of terrorizing him.'

Umer did as he was told. Later the Jew explained that he was only testing our Prophet as he recognized he was a Prophet but he wanted to test his forbearance. He said: "When I saw Muhammad I recognized from his face all the signs confirming prophethood that were mentioned in their scriptures except two. I needed to test his forbearance that it would control his anger and the more harshness that is shown to him the more gentle he is. I did this test and confirmed my suspicions. Therefore I would like you, Umer, to be a witness that I bear witness there is no

God but Allah and I am happy to follow my faith as Muhammad being my Prophet." He also allocated half of his wealth for the poor.

Please know this was related by multiple sources.

I know this is a story you listen to as the man tested our Prophet and when our Prophet saw the terror in his eyes he was tender hearted to him.

Please know we do not wish to scare you with Islam.

Please understand that terror has no place in the propagation of our religion.

Please understand it was because people recognized the merit of the religion and the people propagating it they were overcome.

Please realize terrorism is therefore nullified as a basis of faith. I am sane when I tell you that Islam does not like terror tactics when they are applied on people as was shown by the reprimand given to the companion of the Prophet here in this text.

Please know when you bomb women and children you are propagating your views by this terror.

Please see a requiem for our Prophet.

Please know I never caused terror on anyone to win them over.

In this there is certainty and I would challenge anyone to show he did so. Omar.

Please know if you behave with the bad with wellness they will come around for you.

Please know the following is how man must behave with the ignorant.

Please understand the Word of God on him.

Please know he was a mercy to mankind and he could not reproach man on things, like we do.

Please know he was rich when they had won over people to Islam and they didn't need wealth.

Please see the following caption there,

Please know we have wealth but it is for the poor.

Please know he had to ability to sustain abuses without being offended.

Please understand this,

Please know he was like a father to them in the way of a metaphor.

The end occurs when you think they were not human, like me and you.

Please know they had human intelligence and they could discern greatness in him.

Please see the following hadith where it was communicated how he behaved with those who were rude to him and did not know how to behave any better.

Anas reports: "I was walking with him when he was wearing a coat with a rough edge. A bedouin caught up with him and pulled hard at him. I looked at the Prophet's neck and saw how the edge of the coat left a mark on him due to the rough attitude of the bedouin. Then he said to him 'Muhammad, give orders that I should have a portion of the money Allah has given you.' The Prophet looked at him in surprise and then gave the order for him to be given a share."

Narrated by Bukhari and others.

Please know the forbearance that he did not berate the man on his rough attitude that obviously gave him pain. I know this was his norm.

Please understand this is not put on but actually results because he knew this man was ignorant but would come around if he gave into him.

The end is there for people if they think the companions of the Prophet could not discern greatness and think that he was the leader of a savage bunch of them there in Arabia.

Please know these were men who would cry with grief at their wrongs and know that they would be held accountable for their sins.

Please know they had beards but were otherwise were you, in deeds and goodness.

Please see a requiem for those who think they are different.

Please know we were wrong and now we suffer the loss of intellect that was ours before we blighted him, our Prophet.

Please know you will lose intellect when you say bad things about him rather than recognize his merit. Omar.

Please know our articulation is our beard to you as when you see our repose you know men with beards have intellect as well as you do.

Please know we are asked about deeds.

Please know everything must be in order and neat.

Please know when we do a thing we do it well.

Please understand this,

Please know it is compulsory to keep yourself neat.

Please know that he asked his companions to keep to neatness.

Please know that we are asked about our habits.

Please see the hadith below.

"He who wears hair on the head or in the beard should take care to keep them neat and graceful."

Please know his hair was long and his beard was combed for neatness.

Please know he was commanded that when he did a deed he should do it well.

I ask you to judge me. Am I not neat and graceful?

Was this the reason you could not imply mental disease in me? Omar.

Please know our sanity is our scent as you would think us barbaric thereby.

Please understand this,

Please know to keep ourselves neat and clean and lightly scented is in the sunnah of the Prophet.

Please understand this,

Please know our Prophet loved a nice scent.

Please know when he was offered a gift of a scent he never refused this gift.

Please know there were traces of scent wherever he passed by.

Please know it is good to be sweet smelling.

Please know he and his wife would place scent on each other.

Please know this is the reason we apply scent in our prayer area.

Please apply it on yourself. Omar.

Please know the law needs a semblance of sanity to see the if law is applicable to you when men take flight for another woman.

Please understand this idea prevails in Muslim country where it is successful in preventing bastardy in a culture where promiscuity occurs.

Please know this verse from chapter four or The Women.

Please know we cannot think of a better way to remedy the problems of the west.

Please know I am an advocate of the one marriage rule for men here however it is better for them to marry another women when the flight to adultery occurs.

Please know these are exceptional circumstances here where a man will leave his wife for another woman but it does occur and rather than the wife losing her husband he has the option of another wife where the family would not break up.

Please know this is the exception as sanity has occurred and men do not necessarily want to leave their wife for another woman.

The end occurs when you think this is sedition. It is an avenue for the thought to grow into law if acceptable by man and woman. I know I am held accountable for minor details of law while nearly everybody discusses these things amongst themselves. I am safe as this idea can formulate into law if you wish it in your culture, rather than the loss of a family unit. Omar.

Nisa.

4:3 And if you fear that you cannot do justice to orphans, marry such women as seem good to you, two, or three, or four; but if you fear that you will not do justice, then (marry) only one or that which your right hands possess. This is more proper that you may not do injustice.

Please see the deportment of him in full splendor of light.

Please know our Prophet was in excellent health and was in complete control of a people in a gathering.

Please know our Prophet's face was like the full moon.

Please know he had a reddish hue.

Please know his cheeks were straight. His eyebrows did not meet in the center and were full.

Please know his lips were full.

Please know he walked with an assured gait and when he talked to somebody he would turn completely to face him,

The end occurs when you think he is ugly.

Please know he was considered beautiful to view.

Please know his countenance was calm and assured,

Please know he was impeccably clean and had a nice odor. I know he would shave of excess body hair regularly from his pubes and under his arms.

Please know his deportment was calm and assured.

Please know this,

Please know his companion said they had never seen someone smile as he did.

Please know he would smile often,

The end occurs if you think he was stern and hard-hearted. Ure son in repose knows it is safe to say that his demeanor was like that of the sun.

Please know by that I mean he was bright and engaging.

Please know this,

Please know he never broke out in an angry tirade with his wife,

Please know calm,

Please know it is peace without.

Please know he mended his own clothes, milked his goat and tended to the things his wife wished him to. Omar.

CHAPTER SIX

PEARLS FROM MYSELF

Please know I am an Ahmadi heart,
Please know it is no different from other hearts that love the truth and are willing to change dogma in themselves,
Please understand dogma for a while,
Please know it is belief that is blind and fixed,
Please know it is over for those who are not willing to listen to reason,
Please know there is no dogma that weighs so heavily on one that there is 'no god but Allah.'
Please know I am sane that dogma must have peace in the heart for some,
Please know if it creates doubts then it is false,
Please know there is a need to be upfront about it,
Please know we know in our heart's repose if we lie or tell the truth,
Please say a prayer that you come out true,
Please see my following posts,

Please maintain the divorce decree as a part of your marriage contract in case you fall later, both groups.
Please consider this to be an agreement between the partners at the time of marriage and keep it as a part of marriage vows you have thus ensuring an equitable relationship in marriage clause here.
Please see this will prevent unnecessary divorce from happening in this culture where greed may play a role in divorce proceedings and this act of giving this law here is a gift to married women in that it will preserve their marriages if a flaw results in it as usually in this land the guilt is on both hands and forgiveness should result by law of sanity

in us they say to each other but it is so if divorce is to take place then greed should not be in the equation.

Please see the divorce law there is sane and is fair to both in that marriage is pursued once it is over with ease in that situation.

Please see this verse from the Quran that you treat them with kindness when you divorce her and so it is that amicable relationships are maintained there, especially if children are born to her, then there is no leeway on excuse of this situation of good fellowship be maintained on both ends but it is so many times there is evil there and relationships are strained in it but try to complete the term of 3 courses if at all possible so repair may result and if there is any love there try to keep it with you as in this culture guilt occurs with both usually.

Please know the husband's decisions are more sane and he is the breadwinner on many occasions and he should be obeyed in regard to the children even if they are kept with her as a father is naturally inclined to discipline and more strict with her and him in their rearing and so he should have the final say regarding their discipline and rearing matters as well, especially if monetary decisions are to be made for them, but a mother's heart is to relent to the child in things they want and that is not good for family structure, in other words the father should remain as the head for the child as the Quran says he is a degree above in decision matters for them but it is so in this land joint custody is pursued but courts should give leeway for the father's final say in matters of divorce parents with them.

Please know the limits of Allah are good companionship in things related to a marital home but if peace cannot be maintained it is better to separate or divorce but give leeway to repair issues that may occur and if they insist on it, divorce there, the mother should take the child with her until the matter is settled but she should not stay with him in her house not if he has made payments on the property, and in divorce in Islam she takes her assets with her and he keeps things he has paid for but he should be generous and gift her on depart door especially if she has borne him some kids, that is honorable by him and will give her peace too.

Please see that there is no alimony but until iddat or the courses not but three months have elapsed he should pay her support of a reasonable amount to maintain her expense and the children too and the upkeep of the children is always the father's responsibility there.

Please see that alimony is curtailed after the divorce takes place as she is not providing sex to him and not maintaining her home with him and he is encumbered not in this issue as he may want to marry again and he does not need to support two wives in that sense she is still a wife to him if he supports her and that is not correct for them.

Please know the assets are not divided but things that are paid for are kept but gifts are relinquished usually, but if she seeks divorce then she is to return gifts to her by law we have especially the marriage gift that is transected at the time of nikah or marriage to her.

Please know Allah does not like divorce to happen but sometimes it is necessary if there is hatred between the two partners but it is true this saying from Prophet Muhammad that of all the things He permits Who is their Creator He likes divorce the least so there you have it try to repair the situation but if not part on good terms with remembrance of the good times we spent together and reared a family, if that applies to them, but it is so in Islam the right of divorce is given to the husband and not the wife, why, because she is fickle and gets hurt easily and men sense when divorce is necessary more easily while women in their anger take drastic action like getting the police involved or something of that nature as is well known in this country but in our lands she usually leaves home with the children when the waiting period is over and repair hasn't occurred.

Omar.

Al-Baqarah

2:227 And if they resolve on a divorce, Allah is surely Hearing, Knowing.

2:228 And the divorced women should keep themselves in waiting for three courses. And it is not lawful for them to conceal that which Allah has created in their wombs, if they believe in Allah and the Last Day. And their husbands have a better right to take them back in the meanwhile if they wish for reconciliation. And women have rights similar to those against them in a just manner, and men are a degree above them. And Allah is Mighty, Wise.

2:229 Divorce may be (pronounced) twice; then keep (them) in good fellowship or let (them) go with kindness. And it is not lawful for you to take any part of what you have given them, unless both fear that they cannot keep within the limits of Allah. Then if you fear that they cannot keep within the limits of Allah, there is no blame on them for what she gives up to become free thereby. These are the limits of Allah, so exceed them not; and whoever exceeds the limits of Allah, these are the wrongdoers.

2:230 So if he divorces her (the third time), she shall not be lawful to him afterwards until she marries another husband. If he divorces her, there is no blame on them both if they return to each other (by marriage), if they think that they can keep within the limits of Allah. And these are the limits of Allah which He makes clear for a people who know.

2:231 And when you divorce women and they reach their prescribed time, then retain them in kindness or set them free with kindness and retain them not for injury so that you exceed the limits. And whoever does this, he indeed wrongs his own soul. And take not Allah's messages for a mockery, and remember Allah's favor to you, and that which He has revealed to you of the Book and the Wisdom, admonishing you thereby. And keep your duty to Allah, and know that Allah is the Knower of all things.

Please see the divorce law in Christianity is similar to Islam in that supervisory role is the fathers domain.

Please know the Nisa is done widely now in married couples who don't want to go through court proceedings in case of divorce but it is still necessary for them to bear equanimity to each other in case they go separate ways and it so occurs children are an issue of content not but the law in Christian land has always been that the father gets custody rights and supervises visitation with her mother they have, but it is so the mother is a better parent in this land so allow her leeway to live with them with supervisory role given to the father still as he has more acumen for the child in regard to visitation and holiday schedule, but that said it is better to stay with the child in his or her wishes as well for him, and so it occurs that Christianity is sane to pursue in their divorce decree in this land for you, and Islam is similar, custody rights are with the father for the most part and if they separate then the child must stay in the father's home town by law as the father must oversee his or her care.

Omar.

Please know yourself as a believer when you submit to Him Who created you.

Please know we are complete when we pray for you and them who think it is okay to wait.

Please see the opening chapter of the Quran,

Please see that we say this prayer several times in each of our daily prayers,

Please know why,

Please know we wish to be the guide of you.

Please understand how,

Please know if we are on the right path then we will guide you who are astray.

Please know I don't mean that in a demeaning sense but the facts are the facts.

Please know you had left your religious edicts and were leading the life of apostates.

Please know how,

Please know you don't follow the law.

Please understand how this makes you an apostate,

Please understand how could you be a submitter to Him with no law that you follow.

Please know that is like a Muslim who has a law but does not submit and does what he wishes and says he is a Muslim,

Please know in the same sense you are a follower of him who is Jesus to you in name only as you do as you please and not as he says.

Please know I don't mean to demean you; only tell you facts of your religion,

Please say a prayer for me that delineates religious belief for you and Muslims alike.

Please know you can say you are Christians or Muslims by my leave but it does not hold water with Him and His Prophet and his companions,

Please see the reality in this world,

Please know it will be too late in the next. Omar.

The Fatiha.

1:1 Praise be to Allah, the Lord of the worlds

1:2 The Beneficent, the Merciful,

1:3 King of the day of Requital

1:4 Thee do we serve and Thee do we ask for help.

1:5 Guide us on the straight path,

1:6 The path of those upon whom Thou hast bestowed favors,

1:7 Not those upon whom wrath is brought down, nor those who go astray.

Please know to rancor my heart but not my deeds as I am careful not to supersede him who is my Prophet.

Please know rancor is her who hates me,

Please know in us it is normal to admire my predecessor as we all feel it rise in us.

Please know our Prophet had rancor to some who were better in degrees but knew he was in the position of envy of most.

Please know rancor is sane and we know ourselves through it.

Please know rancor is sane,

Please know it rises within us as people call us perfect and our pride rises,

Please know it is incorrect in us and we must submit he is better than us,

Please know we all have rancor for purpose,

Please know it is to inhibit us,

Please know it rises because it is incorrect to have but we can't prevent it,

Please know we will be cut down for rising above him as he was the best,

Please know Prophet Muhammad was destined to be maqaam e Mahmood,

Please know he is coveted so it is written for us to covet him,

Please know it is evil in me to covet as he is my benefactor but it is so written for all men to vie for him in that position, though we may not want to.

Please know to have rancor to Muhammad is sane but to be jealous is not as he showed his worth during his life here,

Please know we could not have lived the life he did with all its austerity and trials he had,

Please know I have rancor because I wish it.

Please know it is written for us to have rancor to those better than us in caliber and degree,

Please know my mentor Mirza Ghulam Ahmad had it to me as in some ways I am better but in other ways he is superior.

Please know I know this but the rancor rises anyway,

Please know we are all human and the rancor is a part of our make and it will abide until it is clear to you I am not he who is Muhammad to me,

Please know we all have rancor eventually as it is written there we will and it will be removed by Him on the entry to Paradise as we are all equal there,

Please know I said equal in stature as we are all created the way we are though our deeds are different as it is written for us what we are and we can't help it if we are inferior to him who was the best,

Please know my Prophet had the best deeds, then myself as I brought a similar nation to Islam that was of debauched in idolatry to themselves and her,

Please know I say I did it as the credit goes to me actually as we all have a guide from Him but I know it is my worth to give credit to Him

Who turns hearts towards Islam as I do not have that option, neither did my Prophet, who became the ruler thereby through his sagacity and wisdom,

Please know I won because I had the Prophet's intellect with me, not because of myself, because I am plain, simple, fool to you, while I am sagacious as well, though less than others you think. Omar.

Types of revelation.

Please know I am a saint who guides you aright to the truth of a matter by the will of my Creator and His Prophet Muhammad, on him be peace.

Please see this verse that talks about revelation from the chapter The Poets.

Please know it is three types.

Please know the lowest form of communication is what occurs in our instincts.

Please know it is similar to animals and they know how to act according to their instinct.

Please know it is also called a hasty suggestion,

Please know sometimes we are certain of a certain thing based upon a hunch.

Please know our Creator guides all of us.

Please understand our heart is a repository of truth,

Please realize this,

Please know the more truth we embellish ourselves with the more our hearts are receptive to guidance.

Please see if we can get to the truth without revelation,

Please know it is not possible and our God guides us to the truth through His prophets to whom He gave guidance.

Please know this guidance comes forth in the shape of a book.

Please know all the prophets are given books.

Please understand this,

Please know some books are conserved hundreds of years after the prophet's demise, while some are not,

Please know the books have to make coherence to us,

Please know there is a reason why the collection of the books was delayed.

Please know it was so that people could use their rationale to see if their books were coherent to people and so that books are not followed blindly.

Please know of all the books the Quran was collected in a systematic manner with scientific principles applied within a few months of the Prophet's demise.

Please know the teachings of the Prophet were different.

Please know there are truths in the Quran that confirm the earlier scriptures.

Please know there are no two diverging truths on a matter as the truth is known and false lies are knocked out by it. If you look at your books with circumspection you will see how errors occurred.

Please know this was the basis of errors in concepts occurring in religions.

Please know the Quran is the attester and it provides a rationale.

Please use it is as a reference for the truth of a factual matter.

Please know there are incorrect practices in Muslims which are not true to the Quran or the practice of the Holy Prophet.

Please know that diverging viewpoints will find the truth in the Quran which is the criterion for earlier scriptures, verifying truths from before.

Please know I have explained the flaws in the reasoning of the Christian church from the revelation I have from Him.

Please know the arguments are clear in my book and are corroborated by the absolute truth of the Quran. Omar.

Al-Shuara

26:51 And it is not vouchsafed to a mortal that Allah should speak to him, except by revelation or from behind a veil, or by sending a messenger and revealing by His permission what He pleases. Surely He is High, Wise.

26:52 And thus did We reveal to thee an inspired Book by Our command. Thou knewest not what the Book was, nor (what) Faith (was), but We made it a light, guiding thereby whom We please of Our servants. And surely thou guidest to the right path —

26:53 The path of Allah, to Whom belongs whatsoever is in the heavens and whatsoever is in the earth. Now surely to Allah do all affairs eventually come.

Please see these verses from Baqarah where it says that disbelief in Allah is akin to take the devil as friend.

Please know the choice is yours, your heart knows when things make sense to you.

Please know it is clear we make the choice to enter Heaven or Hell by our own accord and it is satisfactory there as a reason, the life we lead will be enough as a witness on us and we will be satisfied with the result as we have done our deeds and seen the results first hand.

Please know our heart guides us as to the truth but for ourselves we make the choice of Allah's word versus the devil's handiwork on us.

Please know I present the data to you, it is for you to choose if it is accurate.

Please know we make the effort and God's reward is with us but for you who do not find it accurate is a reckoning as most of it is God's word from the Quran with accompanying data from other sources considered reliable here. Omar.

Al-Baqarah.

2:256 There is no compulsion in religion—the right way is indeed clearly distinct from error. So whoever disbelieves in the devil and believes in Allah, he indeed lays hold on the firmest handle which shall never break. And Allah is Hearing, Knowing.

2:257 Allah is the Friend of those who believe—He brings them out of darkness into light. And those who disbelieve, their friends are the devils who take them out of light into darkness. They are the companions of the Fire; therein they abide.

Please know Islam is perfect and if you say you believe it is correct, it is enough to win you acclaim as Muslims but won't win you Him until you submit and faith enters your heart.

Please see the following caption with me.

Please know there is no God but Allah and Muhammad is His Messenger is the edict we have to prove to Him by our deeds and our struggle here on earth and it is not like some who say it is enough for Paradise to occur.

Please see these verses from the chapter The Apartments or 49.

Please know the onus is on us to submit.

Please understand this,

Please know we must believe in the truth from Him and show our belief with our deeds.

Please understand this,

Please know if our deeds are not what our words are then we are guilty of hypocrisy.

Please know it is not enough to say we believe while you do not if your deeds are empty of Him.

Please know He says in the Quran that if you love Him then obey Allah and His Messenger.

Please know love is a very basic emotion and He requires more of mankind.

Please know you lay no obligation on Him,

Please understand this,

Please know you cannot enter Paradise without His pleasure in you.

Please know the onus is on you to prove your worth and to show that you are capable of pleasing Him.

Please know to say the words, you believe, is the first step.

Please know there is no Paradise here.

Please know the second stage comes when you submit to His commands,

Please know you may be forgiven here then.

Please know when faith enters your essence then you enter Paradise.

Please know I weep for you,

Please know there are some here who don't know the first stage of survival.

Please remember you used to live lives of apostates for the most part here in this country of yours. Omar.

Al-Hujurat.

49:14 The dwellers of the desert say: We believe. Say: You believe not, but say, We submit; and faith has not yet entered into your hearts. And if you obey Allah and His Messenger, He will not diminish aught of your deeds. Surely Allah is Forgiving, Merciful.

49:15 The believers are those only who believe in Allah and His Messenger, then they doubt not, and struggle hard with their wealth and their lives in the way of Allah. Such are the truthful ones.

49:16 Say: Would you apprise Allah of your religion? and Allah knows what is in the heavens and what is in the earth. And Allah is Knower of all things.

49:17 They presume to lay thee under an obligation by becoming Muslims. Say: Lay me not under an obligation by your Islam; rather Allah lays you under an obligation by guiding you to the faith, if you are truthful.

Please know I am scared for you since you tempt Him by denying His worship.

Please see that we avoid Hell as the turmoil there will be unlike any on earth.

Please see these verses from the chapter The Beneficent or 55.

Please know the creation of man is for a destiny with Him.

Please know we each are supposed to submit to Him,

Please know in return He will forgive and elevate our status.

Please know every entity He creates is precious.

Please know He creates us so we worship Him.

Please know He gives us leeway if we don't.

Please know eventually we will submit willingly.

Please know for some it will be on earth.

Please know if they don't here they will have a reckoning with Him that will be severe.

Please know after suitable modification of our thought where we will submit we will be raised to our Heavenly abode.

Please know the turmoil of Hell is best avoided by submitting here The end occurs if you think you will tempt fate by going to Hell.

Please understand the turmoil of Hell,

Please know it is as if you are blasted out of existence and created anew.

Please know you cannot die there.

Please know this process will go for eternity unless you submit.

Please know we cannot know the turmoil of Hell but a few moments there will make you think you never saw any good here on earth.

Please say a prayer that since you have to submit you might as well do it here on earth, before you die.

Please know there is no going back to submit once you exit here,

Please know the reality,

Please know you are going to die,

Please understand life,

Please know it is a test to see who is the best of submitters. Omar. Al-Rahman.

55:26 Everyone on it passes away —

55:27 And there endures forever the person of thy Lord, the Lord of glory and honor.

55:28 Which then of the bounties of your Lord will you deny?

55:29 All those in the heavens and the earth ask of Him. Every moment He is in a state (of glory).

Please know your law books are correct but your people are corrupt who implement them.

Please know our courts are not fair to the poor and those of minorities.

Please know this verse.

Please know it is from The Apartments in the Quran.

Please know there is no distinction.

Please know the family you belong to carries no weight with Him.

Please understand that our creed and nationality is of no basis of distinction with Him and those in Heaven and the righteous in the world.

Please no there is no class distinction.

Please see is this not the universal law of mankind that was taught to mankind?

Please know your law here allows this but your people lag behind.

The end occurs when you give leeway to the rich but demolish the house of the poor.

Please know the metaphor here.

In this is reality that you do not follow the law book in your courts.

I hope you bear heed and use this as your sole criteria for judging mankind. Omar.

Al-Hujurat.

49:13 O mankind, surely We have created you from a male and a female, and made you tribes and families that you may know each other. Surely the noblest of you with Allah is the most dutiful of you. Surely Allah is Knowing, Aware.

Please know Islam is fair to you and allows you peace as you come through in it.

Please know we are responsible if we give in to the harpings of others.

Please see these verses from The Family of Amran.

Please know this is true in this land where a party of you believers are being dissuaded from following the precepts of Islam by your family.

Please know this,

Please know the truth of the Quran is apparent to people and it is their family and friends that tell them otherwise.

Please know the truth will precipitate towards the heart and settle there and if there is any good in a person it will be accepted.

Please know it shows the worth of a man if he accepts the truth when it is apparent to him and it does him credit when he does so.

Please know we must try to acknowledge truth when they occur in our thoughts as to deny them is to be a hypocrite.

Please know you should encourage the truths when your youth show an inclination to believe.

Please know there are many in mainstream Islam that are like us in Ahmadiyyat that have values like you and me.

Please know we hope to have a good family and friends with us and we hope for the usual aspirations that mankind has. Omar.

Al-Imran.

3:69 A party of the People of the Book desire that they should lead you astray; and they lead not astray but themselves, and they perceive not.

3:70 O People of the Book, why do you disbelieve in the messages of Allah while you witness (their truth)?

Please know our outcome depends upon how we live our lives here.

Please know the affectionate will have a good outcome.

Please know this article is in reference to the travailties of time and that fame is evanescent.

Please know our companions will pass on and they will be remembered by us for a period then we will move on as well.

Please know that it is in the Hereafter that we are remembered.

Please know the affectionate are remembered fondly,

Please consider this,

Please know your destination is going to be where your companions are. If they were good you will be in a good place.

Please understand in the past for the most part your companions were not righteous as there were few people who had that quality in them then.

Please understand this,

Please know on the Day we are judged the majority of the people will be the denizens of Hell not, but few will make it Heaven unscathed, some will wait there for Heaven to occur but some will go there where their destination awaits them,

Please see it is those who go for reform there to Hell of the Hereafter,

Please know why?

Please know there are many who observe the truth now but a few still deter, it is these that are referred to here,

Please know they were given options and chose to ignore the truth and live on with their companion who deters you.

Please know this is a crime with Him and He expects us to grasp what is true.

Please know you do it to yourself.

Please know you have a choice to hold on to the truth or live in ignorance.

Please know you make your choices and your destination will transpire.

Please know the heart observes the truth. We act to ignore it or grasp it. I know you make the choice of choosing your destination.

Please choose your companion with care, he will lead you astray if he is not truthful to you about us in Islam for you that you like.

Please deter him who is untruthful there.

Please know you deter him for your benefit to occur, he will deter you there and you won't enter with us your final destiny to you. Omar.

Please know friendly relationships are permitted between you and others not of your faith.

Please know this verse that friendly relations can exist between you and the People of the Book as long as they don't harm you.

Please see these verses from the chapter The Woman Who Is Examined or sixty.

Please understand the words here,

Please know our Creator permit the friendly relationships with people of other faiths.

Please understand it is a misunderstanding amongst Muslims that there is no friendly relationships between unbelievers and those who submit.

Please see the following caption there.

Please know these are friends who help me.

Please understand this is our Prophet's heart.

The end occurs when people think he fought people because of their religion. In this there is certainty that there were many women and men who protected him. I know he took refuge from the enemy in them. It is ill-conceived that they were friendly for a need only as this continued even when he was secure.

Please know we strive to be friends but sometimes we fail as they show enmity rather than solace to us. In the hereafter some will come through and some will die as unbelievers.

Please know a requiem for me.

Please know I tried to do as the Prophet did and succeeded. Omar. Al-Mumtahanah.

60:7 It may be that Allah will bring about friendship between you and those of them whom you hold as enemies. And Allah is Powerful; and Allah is Forgiving, Merciful.

60:8 Allah forbids you not respecting those who fight you not for religion, nor drive you forth from your homes, that you show them kindness and deal with them justly. Surely Allah loves the doers of justice.

60:9 Allah forbids you only respecting those who fight you for religion, and drive you forth from your homes and help (others) in your expulsion, that you make friends of them; and whoever makes friends of them, these are the wrongdoers.

Please know your defeat results when you hear the bitter one against you as he berates you for understanding we are correct as to the perfect nature of the faith of Islam.

Please know the ignominy of defeat is from the accursed one who puts doubts in the hearts of mankind even though they recognize the truth in it.

Please see these verses from the Quran.

Please know that our Prophet never killed anyone for leaving the religion of Islam.

Please know apostasy as we know it was negligible in those times and the instances it was reported nothing was done to those who turned away. Our Creator here states the punishment for leaving one's religion of Islam is Hellfire.

Please know the law of killing an apostate is derived from a hadith and needs to be rejected as it contradicts a law of the Quran that there is no compulsion in faith. I know the hadith is well rooted however it appears to relate to those who were guilty of treason where they joined the enemy camp in an attempt to kill the believers as they knew the secrets of the army. I know this concept is gaining ground and eventually people will not be killed for leaving Islam as their destination is known and it is up to Allah to do the needful for them and cleanse them of denying the truth after it had entered their heart. In the event that they increase in disbelief they will not find any avenue of peace as ransom will not be accepted and their deeds will be in vain.

Please know God is kind and knows that doubts occur in the hearts however on this matter He is strict as to deny the truth is the opposite of the peace we have in it and people should be encouraged to seek solace after they have doubts appear rather than lose themselves in the ignominy of defeat from the accursed one, the devil to one. Omar.

Al-Baqarah.

2:217 And whoever of you turns back from his religion, then he dies while an unbeliever—these it is whose works go for nothing in this world and the Hereafter. And they are the companions of the Fire: therein they will abide.

Al-Imran.

3:90 Those who disbelieve after their believing, then increase in disbelief, their repentance is not accepted, and these are they that go astray.

3:91 Those who disbelieve and die while they are disbelievers, the earth full of gold will not be accepted from one of them, though he should offer it as ransom. These it is for whom is a painful chastisement, and they shall have no helpers.

Please know the prodigal have a heaven if they but submit.
Please see this verse from the chapter of The Companies or 39.
Please know we are all prodigal in some way or another.

Please know our Prophet and the other prophets come to Him with penitent hearts hoping for His mercy and forgiveness.

Please know we all have a destiny and we all sin in some way. I cannot say which sinner will be forgiven but know it will be the one who comes to Him and admits his fault. I know we are all sinners and we need mercy from Him that He will guide us to the right path of enlightenment from Him. I come to you as a sinner and know that while my sins are less than others in things I cannot think that I am safe from Him if He wishes to punish. It is this verse that gives us the heart to go on.

The end is there for those who think a guilty one is beyond redemption no matter what his or her sin may be.

Please know in the final analysis all He asks from us is to repent to Him and stop the wrong we were doing.

Please know His chastisement is severe if we do not have regret for our sins and plan to continue on with them. I know He is a loving God and He wishes for us to come through and better our state so that we may enter our Heaven with our representative from Him.

Please try to pray to Him alone as He does not like it that you should call on others while He is the sole Arbitrator for mankind.

Please know the prophets can intervene only after He decides to permit them. Omar.

Al-Zumar.

39:53 Say: O My servants who have been prodigal regarding their souls, despair not of the mercy of Allah; surely Allah forgives sins altogether. He is indeed the Forgiving, the Merciful.

Please know polygamy is an avenue for vice to end in the world.
Please know we must persevere in defending our faith.
Please see the following verse from the chapter The Women or four.
Please know the moral chastity of the state was at stake.
Please know war caused an excess of widows.
Please know if women are not in the married state it will lead to vice.
Please know the orphan had to be taken care of.

Please know they need food and shelter but the primary objective in allowing polygamy was to take care of them and not let vice spread in the community which results when there is an excess of unmarried women.

Please know our Creator knows us and knows in extenuating circumstances leeway has to be made.

Was this the reason you had prostitution in your societies after wars?

Please know it is.

Please know you cannot keep pure when the children have to be fed.

Please know every human has the sexual urge.

Please be considerate when you see this happen that man marries another rather than shedding his family from before.

Please say a prayer that God may guide you aright and you may see truth was the motif of Islam,

Please know the early Christians and the Jews allowed polygamy.

Please know it was prevalent in the world.

Please understand man does not know more than his Creator. Omar. Nisa.

4:3 And if you fear that you cannot do justice to orphans, marry such women as seem good to you, two, or three, or four; but if you fear that you will not do justice, then (marry) only one or that which your right hands possess. This is more proper that you may not do injustice.

Please know the handmaidens and slaves of Allah know it to be true, His promise for you.

Please see a caption here.

Please know the error occurs when you ignore Him and enter perdition.

Please see these verses from The Cow or chapter two.

Please know this is the edict we live by.

Please understand we cannot control what the other thinks.

Please realize our Friend is Him Who creates and then perfects.

Please follow Him to Paradise.

Please know we are only guides to you.

Yours truly knows there is a reckoning and I prepare myself for it.

Please understand we all have faults and it is a gradual amelioration of our faults that we strive for.

Please understand there are men and women who have perfected themselves.

Please know that is our goal.

Please know perfect,

Please know it is to follow the Prophet's car to you on my page to you.

The end comes to those who do not care how we do in the Hereafter.

Please know they will have a hard reckoning with Him and may enter The Hellfire.

Please know it is not a pleasant place. Omar.

Al-Baqarah.

2:256 There is no compulsion in religion—the right way is indeed clearly distinct from error. So whoever disbelieves in the devil and believes in Allah, he indeed lays hold on the firmest handle which shall never break. And Allah is Hearing, Knowing.

2:257 Allah is the Friend of those who believe—He brings them out of darkness into light. And those who disbelieve, their friends are the devils who take them out of light into darkness. They are the companions of the Fire; therein they abide.

Please know to berate yourself when you do wrong as that is the human in us.

Please see the passage from the Quran from chapter 69 or The Sure Truth.

Yours truly has a dream.

Please know it is to emulate the Prophet in delivering the message to you.

The end is there for those who think it is useless to deliver the message as America will not change.

Please know this is incorrect and America prays to Him, by and large, and knows Jesus to be a servant of His Grace.

Please know on other issues I know I am on firm ground and it is relayed to me that you have abdicated your views on sexual mores, prevalent previously.

Please know I have delivered the message faithfully thus far and hope to continue to do so in the future as well. I know the Prophet's job was more comprehensive. I am only his slave and my job is not as daunting or hard as you were subservient to me and expected me to emerge and teach you the truth of Islam to you.

Please say a prayer for me that I continue in the same vein and I can convince people about the beauty of Islam, whereby your Hereafter is reckoned.

Please know we must serve humanity and not ascribe partners to Him. I know it is a complete human who never bowed down to idols.

Please know Abraham was next in degree of steadfastness and perseverance in what was right with Him. I know these men are examples to humanity.

Please know to be a complete human we need to ascribe traits that these two humans had. We all falter and we are raised in degree when we leave something wrong for what is right in us.

The end is there for those who think we consider one prophet better than another except in degree of submission they had. But nay, they are all honored servants in the eyes of their Creator.

Please try to say a prayer for yourself and others as there are many animal-like traits prevailing here as yet in some of you but many are human and admit their fault in things.

Please know there are three stages of mankind. The lowest is the animal-like stage where we do things and our conscience does not berate us. The next stage is the human-like stage where our conscience berates us when we do something wrong and we correct ourselves or improve our worth. The last stage is the highest and involves a state of peace in us. It occurs when we see humanity for what they are and attempt to help them through our teachings. Omar.

Al-Haqqah
69:40 Surely, it is the word of an honored Messenger,
69:41 And it is not the word of a poet. Little is it that you believe!

69:42 Nor the word of a soothsayer. Little is it that you mind!
69:43 It is a revelation from the Lord of the worlds.
69:44 And if he had fabricated against Us certain sayings,
69:45 We would certainly have seized him by the right hand,
69:46 Then cut off his heart's vein.
69:47 And not one of you could have withheld Us from him.

Please know religion is only for Allah and there is no compulsion in faith is the dictum we follow in this land.

Please know religion is only for our Creator,

Please Him and allow them to pray as they wish as there is no compulsion in faith,

Please know there was religious freedom at our Prophet's time and they were allowed idolatry under his rule.

Please know he is immaculate and the custom of not allowing them is a later custom based on a hadith that they should not be allowed there in Saudi Arabia.

Please know the underlying principle is ignored that there is religious freedom as the compulsion is decried and the Prophet's example is to be followed.

Please know scholars know this but make an exception,

Please know it is not right to make an exception.

Please know it is the government's duty to protect the places of worship and this country has that law in place.

Please understand our Prophet and his caliphs stayed away from praying in churches and the places of worship of other faiths. In this there is sanity as one can see Muslims wishing to usurp the property as their own. In this there is clarity of thought in that the places of worship are to be protected by the government in charge of these buildings and should not allow baser instincts to prosper where a minority could be forced out of their prayer area. The Quran tells us we must protect the prayer areas of the People of the Book but the principle applies to all religious denominations living in Muslim lands.

I should be pleased but it is not correct that there in Pakistan and the Middle East Christians and Jews are inhibited while in this land they are allowed religious freedom.

Please know that our Prophet did not recommend Muslims praying in churches or cloisters. Omar.

Al-Hajj.

22:40 And if Allah did not repel some people by others, cloisters and churches and synagogues and mosques in which Allah's name is much remembered, would have been pulled down.

Al-Baqarah.

2:193 And fight them until there is no persecution, and religion is only for Allah.

Please know it is not the birth of a prophet we should celebrate but their life with knowledge of their character and deeds.

Please know we celebrate the life of our prophets but their birth is not real enough for us to celebrate. In this we know is peace as there is no deed that is performed that we should mention in the birth of a prophet while their life is full of things to admire and talk about.

Please know that the birth of a prophet is an august occasion but in Islam it is usually not recommended to celebrate it as it leads to a celebration that is deviant in nature as seen in the present-day Christmas celebrations where the spirituality of Christ is lost. It is the same in Muslim countries where the birthday of our Prophet is celebrated.

Please see the following verses from the Quran depicting the time of the birth of Jesus.

Maryam.

19:22 Then she conceived him; and withdrew with him to a remote place.

19:23 And the throes of childbirth drove her to the trunk of a palm-tree. She said: Oh, would that I had died before this, and had been a thing quite forgotten!

19:24 So a voice came to her from beneath her: Grieve not, surely thy Lord has provided a stream beneath thee.

19:25 And shake towards thee the trunk of the palm-tree, it will drop on thee fresh ripe dates.

19:26 So eat and drink and cool the eye. Then if thou seest any mortal, say: Surely I have vowed a fast to the Beneficent, so I will not speak to any man today.

Please know the Christmas you are getting ready for is something that originated out of a pagan custom of sun worship.

Please understand after the winter solstice the pagans would celebrate the lengthening of the day with a celebration on December 25 to honor their sun god.

Please know according to the Quran, Jesus and Thomas, the twin, were born in September, the time of the harvesting of the dates from their trees.

Please know also in Luke it says the shepherds were tending their flock which wouldn't be the case if he had been born in December.

Please understand these things are not important in Islam and the celebration of the prophet's birthdays is not recommended as it leads to an association with their Creator when we worship them inadvertently. I am inclined to let people celebrate Christmas though I think it is not something we aspire for in Islam. Omar.

Please know women have intellect but in most cases lose interest when they have children.

Please see this verse from chapter two or The Cow.

Please know that transactions in those times were complex as they involved ready merchandise. In this there is certainty that women then did not partake in trade like they do nowadays.

Please understand that this was their norm while your norm is different now and we must live with the times.

Please know I do not abrogate the verse from the Quran but do understand if a woman gets affronted and understand that if she partakes herself to housework the law may be applicable once again. I know transactions are by and large written down now and the point is moot in most cases. Omar.

Baqarah

2:282 O you who believe, when you contract a debt for a fixed time, write it down. And let a scribe write it down between you with fairness; nor should the scribe refuse to write as Allah has taught him, so let him write. And let him who owes the debt dictate, and he should observe his duty to Allah, his Lord, and not diminish anything from it. But if he who owes the debt is unsound in understanding or weak, or (if) he is not able to dictate himself, let his guardian dictate with fairness. And call to witness from among your men two witnesses; but if there are not two men, then one man and two women from among those whom you choose to be witnesses, so that if one of the two errs, the one may remind the other. And the witnesses must not refuse when they are summoned. And be not averse to writing it whether it is small or large along with the time of its falling due. This is more equitable in the sight of Allah and makes testimony surer and the best way to keep away from doubts. But when it is ready merchandise which you give and take among yourselves from hand to hand, there is no blame on you in not writing it down. And have witnesses when you sell one to another. And let no harm be done to the scribe or to the witnesses. And if you do (it), then surely it is a transgression on your part. And keep your duty to Allah. And Allah teaches you. And Allah is Knower of all things.

Please know the purpose of our creation is the worship of His Entity in its entirety.

Please know the caption on His heart.

Please know I am The Beautiful like none other.

Yours truly is an appreciator of Him. We know the essence of our existence is Him.

Yours truly weeps at the immense magnificence of His Being.

Please see the following caption there in the hearts of the companions of the Prophet.

Please know we are pleased if we die for His sake as our very essence beckons us on to do this.

The end is near for those who disdain His service.

Please understand we only live once so let this life be of service to Him and His creatures.

Please know your beauty is in the appreciation of our Creator. Omar.

Please know an animal knows we are His vicegerent and submits as its norm.
Please see the following caption on their heart.
Please know we were created for this.
Please understand it is not wrong to sacrifice an animal for its meat.
Please know these animals are submissive in this role of being sacrificed and they know they will be rewarded by their Creator for being sacrificed. In Heaven they will have a similar role but they will regenerate. In this there is clarity that the reward of a being is never lost by our Creator. I hope we will appreciate meat when we eat it as it has given up life so as to be sacrificed for its food content.
Please understand animals can be slaughtered for their nutritional value however one has to be kind to them in the process.
Please see they are created to be fodder as you can see from their lives in the wild where lions eat gazelles and so forth other animals eat others and they do not mind being a part of this life cycle.
Please see we are kind to an animal when we raise it for husbandry and if we treat it well it will be happy with us and intervene for us on the Day we are judged, just like mankind can do so,
Please see Allah asks us why we do not eat an animal and equates it to following the footsteps of the devil as we gain strength by it and wisdom as well as we see nature is to allow death of animals for us and we must be kind in it, in their kill I mean.
Please know we are strong if we sacrifice an animal in Islam but there are certain conditions in animal slaughter that have to be followed to minimize grief to the animal. This includes shielding it from the other animals so that it does not see its fate before it occurs. In this way we are kind to animals who are sacrificing themselves for us. We are thankful to our Creator who has provided for us as well.
Please know these animals are taken to a place after they die where they await Judgment Day just like humans are to wait for that day. Animals that are sacrificed have a higher status with our Creator than

those that are not sacrificed and animals that are sacrificed in God's name have a still higher degree in the eyes of His Benevolence.

Please know in Islam there is some controversy as to the fate of these animals and others that live on earth. In my view our Creator's mercy is such that once He gives life to a creature of His He will not take it away and He will not annihilate any being. I hope people will realize that just as humans do not like to annihilate any being then so it will be with our Creator. Our Creator's mercy and love is so much greater than ours. Omar.

Al-Anum

6:118 Eat, then, of that on which Allah's name has been mentioned, if you are believers in His messages.

6:119 And what reason have you that you should not eat of that on which Allah's name is mentioned, when He has already made plain to you what He has forbidden to you—excepting that which you are compelled to. And surely many lead (people) astray by their low desires through ignorance. Surely thy Lord—He best knows the transgressors.

Al-Anum also

142 And of the cattle (He has created) some for burden and some for slaughter. Eat of that which Allah has given you and follow not the footsteps of the devil. Surely he is your open enemy —

Please know our status is of slaves on earth.

Please see if you can survive on pennies.

Please know we all need wealth yet it is wealth that hurts us in the end. I would have been sad there as I had much here. I know it is sad but abundance diverts us and we become foolish and spendthrift. I know we are just slaves of our Creator and it is better to know our station and live humbly.

Please understand this is correct. In this way we know that we are asked to be patient by our Creator when resources are meager and to persevere with truth telling and honesty in our earnings.

Please know the other statement is accurate as well. The end is there for those who think they will not be altered with wealth and abundance.

It despoils us and makes us fat-headed. It is time to persevere with good deeds as they become hard for us when we are rich.

Please try to realize the rot that sets in with wealth. Our egos reach a pinnacle.

Please know we were meant to be slaves with few possessions. It is our peace we live with when we are so. When we come to earth we are empty handed and when we die, we are so. I hope you realize that everything here belongs to our Creator. We have possession for a while. It is best not to despoil ourselves with abundance but to live simply. It is moderation we seek. Omar.

Please know the nature of law with us is man maintains the women with him.

Please see this verse from chapter The Women or four.

Please know that our Prophet had indicated that the property of a man was meant to be used for the welfare of the women and child.

Please know he categorically states that the man is to maintain the woman with his wealth. In this there is certainty that I have done so with my wife and then with my mother and sister when they came to live with me.

Please know I am just and only ask for justice to be done and I be allowed to live with the laws that I live with. Omar.

Nisa.

4:34 Men are the maintainers of women, with what Allah has made some of them to excel others and with what they spend out of their wealth. So the good women are obedient, guarding the unseen as Allah has guarded.

Please know reality is to keep the words of the Quran in perspective in your lives.

Please understand our Prophet had a child he adopted.

Please know he was asked to change his name to his father's name who was in reality his father.

Please know these verses.

Please understand our words do not take the place of reality.

Please understand that we cannot adopt in reality as the children were born of another parent.

Please know that is the reality and if we give them our name they should know they are not ours in reality.

Please know spiritual matters take precedence and form the basis of reality.

Please understand Zihar.

Please know it was an Arab custom when he would declare his wife to be his mother in sexual relationships and would stop sleeping with her. It was not real and was abolished by Him.

Please know the same stands for our adopted sons and daughters.

The end occurs when you fight this.

Please know the wives of our Prophet are our mothers in spirit. In reality they are not.

Please know the Prophet's wives would cover themselves from their companions as it was not a reality that they were mothers of them.

Please know the early Muslims took their friends as brothers.

Please know they could not inherit from them.

Please keep reality in perspective as it will give a solid foundation with your child.

Please know these verses are from the Criterion or the Quran, from chapter thirty-three.

Please understand criterion,

Please know it is the standard format for mankind. I know we need something in life by which we judge by. Omar.

Ahzab.

33:4 Allah has not made for any man two hearts within him; nor has He made your wives whom you desert by Zihar, your mothers, nor has He made those whom you assert (to be your sons) your sons. These are the words of your mouths. And Allah speaks the truth and He shows the way.

33:5 Call them by (the names of) their fathers; this is more equitable with Allah; but if you know not their fathers, then they are your brethren in faith and your friends. And there is no blame on you in that wherein you make a mistake, but (you are answerable for) that which your hearts purpose. And Allah is ever Forgiving, Merciful.

33:6 The Prophet is closer to the faithful than their own selves, and his wives are (as) their mothers. And the possessors of relationship are closer one to another in the ordinance of Allah than (other) believers, and those who fled (their homes), except that you do some good to your friends. This is written in the Book.

Please know the first choice is yours and the follow-through is His to make you amend your ways.

Please see a requiem for me,

Please know I could not come through as advised and had a fall.

Please see I was advised by my Prophet not to pursue a date but did, the urge was too strong in me and I fell there eventual ways with her, so it occurs I am not the first of submitters but learnt to obey him who was Prophet there,

Please know our Creator revealed these words in the Quran here to the Prophet's heart when he was in the cave Hira,

Please know them,

Please know the first injunction was to seek knowledge that is propagated by the pen,

Please know our Prophet was unlettered,

Please understand this,

Please know it was to indicate to him that some people cannot submit to their Creator as he could not.

Please know this,

Please know he was asked to do something he had an inability to.

Please be gentle when they commit a crime,

Please know man,

Please know they must make an effort and if they fail it is decreed for them,

Please know our Prophet was quiet when people could not come through,

Please know this is in spite of the law.

Please know eternity,

Please know man will be pleased there,

Please know some things are fate and our Prophet told us not to cry over spilt milk,

Please know our job is to give you the choices,

Please know you make them with your own volition,

Please know our Creator is merciful and will guide those who don't come through,

Please know punishment is written.

Please make your choices wisely,

Please know they affect your Hereafter.

Al-Alaq.

96:1 Read in the name of thy Lord Who creates —

96:2 Creates man from a clot,

96:3 Read and thy Lord is most Generous,

96:4 Who taught by the pen,

96:5 Taught man what he knew not.

Please know we turn away with aversion from the truth when we don't accept it for ourselves.

Please learn the lesson of life,

Please know it is to tell you the truth,

Please know the truth is apparent to us and it is for us to submit to Him.

Please know of this verse from the Quran from chapter four or The Women.

Please know it is the characteristic of a hypocrite that when he sees something good from his Prophet he turns away.

Please know that it is true,

Please understand our Creator puts aversion in the hearts of people who He does not wanted to be guided to the truth,

Please know why,

Please know it is because their deeds are corrupt and they are not ready for solace from Him,

Please know they themselves don't wish it,

Please know He would guide them if they but had the heart to submit to Him,
Please know the deeds of theirs need to be in order.
Please know there were some men who never accepted Islam, even when it was ascendant,
Please know that is what the seal is,
Please know our Creator is only making it occur.
Please know if we repent we would be saved,
Please know some never learn in this life. Omar.
Nisa.
4:61 And when it is said to them, Come to that which Allah has revealed and to the Messenger, thou seest the hypocrites turning away from thee with aversion.

Please know we all make our choice, Heaven or Hell.
Please know our Creator is kind for us to come through.
Please see these verses from the chapter The Immunity.
Please know this,
Please know Allah accepts the repentance of His servants.
Please know this is because He decides,
Please know He is the Creator of mankind,
Please know each has its destiny,
Please know He has vouchsafed it, Heaven or Hell.
Please know why?
Please know the progeny of mankind has a characteristic for some,
Please know they don't want to submit,
Please know He knows that in His foreknowledge.
Please know it is written for us.
Please know He knows why it is so.
Please know it is because of the sins that have a precedence with them,
Please know a believer submits,
Please know he forsakes sin,
Please know he wishes to please,
Please know he cries at wrongs.

Please know he forsakes his pleasures for Him,
Please know it is written. Omar.
Al-Bara'at.

9:104 *Know they not that Allah is He Who accepts repentance from His servants and takes the alms, and that Allah—He is the Oft-returning (to mercy), the Merciful,*

9:105 *And say, Work; so Allah will see your work and (so will) His Messenger and the believers. And you will be brought back to the Knower of the unseen and the seen, then He will inform you of what you did.*

9:106 *And others are made to await Allah's command, whether He chastise them or turn to them (mercifully). And Allah is Knowing, Wise.*

Please know we are made fit by life in this world if we but try to fathom the reason of the trial we are placed in, in heaven on earth.

Please know Him as He is your advocate.
Please see these verses from the chapter The Bursting Forth or 84.
Please know the purpose of man,
Please know the trial that befalls him,
Please know the test that occurs,
Please understand this,
Please know without the trial we cannot prove our worth,
Please know that if we are tested not, how can we excel,
Please know the exam is hard for us but those that succeed are relieved at the result.
Please know life is a test for us.
Please know God sends us tribulations to make us see and hear.
Please know when we do so our heart reforms and learns,
Please know our life is not meaningless,
Please know we were not created for fun and gaiety but to know Him and ourselves.
Please know we must see the reality of the world and know that it is evanescent.
Please know Him.
Please know you do so by toiling.

Please know we gain in intellect when we are made fit.

Please know the bursting asunder is ourselves.

Please know when we kill our previous opinions we make new opinions and grow and become fit.

Please know our Prophet said "kill yourself before you die."

Please know he did not mean suicide but to kill your falsehoods.

Please know our destiny is to toil here.

Please know it is good to take Him with us on our journey to Him,

Please know He is peace to us,

Please know our journey can be peaceful.

Please say a prayer that you can keep Him with you,

Please know the journey is arduous but the reward is the most joy you can imagine,

Please know Islam is the armament of peace you need on this journey,

Please know we thank Him,

Please know there is no burden too severe for us,

Please know if you think it is fun and games you are here for then perdition is your home,

Please know I care for you and hope you will keep Him with you, inshallah or God willing you will. Omar.

Al-Inshiqaq

84:1 When the heaven bursts asunder,

84:2 And listens to its Lord and is made fit;

84:3 And when the earth is stretched,

84:4 And casts forth what is in it and becomes empty,

84:5 And listens to its Lord and is made fit.

84:6 O man, thou must strive a hard striving (to attain) to thy Lord, until thou meet Him.

84:7 Then as to him who is given his book in his right hand,

84:8 His account will be taken by an easy reckoning,

84:9 And he will go back to his people rejoicing.

84:10 And as to him who is given his book behind his back,

84:11 He will call for perdition.

84:12 And enter into burning Fire.

Please know bastardy has to be prevented in a community by multiple marriages if the need be.

I agree nikah is sunnah of our Prophet and ordained by God. It is the panacea for peace to occur in a relationship as without it there would be strife and hardship.

Please know we are married when the marital physical contact begins. I am surprised at you in this country that you used to discount marriage. It is essential for a relationship to prosper and gain acclaim.

I am hopeful that people will see through this sentiment that it makes no difference.

Please know it is sad for me to see children born out of wedlock. They need a parent there who they know is married to their mother. I know this as a fact that children perceive marriages better than we do as adults.

I am safe in this that there will always be strife in a relationship without the marriage knot being tied as it makes us think we can dispense with the partner since we are not married. I know this emotion occurs in couples.

In the end we choose our own destination. Whether to be law abiding and therefore enter Heaven or the converse.

I know we make choices.

My heart was sad when you didn't make the choice ordained by God as correct for you here on earth.

Please know you are adept now to take him in marriage if you wish to keep him.

Please know Nisa prevails you. Omar.

Please know the cool shade of the world is pleasing for me rather than the contrast of having hellfire when our Creator thinks us unworthy.

Please know this,

Please know our Prophet was a wayfarer who stayed awhile in the cool shade of the world then moved on to travel again.

Please know this is the way of humans.

Please understand they have a soul which will travel after this life.

Please understand this,
Please know that we are only in the world for a while.
Please understand we are bereft of belongings when we travel and only have our companions in heaven that occurs there in our waiting area.
Yours truly is a traveler who rests in the cool shade of the world as well.
Please know this world has a cool shade for some who forsake it.
Please know the opposite of the cool shade is the sweltering heat of hell.
Please understand this,
Please know we must be aware that if we commit sins our world is hot, as hellfire is kindled here and manifest in our Hereafter.
Please know what it means to travel,
Please know it is an experience we experience. Omar.

Please know we all need the stick as a deterrent so don't berate Him on the issue as you would not come around without it.
Please know we all need the carrot to entice us but later we do it for Him because we love Him.
Please understand psychology,
Please know it is to use the carrot and stick approach with mankind.
Please know man is strange.
Please understand this,
Please know that he does not want to understand the truth for fear of losing his liberty.
Please know when he does perceive it in his heart he still denies it with his tongue.
Please know the carrot,
Please know it is blessings from Him,
And the stick is His wrath which causes disquiet there.
Please know He understands you.
Please know without the fear of Hell you would not come through.
In this there is certainty that He encourages you to come around and be with Him in Paradise. Omar.

CHAPTER SEVEN

AHMADIYYAT

Please know Ahmadiyyat is a movement in Islam that teaches the principles of brotherhood in Islam,
Please know it teaches diverse topics that are different in mainstream Islam like the death of Christ,
Please know it has several branches, the one I belong to Illihoon ideology,
Please know it has adherents and detractors,
Please know it is Islam taught to us by Prophet Muhammad in direct communication, through sainthood,
Please know there are many hidden pearls there,
Please know it was not meant to be a sect but became one through a series of events,
Please know it is a thought movement,
Please know it has acceptability in some countries.
Please see a series of articles that accompany this text.

Please know the Ahmadiyya Jamaat of Illihoon fulfills the criteria of mubashiraat.
Please know I am an Ahmadiyya aqaid holder.
Please understand that means I consider us to be the correct ideology in Islam.
Please know I pray with mainstream Muslims as our principles of faith are identical.
Please understand there are people who do not understand my claim for sainthood as there is a view in mainstream circles that there can be no communication after revelation to Prophet Muhammad.

Please know this is a fallacy and many people have reported seeing our Prophet in dreams with communication to them,

Please know also there is no bearing in these views that revelation is curtailed after him in that sainthood was vouchsafed by our Prophet in his statement that after he passed away there will be partial Prophethood left which include true dreams and visions- Mubashiraat. I am quoting a true hadith of the Prophet here.

The element of communication from our Prophet does not end. He said in a hadith that the person who sees him in his sleep is vouchsafed Heaven signifying this form of communication I have will continue onwards.

Please know there is a hadith in Bukhari that signify people can see him in the awake state as I do. Omar.

Please know I am a Sufi as well, as my mentor was, but fulfill strict criteria of orthodoxy.

Please understand I am a Sufi saint like those before me were. I do not abdicate Ahmadiyyat but know my mentor was a Sufi saint as well.

Please understand Sufi indicates mysticism which has existed in all religions when we know there is an inner connection with God.

I am sad at the state of affairs of organized religion as it has lost attraction for some of its adherents due to blind belief in edicts from scholars nowadays.

Please know we are answerable to Him and He admonishes us to do the right thing for our own safety.

Please understand mysticism is an ancient art and was practiced by the people who followed the Torah, and Christians alike. Our Prophet was a mystic even before prophethood was given to him as he used to seclude himself from people and retire to the cave where he first received revelation from the angel. I know this art of religion existed there in the People of the Book as there is mention of this in their literature.

Please know not all mystics are accurate and due circumspection has to be applied to them to see if they meet credibility with the religion they follow. I know mystics have existed in Christianity and Judaism and it is my impression that it is very widespread in different religions as there are good people who are in touch with God or His emissary to them. I am confident that people will see me as a mystic from Him as I write with precision and accuracy.

Please know we are united in one body and if we understand our differences we will realize how similar we are. Omar.

Please know my service in Islam is clear to you.

Please understand the duty I put is for you to emerge from your hole and greet us in the shade of swords.

Please understand the metaphor here as I don't wield a sword.

Please understand this verse from The Apartments or chapter 49.

Please know no one is better because of his lineage or caste or tribe or nation.

The end occurs if you think you are better than me.

Please understand why.

Please know I gave up my career to be here preaching to you Islam that you understand is fair and that which has equanimity to you. I am the most observing of duty as I do as I am told which is something you cannot bear here. I know you think this mental disease but if it is you have to prove it me. I know sainthood is hard for some but for me it is easy and comes naturally as I have been experiencing it for thirty odd years. Omar.

Al-Hujurat.

49:13 O mankind, surely We have created you from a male and a female, and made you tribes and families that you may know each other. Surely the noblest of you with Allah is the most dutiful of you. Surely Allah is Knowing, Aware.

Please know these are complex terms used for teaching repose in Him is what we strive for in our efforts to show you we are one with Him when we do tasks for Him.

Please know it is over and you have learnt my imamat is sane for you and needs to be adopted,

Please know Muhammad Ali was another imam,

Please know he was blessed with an intellect that was acknowledgeable.
Please know he was a child prodigy of immense caliber.
Please understand he learnt by himself as I have and he was interested, as I am, in deen of Islam,
Please know it is inherent in us to learn,
Please know you like him immensely as he is your intellect.
Please know we are all facets He creates.
Please know I am an imam as a facet and my Prophet was a prophet of His.
Please know he was perfect though but still a facet,
Please know in the future you will be all Imams of sorts and you will learn me,
Please know it is saint you serve here.
Please know I am a leader though and one you respect and admire for my integrity in sticking to my guns and exposing government corruption.
Please know we are all facets of Him when we submit to Him.
Please know He is me in the metaphor.
Please know this,
Please know He has become united with us,
Please know saint,
Please know we bend or else we fail.
Please know He is 'We' when we work for Him,
Please know this is a title and not actual as it is in the metaphorical sense.
Please know He wishes to honor us as Him when we are His extension,
Please know we are not God and we should be named our name,
Please know there is no God but Allah or God or whatever you wish to call Him, our Creator.
Please know he is a celebrity who knows me,
Please ask him,
Please know the world has a new awakening about Islam through me,
Please know this,

Please know the multitude will occur there when Mecca accepts me as their Imam,
Please know they will.
Please know they have seen caliber that they know exists only in the Ahmadiyya group of his,
Please know I include my mentor, Mirza there, as he is them in our group of Illihoon ideology.
Please know why,
Please know it is because they call him a star who was like a prophet,
Please know him,
Please know he is my colleague and he did not lie when he grew old,
Please know this,
Please know he was careful to an extreme,
Please know the word is out,
Please know he was prophet as a metaphor, which is not one,
Please know he was not real as one,
Please know he was a saint,
Please know he was like Christ, as I am,
Please know I still use the metaphor,
Please know he gave me impetus,
Please know he was not guilty and they have fabricated it that he used the word prophet for himself in the actual sense though in his earlier writings it did appear as such when he named him as one but we know he always said he who is Muhammad there was the last one the world will see and upheld his law there.
Please know the metaphor is not real and means another state,
Please understand me,
Please know I am like him, in repose to Him,
Please know we work as a team and our Leader is God,
Please know repose,
Please know it is Him we work for and we are one with Him,
Please know this,
Please know I am His repose,

Please know He is our Master and we are the slave who serves Him only,

Please try to see reason in that we don't associate out of reason like you do with Jesus,

The end occurs when you say god to him or to any entity other than the Creator,

Please know we are Him but He is not us in the sense of actuality or reality,

Please know our soul is from Him but we cannot be called Him since that is a facet only or Him partially in us,

Please know He, in His entirety, is on His throne in Heaven,

Please know we, as a facet, are only part Him when we are Him in intent or our resolve of things,

Please know when we dissipate ourselves our repose occurs, which are thoughts from Him,

Please know if we follow through and do His bid we become Him or develop His characteristics in us.

Please know we are 'We' with Him when we obey Him in that we are His slaves,

Please know we fuse with Him but He does not become us,

Please know He is the Mother Ship and we are His extension, as creatures of His,

Please know fused as one Entity, yet separate,

Please know this,

Please know the saints wish to be us when they say they will annihilate themselves and be with Him.

Please know it is a spiritual state in that they have no will of their own is what it means to annihilate ourself and we remain separate as kings and queens of His,

Please know this,

Please try to remove the boundaries that block, and become Him, like Jesus was as he told you he did His bid and not his and so forth became an extension of Him.

Please know it can be done. Omar.

Please know you are on Araf with me and your destination is sad unless you fill your repose with His ways.

Please understand what Araf is and to whom it belongs to. It is the highest intellect today and it refers to those people who have understood our literature.

Please know they have understood me in this country and now it remains to be seen where they descend to or arise with a new awakening to be with the prophets and saints. In this there is certainty that the intellect of Mirza Ghulam Ahmad was combative and precise, while his helper, my grandfather, had a vast depth and breadth of knowledge, and my knowledge is deep and precise.

Please realize if you read our literature with the understanding that it is meant to convey you will be on the plains of Araf with us. I know this is complex but suffice it to say that our group's intellect is at the third highest pinnacle in the world after that of Muhammad to me and then Jesus to his follower and so forth other teachers as well who are taught by them in dreams to us, like I am here.

Please know if you enter it with us you will be in a high Heaven with the scholars of Islam who teach you things through the ages. Omar.

Please know the wise take on a challenge from your judiciary when you deny me peace by calling me unwell.

Please know our Prophet was a sign to mankind in many ways,

Please know his wisdom was consummate and he won every argument, as I have here,

Please know do your bid if you wish your peace,

Please know Islam is here and you won't be able to stop it from spreading,

Please know you are a nation of intellect and recognize merit in me and will in others in Islam,

Please know I have converted hearts through my efforts and my sign is you took the shahada worldwide.

Please know the church groups see this sign,

Please know this is the sign that their overthrow was imminent,

Please know we are a shatail qamar group where the sign was given to us.

Please know my book on Facebook is read as a sign to you and my master's thesis of Islam occurred from Muhammad to us,

Please know I speak of Mirza here,

Please know his history compilation is with you in his archives,

Please know he brought to clarity Prophet Muhammad's teachings from Him, our Creator, as I have brought you Islam here from the agency of my Prophet.

Please know we are one body in Ahmadiyyat,

Please know he is companion and we live in peace there,

Please know he guides me to tell you things from Him,

Please know we are both Allah's angels,

Please know He is our knowledge source,

Please know we were raised to raise you through teaching with the pen,

Please know Muhammad Ali is our savior and will bring the Muslim world to us.

Please know you know me magical but I am sane and don't write from him, the devil.

Please know He is my author and He gave me the page.

Please know He will give you a moratorium,

Please preach if you wish but don't blaspheme Him or His Prophet.

Please know He has asked me to fight you with my intellect if you do so,

Please know I use a pen though and the intellect is his, my Prophet. Please Him,

Please know He is exacting and terrible in conflict.

Please know I ask for your peace with me,

Please let me be.

Please do your bid though if you wish otherwise. Omar.

Qamar.

54:1 The hour drew nigh and the moon was rent asunder.

54:2 And if they see a sign, they turn away and say: Strong enchantment!

54:3 And they deny and follow their low desires; and every affair is settled.

54:4 And certainly narratives have come to them, which should deter—

54:5 Consummate wisdom—but warnings avail not;

Please know the Ahmadiyya Jamaat worked in unison to you to bring you the teachings of Muhammad as you saw fit for you.

Please know the metaphor to be one in repose to Him,

Please know that is what we three are in the Ahmadiyya Jamaat,

Please know we all work for Him,

Please know we are one though different,

Please know these are metaphorical terms,

Please be in one with Him,

Please do His works and further my cause in bringing Islam to people,

Please know you are then a servant who walks with the legs of Allah and talks His words as our Prophet indicated what a servant is like myself,

Please know we use the metaphor as it was used before,

Please know I am your son in repose to Him and wish you well.

Please know my mentor Mirza Ghulam Ahmad was a Sufi as well.

Please know his prophethood was in the metaphorical sense and he did not wish to be called one,

Please know he wrote this in his last book,

Please know if one commits a mistake before it can be assuaged if one asks for forgiveness and repents though he was led to say it as I was in the following line what I state here,

Please know I committed a similar error when I said I was an emissary from Him,

Please know we both ask forgiveness from you but sometimes our thinking was not clear initially,

Please know there is no prophet after Muhammad that the world will see, we both say that to you in our final word there,

Please know other saints have called themselves prophets but it was in the metaphorical sense, though they may have misunderstood the issue as well.

Please know within the Christian lore there are examples as well but their words were misconstrued to give them actual prophethood,

Please know the Quran is clear that Muhammad is the seal of the prophets,

Please indicate disfavor to those in Islam who still try to portray prophethood in us while we use the metaphor,

Please understand me,

Please know I am careful to an extreme about these issues but I am human,

Please know to forgive is sane,

Please know our works,

Please know we have given you Christ as he actually lived and died,

Please know we have converted him from a God to you to a prophet of His,

Please know we teach you his works so that you understand him,

Please give in,

Please know we are responsible for Islam to be the predominant religion in the world,

Please know it has occurred and the facts will come out, just as they did for the belief their God was One,

Please give accolade to the one who translated the Quran for you. Omar.

Please know the highest form of communication is when the Prophet communicates to you so you become a messenger of his to them.

Please understand Syria is a country our Prophet warned us about but it is not the Syria where Assad reigns though it has some characteristics that are similar.

Please know he referred to a Christian Syria which was under the Roman Empire though people there don't succumb as yet to me either. In this way we know he referred to the Christian countries. In the later days the saint Dabbat Al-Ard will emerge and will teach religion to the people of Syria or the Dajjal or Antichrist nation.

Please know he will continue the work of the Prophet before him in the Messiah clan and eventually they will come to Islam. In this there is clarity that I am Dabbat Al-Ard and I am the spearhead of the movement.

Please know Syria is a land where my literature is rife however they feel I am an Ahmadi and therefore different from them. I know I am an Ahmadi believer but my heart is with Muhammad, on him be peace.

Please know Ahmadis are Muslims with the same ideology of Islam like the other Muslims but have certain characteristics that make them different.

Please know they believe my mentor received revelation in the form of visions and other ways as well. I know we consider this to be revelation of the saints but one characteristic is that they have the prophethood of Prophet Muhammad in them. I know this occurs but it is difficult to explain and needs to be experienced. I know I write with clarity from him so it is a dream communication that is clear and distinct. I know it differs somewhat from other Sufi saints and is a high level of communication. Omar.

Please know Al-Dajjal is queer to you as he is a man but in the metaphorical sense of the word.

Please know Dajjal is one eyed,

Please know it is a metaphor for one who is spiritually blind and materialistic.

Please know it has started his car and my car is inhibited,

Please know they will do it again that my car is heisted again and again by them,

Please know they have power to do it and it must be done they say.

Please know I have achieved it and they know he is dead who is Isa Ibn Maryam,

Please know the facts is it all fits in,

Please know as I explained in my book there is no reason to be in disguise for a dead man raised to life,

Please know you can only die once.

Please know it is in spirit form we are raised but the gospel is clear in that regard he was flesh as he asked Thomas to put his hand in his wound and ate fish with hunger.

Please know it makes sense to a believer that he was unconscious and he survived it.

Please know the word death also means unconscious in Hebrew so they are used with interchange,

Please know Jesus knew this and prayed that he may be saved in the garden of Gethsemane in the evening before the crucifixion as he knew the term meant both things,

Please know the scholar knows to check the data.

Please know it is over and you have read me,

Please Him and be open about it.

Please know we ascribe to peace when we tell you you have amalgamated it and you realize the Quran is revealed,

Please know it all fits you say.

Please know the Quran was monotheistic and they told you it was idolatry with Allah being a moon God,

Please see what liars they are in churches on you,

Please know you know because you read him in the church literature they give you.

Please know Yahweh was only a name for Him Who creates, from the Bani-Israel perspective,

Please know He was their God and did not permit another.

Please know Allah is similar and the one Who creates according to the Quran's teachings on us,

Please see what liars they are who say otherwise that your God is the Creator and He is not, the Muslim God to you,

Please know Jesus was similar in message and told you to worship Him, not himself.

Please know who will you believe, him, or them in churches on you.

Please know all your prayers were directed to Him there,

Please know so were his and he cried longingly for His succor.

Please know it is false to claim he called himself Him in the actual sense as he could not answer prayers, therefore his repose was His.

Please know the testimony is damning for them where he explained the metaphor was him and he did not commit blasphemy for them,

Please know he used the metaphor adeptly, seeking His repose.

Please know Allah permit him but he realized it was dangerous and stopped as documented in the gospel there,

Please know Allah permit the gospel to emerge after the others where the metaphor was explained so that you would have peace and come to the Quran when I explained it as your church goers were recalcitrant and said the Quran was evil and devil worship though they knew better as they recognize it as their own book,

Please know some of them kept you away from it through deception, a characteristic of Dajjal who creates subterfuge and deceit in his dealings,

Please know Muslims know I am Dajjal's metaphor as I speak to you in your materialistic language and am one eyed they say, but my spirit is okay.

Please know I am one eyed in spirit as the eye that shines is the right one and I have left worldly pursuits so my left eye is shut.

Please know my car is sane for you to show you wealth will be permitted to you.

Please know I offer Heaven to a believer and Hell is their due if they ignore it what I teach.

Please know I am not evil to you and am a well-wisher taking you to Heaven by Prophet Muhammad's car when it is used.

Please know he said if they were alive, the Prophet Jesus and Moses, they would have to use his car or follow him,

Please know the same applies to you.

Please know I am a car in reverse as they will admonish me if I continue to teach he is Dajjal who uses subterfuge,

Please know he is but I am quiet from here on as you call him that openly in your homes and workplace. Omar.

Please know a manufactured good is pleasing to one but takes away from His remembrance.

Please know a manufactured good is ingenuity but it takes one away from the appreciation of the Creator and they are pleased with it,

Please know they think they are self-sufficient and don't care Him in their lives,

Please know it is this pragmatism that occurs and He is ignored, Please Him,

Please know they are in need and don't realize He won't come through until they are obedient to Him,

Please know it is secular pragmatism that is the death knell of a society as sexual promiscuity occurs and abortions are commonplace,

Please know this is because they have taken God out of their lives when they ignore Him,

Please know this is Dajjal or Antichrist as Christ taught differently and said to follow Him in your deeds,

Please know he prayed in fervor and was ardent with Him.

Please know this verse we are mortals.

Please know this is surah Kahf.

Please know all mankind is so.

Please know our Prophet was the best of created beings and he was asked to say so.

Please know I have showed you through literature that we come from ejaculate and so are lowly in essence but people can be high with Him as well.

Please don't elevate him to rank of God since he was lowly extract of her and him,

Please know we must ascribe to peace if you think he is divine but the evidence is incontrovertible on my page as he himself never ascribed divinity to himself.

Please know Matthews 4:10.

Please know he was born of man, in his own words.

Please him,

Please know he does not like it you call him divine,

Please know it is all false what you say about him as I have shown you his words from your book.

Please know don't do it as he in anguish,

Please know so is Muhammad when they call him things he is not as Muslims are akin to exaggerate him as well.

Please know a great personage is not your God that he can intercede for you, as indicated here where it says do not take him for caretaker or friend in preference to Him, your Creator.

Please know when you do so you lose Him,

Please know it is over and you don't give him preference like you used to.

Please Him,

Please know material things are good if they don't keep you away from your duty to Him,

Please know He knows you and you don't give preference to them but you ignore Him,

Please know your Hereafter has a balance or a scale to measure you in your deeds you do,

Please know why?

Please know it is because you care about yourself,

Please know it is because you care you come forth with me and admonish him who creates,

Please know he creates you as your anger occurs with him when he calls me mad,

Please know they know how to create,

Please know they created him as God to you,

Please know they created goodly manufacturers and called them good and wholesome,

Please know they innovate things but they lie,

Please know some things they don't but they lie that I am unwell.

Please know they are upset, you see through them and know my literature speaks for itself.

Please know you know it occurred as I say here on my page and it was confirmed by you.

Please know don't take me God,

Please know that is because I make mistakes,
Please Him,
Please know there is no god but Him in whom you have repose that He will take you there now that you submit to Him alone,
Please know it is not enough and your deeds have to be in order,
Please know you have a balance waiting,
Please Him and defend me with him who admonishes you for fighting the issue of Godhead in him,
Please make them melt,
Please be my soldiers or combatants,
Please be Christ's family as I fight for you in the Hereafter where me and my Prophet will intervene for you.
Please take me to be a friend but not caretaker as I can't intervene in that way.
Please know I am a mortal and am powerless with Him and He will do with me as He pleases.
Please know a prophet is friend but not in preference to Him Who allows them to intervene when He permits,
Please know they have no power to intervene until He lets them.
Please know we must ascribe to peace to you.
Please know Dajjal is a goodly manufacturer to the exclusion of Him,
Please know money becomes your God and human concerns become meaningless,
Please know He is Antichrist as Christ did not teach this,
Please know it is a product of your nation that started when you took him to be your savior and not the Creator,
Please know you thought he would intervene for you,
Please know you thought there was no accounting so you did it and took manufacturing good to be your God,
Please know you made it the end-all and be-all of your existence and you took God out of the equation,
Please know money became the bottom line and the end justified the means,
Please know that's why He says you are Dajjal here,

Please know there is no God there in their conference rooms,
Please Him and give to the poor and feed the destitute,
Please know you are better now that God has appeared to you in His understanding to you and you don't worship man,
Please know the left eye is materialism,
Please keep it but develop the right one,
Please pray and give,
Please obey Him in your works,
Please follow His law that tells you not to be pragmatic with remnants of atheism in it and deny sexual contact outside the marriage tie as He does not permit it. Omar.

Kahf.

18:102 Do those who disbelieve think that they can take My servants to be friends besides Me? Surely We have prepared hell as an entertainment for the disbelievers.

18:103 Say: Shall We inform you who are the greatest losers in respect of deeds?

18:104 Those whose effort goes astray in this world's life, and they think that they are making good manufactures.

18:105 Those are they who disbelieve in the messages of their Lord and meeting with Him, so their works are vain. Nor shall We set up a balance for them on the day of Resurrection.

18:106 That is their reward—hell, because they disbelieved and held My messages and My messengers in mockery.

18:107 As for those who believe and do good deeds, for them are Gardens of Paradise, an entertainment,

18:108 To abide therein; they will not desire removal therefrom.

18:109 Say: If the sea were ink for the words of my Lord, the sea would surely be exhausted before the words of my Lord were exhausted, though We brought the like of it to add (thereto).

18:110 Say: I am only a mortal like you—it is revealed to me that your God is one God. So whoever hopes to meet his Lord, he should do good deeds, and join no one in the service of his Lord.

Please know your government has been good to me despite its failings and attempts on my life.

Please know your president has melted but his law has not,

Please know he created homosexual car as norm while it is with him, the devil as norm for man.

Please see these verses from surah Kahf or The Cave.

Please know Godhead in man is their creation in the church.

Please know it is Dajjal they create as he is a liar.

Please know he conceals the truth with lies.

Please know it is not your government that is Antichrist anymore as they have melted and want it to come out that man is man and not divine,

Please know they see sanity is clear mindedness,

Please know they want their people to develop.

Please know they are kind to me and let me live while your church wanted me gone,

Please know they are the Dajjal in your community as they continue with Christ being God.

Please know they will fail as you will fail them,

Please know it is written that I am like Christ fighting Antichrist.

Please know I bring Islamic principles to you and show you Christ was a Muslim like me having Islamic precepts, not those of Paul and others who created divinity in him,

Please know the Quran is a book with no crookedness,

Please know its precepts are clear and will give you light,

Please know Islam,

Please know it is not Middle East, so ignore them some,

Please know they have Dajjal elements and cover the truth with lies and subterfuge.

Please know they declared him a Non-Muslim,

Please know my mentor was like Christ before me and had a similar repose.

Please know, however, I am the one foretold as Isa and I have done it as your trinity is over in the eyes of people who don't worship Jesus as God anymore,

Please know I have done it, not him, though he is my mentor and I use him,

Please know I took the hit with your government agencies as they declared me bankrupt to you and you thought me unwell.

Please know they converted, though, as they read my literature.

Please know they melted and the people followed.

Please know your government is similar and has read me and now let me teach as it is good for you.

Please know they melt in an obvious way.

Please know the church is left and they are recalcitrant some but are getting better,

Please know you will melt them as you find my literature tenable and you love Him,

Please know He loves you in return but wants your obedience,

Please know you have stopped it and get married now as a norm.

Please know women will have to cover though as He doesn't permit them nudity.

Please know I am kind to you and know you are gradual in some things but He knows what is best for you.

Please take Him to be your God and trust Him,

Please know He has prepared Heaven for your leisure and wants you with Him,

Please don't lie about him,

Please know to use the Quran as a reference,

Please know it has precepts that train you for Him,

Please know it will perfect you for life in the Hereafter,

Please Him,

Please do not deceive anyone,

Please know that is a Dajjal element and you know he was man,

Please know you know. Omar.

Kahf.

18:1 Praise be to Allah! Who revealed the Book to His servant, and allowed not therein any crookedness,

18:2 Rightly directing, to give warning of severe punishment from Him and to give good news to the believers who do good that theirs is a goodly reward,

18:3 Staying in it forever;

18:4 And to warn those who say: Allah has taken to Himself a son.

18:5 They have no knowledge of it, nor had their fathers. Grievous is the word that comes out of their mouths. They speak nothing but a lie.

Please see my take on this as you know these events transpired after you took the shahada.

Please know Dajjal has been foretold in literature as one eyed,

Please know his spiritual eye was blind and materialistic eye was bright,

Please know he controlled world events by offering heaven to his friends,

Please know he sanctions nations that go against him,

Please know some he destroys by invasion,

Please know he can create fire through his ridicule like he did to me when he told them I was mad,

Please know this was the fire from heaven foretold by Prophet Muhammad,

Please Him,

Please know he has melted after you realized Islam was correct and these were metaphors he used,

Please know the Quran is now established in your land as the validator of past scriptures.

Please know you consult it,

Please know world peace is occurring as wars are abrogated for peace talks and sanctions, if needed.

Please know Isa suffered because of the sins of people,

Please know it is similar for me,

Please know the people sinned against me and took away my license even though I was only teaching Islam to them, something permitted in the statute law of this country.

Please Him,

Please know they sinned when they told them to commit me so as to discredit me with them who were converting,

Please know they sinned when they approached them to finish me off now that Islam had occurred.

Please know at Western State they fed me a toxin in my tray where I started crying uncontrollably and then became ashen and passed out nearly.

Please know I was ready and said my shahada,

Please know I recovered my strength instead of dying,

Please know I banged the door indicating my displeasure for keeping me there and they gave me a shot with more toxin in it.

Please know they relented after that and realized they could not kill me,

Please know however they used to feed me polonium in my meds as well and in jail attempts were made as well with salve on my handcuffs to me,

Please remember I had challenged them that they would never kill me so they agreed to try.

Please know people came to my rescue,

Please know now you know there were past attempts as well as well as future ones I presume.

Please know it was the sins of people that did this to me,

Please know most of you have melted though and wish me well.

Please know the hadith of our Prophet is fulfilled and Dajjal has been overcome and is us.

Please know you wish me well. Omar.

Please see the book of Daniel is of some relevance to you as the four beasts of Islam come into play here.

Please know the book of Daniel is correct in its content as a dream,

Please know he thought they were possessed and that is why it scared him,

Please know it is clear Jesus is son of man to you and in Daniel's interpretation he is as well.

Please see the book of Daniel,

Please know chapter seven is about the four beasts of the book of revelation,

Please know our Creator knows Daniel's dream was wrong in its content as the beasts are good.

Please know he was a pious man but sainthood was limited in him to think that he was a prophet.

Please know there were many prophets who had limited sainthood and he was one of them and was perturbed unnecessarily as it was a dream he misinterpreted,

Please know they were pious slaves as indicated in the book of revelations where they are depicted as four horsemen,

Please know it is accurate to say Christianity ended with them so John depicted them as evil.

Please know it was John the Baptist who wrote the book of revelations; it was misconstrued to indicate the apostle when the name John appeared on the manuscript,

Please know I am John's disciple in the future and will tell you more, suffice it to say they were evil to her who intends to hurt me for this post now that the Christian church has been abrogated by me in the public view to you.

Please know messenger,

Please know it is one who abrogates law for another,

Please know it was Allah's servant who changed the divorce law for you as it was onerous and unbecoming,

Please know it was done as he saw my condition with him when I tried to bring law into it from another country,

Please know I was demolished by them,

Please know you have an unfair society and he got away with it though the judge did see jail for doing this to me that he took my kids away from me when I traveled forth on vacation with them,

Please know you have a recusement charter for unjust procedure,

Please know I was refused it and was demolished publicly.

Please see what your government does to me as I brought you Islam with clear minded intellect,

Please know this is unjust procedure they do to me in public in this country,

Please know I was demolished then as I rose against a judge and they put me in jail, then relented,

Please know I had a law my wife was a signatory to.

Please know the president's car was behind it but the state was averse as well and crucified me by shutting my practice down when they asked for a mental state examination,

Please know they relented but the damage was done as my practice suffered as I was bipolar to you while sainthood occurred in me and I was following through as they did tell me to.

Please know this is the kingdom I establish.

Please know the kingdom is where my law is supreme,

Please let me advise you on law; I am a law-giver to some until they adopt it universally,

Please know I am the bear you please me with and I have three women with me,

Please know one is my mother, the second is my wife and the third is my daughter,

Please know all three are in my control and eventually will come to me willingly, as my mother has who advises me from heaven,

Please know my father Mirza there is the lion garb as indicated in the book of revelations and his power is over for now but will reemerge when Islam is established by him in his teaching to us in Islam,

Please know my son is the fourth beast who is fierce and ferocious as he will become so with the passage of time when his disease remits.

Please know his kingdom is Islam worldwide and he continue my deen of Islam to the West to them in the East and elsewhere where it is established on Ahmadi aqaid,

Please know the leopard is my grandfather,

Please know he will wield a sword which he destroys nations and you will read him and his work the Holy Quran I recommend for you.

Please know world dominion is his through his Quran which you peruse already.

Please know an entity like Jesus will emerge as the ruler,

Please know son of man is for him but it is not Christ, just someone in his mold.

Please know his spirit will rule till the world is over,

Please know he is my mentor who will rise from the ashes after my book receives acclaim in the public sector.

Please know he is known as man to you.

Please know we are all man in Islam or in other words Adams of His as we bring about revolution, like he did,

Please know Jesus is son of man as well as are we all and it is to signify son of man foretold here is only a human,

Please know you call him otherwise though you know now he was metaphor Him and his true title in scripture is son of man, signifying an earthly father.

Please know this is a sign for some that the scripture called him that word and he himself adopted it to signify unity of beliefs that he was man.

Please know I am like Jesus entity and am told to say that I am the one foretold here as the one like him in whom you have repose and my law will remain with you for the end of time with his teaching of Ahmadi aqaid, who is my son,

Please know it is Mirza who taught us so his spirit will rule,

Please know I am the law giver and my son's rule will establish it as correct for you.

Please know my ex will come to know Islam and will rule him, my son, with Ahmadi principles after I leave her.

Please know life is short for some but I will leave her after a long life,

Please know the pressure is here to conform so this is my opinion, take it or leave it, but we are the three horsemen in your world view already. Omar.

Book of Daniel.

1 In the first year of Belshazzar king of Babylon Daniel had a dream and visions of his head upon his bed: then he wrote the dream and told the sum of the matters.

2 Daniel spake and said, "I saw in my vision by night, and, behold, the four winds of the heaven strove upon the great sea.

3 And four great beasts came up from the sea, diverse one from another.

4 The first was like a lion and had eagle's wings: I beheld till the wings thereof were plucked and it was lifted up from the earth and made stand upon the feet as a man, and a man's heart was given to it.

5 And behold another beast, a second, like to a bear, and it raised up itself on one side and it had three ribs in the mouth of it between the teeth of it: and they said thus unto it, 'Arise, devour much flesh.'

6 After this I beheld, and lo another, like a leopard, which had upon the back of it four wings of a fowl; the beast had also four heads; and dominion was given to it.

7 After this I saw in the night visions, and behold a fourth beast, dreadful and terrible, and strong exceedingly; and it had great iron teeth: it devoured and brake in pieces, and stamped the residue with the feet of it and it was diverse from all the beasts that were before it; and it had ten horns.

8 I considered the horns, and, behold, there came up among them another little horn, before whom there were three of the first horns plucked up by the roots: and, behold, in this horn were eyes like the eyes of man, and a mouth speaking great things.

9 I beheld till the thrones were cast down and the Ancient of days did sit, whose garment was white as snow and the hair of his head like the pure wool: his throne was like the fiery flame, and his wheels as burning fire.

10 A fiery stream issued and came forth from before him: thousand thousands ministered unto him, and ten thousand times ten thousand stood before him: the judgment was set, and the books were opened.

11 I beheld then because of the voice of the great words which the horn spake: I beheld even till the beast was slain, and his body destroyed, and given to the burning flame.

12 As concerning the rest of the beasts, they had their dominion taken away: yet their lives were prolonged for a season and time.

13 I saw in the night visions, and, behold, one like the Son of man came with the clouds of heaven, and came to the Ancient of days, and they brought him near before him.

14 And there was given him dominion, and glory, and a kingdom, that all people, nations, and languages, should serve him: his dominion is an everlasting dominion which shall not pass away, and his kingdom that which shall not be destroyed.

15 I Daniel was grieved in my spirit in the midst of my body, and the visions of my head troubled me.

16 I came near unto one of them that stood by, and asked him the truth of all this. So he told me and made me know the interpretation of the things.

17 These great beasts, which are four, are four kings, which shall arise out of the earth.

18 But the saints of the most High shall take the kingdom and possess the kingdom forever, even forever and ever.

19 Then I would know the truth of the fourth beast, which was diverse from all the others, exceeding dreadful, whose teeth were of iron, and his nails of brass; which devoured, brake in pieces, and stamped the residue with his feet;

20 And of the ten horns that were in his head and of the other which came up, and before whom three fell; even of that horn that had eyes and a mouth that spake very great things, whose look was more stout than his fellows.

21 I beheld, and the same horn made war with the saints and prevailed against them;

22 Until the Ancient of days came and judgment was given to the saints of the most High; and the time came that the saints possessed the kingdom.

23 Thus he said, The fourth beast shall be the fourth kingdom upon earth, which shall be diverse from all kingdoms, and shall devour the whole earth, and shall tread it down, and break it in pieces.

24 And the ten horns out of this kingdom are ten kings that shall arise: and another shall rise after them; and he shall be diverse from the first and he shall subdue three kings.

25 And he shall speak great words against the most High and shall wear out the saints of the most High, and think to change times and laws: and they shall be given into his hand until a time and times and the dividing of time.

26 But the judgment shall sit and they shall take away his dominion, to consume and to destroy it unto the end.

27 And the kingdom and dominion, and the greatness of the kingdom under the whole heaven shall be given to the people of the saints of the most High whose kingdom is an everlasting kingdom, and all dominions shall serve and obey him.

28 Hitherto is the end of the matter. As for me, Daniel, my cogitations much troubled me, and my countenance changed in me but I kept the matter in my heart.

Please know burooz is a nonentity in itself and connotes the prophesy of Prophet Muhammad comes to us.

Please know Ahmadiyyat is served here by explain these terms of communication from Prophet Muhammad are burooz,

Please know it connotes the prophesy of Prophet Muhammad came to us.

Please know we ourselves are not prophets but take him with us and our caliber appears to be that of Prophet Muhammad but it is actually him who communicates facts so they appear prophesy.

Please know it is as if prophesy is coming to the world through us but it is not and the credit goes to him for world reform, something he was vouchsafed with in that he will make it prevail over faiths of a diverse kind.

Please know we are the helpers of Him and the Prophet.

Please know we can take the blame somewhat for using the word prophet in the metaphorical sense and I apologize for that as it causes disquiet in you; the common Muslim man on the streets of our countries. I know we are asked to say it as it lets people know our caliber as saints in that we are communicated by the Prophet Muhammad, whose views we represent. This is a Sufi concept called burooz and I know the common man is unfamiliar with this term. I hesitate to explain any more as I have done so in the past but suffice it to say that both of us are in a burooz state and we represent him. We are not prophets as prophethood has ended with Prophet Muhammad, on him be peace for that event.

Please understand I am a poor communicator myself and whatever gift I have is from Him and the Prophet's grace visits me regularly.

Please know my insight is my own but it is well developed.

The end occurs who think I am a hypocrite as hypocrites don't pray and don't cry at the state of ailing mankind. I am surprised at you in the Muslim world that you don't see me and my mentor as Muslims even after I have explained the burooz as a metaphor and deny that after my treatise here you don't see but you deny out of a jealous state. Omar.

Please know I am a mirror image of him, my Prophet, and you will see I am clear in intellect when I tell you this.

Please know the Pakistani mindset is complex. On the one hand they appreciate my claim of being a saint who brought Islam to the West and yet they are upset that I promote Ahmadiyyat teachings as correct for them.

I am surprised such minor differences can cause so much dismay in them while all our articles of faith such as belief in One God and Muhammad as His messenger as well as belief in the prophets, and their books is the same. We believe in the finality of Prophet Muhammad as the last prophet the world will see, and in the Day we are resurrected for our deeds, as we do in angels.

Please know I am surprised at your ignorance that people that are alike to you you would consider them to be dissimilar over minor issues like using the word prophet in the metaphorical sense of being his representative only.

Please know this is a God-given right to me to use to show my authority over you as I am a reflection of his wishes to you, the Prophet there.

There is no reincarnation in Islam so I do not believe I am actually him but only him in the sense of a metaphor, so that when you see me, you see him. It is with repose to him that we live in Ahmadiyyat and that is why there are scholars who are jealous of us.

I am sad for you as you understand this but you will lie and say that you don't. I know it is easy to understand and just like our Prophet said in a statement of his that when a servant of His walk, he walks with the legs of his Creator, and when he speaks, he speaks with His tongue, it is the similar with us with our Prophet for the most part and we speak for him and do his bid on us to teach you in Islam as well as Muslims occurring around the world with Ahmadi principles of kinship and friendship as well. Omar.

CHAPTER EIGHT

SOME OF MY TRIALS SUMMARIZED HERE

Please know I have been through many trials but the one I won't forget is the divorce proceeding in 2009.

Please know they had it that I appeared a criminal to them since I wished for a trial based upon a pre-commitment of her family to mine based upon Islamic law we were married under,

Please know because I was adamant I would proceed to a higher court I was sentenced to sixteen days in jail.

Please know I was given a chance to repair so I compromised and settled the case,

Please know the judge in question was recused of my subsequent case,

Please know he was vindictive after being guilty of an error early on in the case,

Please know I had reported him to the Court of Judiciary in Nashville,

Please know generally sentencing is not done in divorce cases,

Please know my next big trial was involving the imam of the Islamic Center who had me arrested on charges of theft which were trumped up as I had admonished him by taking away his computer,

Please know I was the head of the Islamic Center,

Please understand this charge,

Please know he said I stole six thousand dollars of his money that were lying under his bed,

Please know this was a likely story as I was a millionaire,

Please know they issued a criminal summons without investigating it,

Please know this was the time when I was fighting for my rights in court in the divorce proceeding with Chancellor Butler,

Please know this was a serious allegation and they should have questioned me before issuing a summons,

Please give in,

Please know they manipulated me when they arrested me,

Please know my third case in 2009 was when my ex-wife arrested me on charges of violation of an order of protection because my son wanted to live with me,

Please know he was sent back and I was arrested the next day on an order that I did not do any criminal intent.

Please know it was over some emails I sent her,

Please know we settled the charges but my career took a debacle,

Please know I was a practicing physician and it hurt my reputation with them in the administration of the hospital.

Please know they sent me for psychological testing which I passed easily,

Please know I had claimed to be a saint by then,

Please know this is the case history.

Please know in 2013 the imam tried to get me arrested on a false charge of a life threat,

Please know we had a skirmish because they charged me falsely of apostasy to Islam,

Please know he failed,

Please know then he tried to obtain an order of protection,

Please know he failed,

Please know this is case law,

Please know he accused me of stalking and threatening his family,

Please know he lied,

Please understand him,

Please know he knows I am not on good terms with the judiciary and wanted to capitalize on it with this order of protection on him and his family and keep me away from prayer there at the mosque.

Please know the trials I go through because I don't fight dirty like they do.

Please know in late 2013 and 2014 I started propagating my faith in earnest,

Please know I sent my article Godhead as a metaphor to state and government officials,

Please know they received it poorly and committed me, bringing my career to a halt,

Please know I tried to sue the state for my commitment procedure but they suspended my license to practice medicine,

Please know shortly thereafter they committed me twice in succession while I was promoting my literature in Nashville and Memphis,

Please know they used coercion to get me medicated,

Please know I am a stalwart at fighting for my rights and they could not commit me according to the statutes,

Please know then they applied a conservator over me and got me medicated on a permanent basis,

Please know this is my life story as far as my trials are concerned,

Please know in the meanwhile I settled my cases,

Please know my wife and I are divorced now.

Please know I planned to bring up conservator abuse in the courts as threats of commitment went on despite medications they give me,

Please say a prayer for me,

Please know I have brought you One God in your realm as you were interested in my case and read my literature,

Please know Islam has occurred in your hearts as correct for you to pursue,

Please know you have said the edict of Islam,

Please know you understand accountability will occur,

Please know you realize Muhammad was a Messenger of God,

Please know these are no mean achievements and I got your attention,

Please know I rest my case with you.

Please know in September of 2014 they arrested me on a trumped-up charge of terrorism to a school.

Please know it was trumped up and it was passed in court but they succeeded in medicating me by forcing me to follow doctor's orders,

Please know they arrested me by trumping up my statement below. Omar.

Please see my Facebook posts from that time.

Please understand some people have taken my words in the recent statement "remember, children; you are my combatants" in a context not intended. In this there is sadness for me as it was not my intend to imply they are my enemies but to imply that they are my supporters and will fight for my rights for a fair trial proceeding as they recognize merit in my works even if some adults do not. The following statement is meant as a disclaimer to the news media that I am sorry if some confusion arose however in my mind it was meant to convey that children support me and not that I will fight them. In this way I have attempted to allay any feelings of displeasure towards me from the community of people living in this land of ours.

Please understand I am held hostage at the whims of a court as I am not guilty yet they have the power to arbitrarily pass judgment of guilty on me despite the facts that I did not cause a lockdown at the school and was off the school property when it was ordered.

Please know they have this power despite the facts or events that transpire because they find me to have guilt on other issues that they can't prosecute because of the freedom of speech amendment in the constitution.

Please know we have the right to write what we wish without making a threat to anybody else and as I have indicated here saying to children 'you are my combatants' is not a threat to them but only an indication of their endearment to me and my works.

Please understand I have made my position clear and now it is up to your good offices to make sure the statutes are followed and I am not a victim of abuse from the state government as it was clear that somebody engineered the lockdown to say that I was disruptive while I was not in the least as video surveillance showed that day. Omar.

Please know my conservator was a sham procedure you need to fight with me against it.

Please know my conservator case was similar and they used mental disease as an avenue to place one over me without showing any proof of disorderly conduct.

Please know there was no proof that I squandered money yet they took my bank accounts from under my control.

Please know there was no disorderly car on me yet they made him control me as I say they inhibit my car, something allowed to say in the statutes in my freedom of speech act on us,

Please know they had witnesses they say and read my medical records in court, something not allowed in the statutes,

Please know though I had victims who came to testify on my behalf that I was well, they deferred and paid them no heed even though one of them was my psychologist Carolyn Willette who let out I did not need one over me and regret occurred when they approached her with vehemence,

Please know it is inconceivable a person of my intelligence and aptitude in communication be served a conservator notice as such things are protected sanity in law and you have to prove worth beyond conceivable doubt to get it through in court settings, which they did, as law is on their side in state of Tennessee law books and court procedure,

Please know it was this that turned them upside down and they became aghast land for you with the police to back them up in aghast virtue to you,

Please know your courts became the laughing stocks of the world for what they were doing with me in conservator court,

Please know they used the conservator to commit me repeatedly to suit the whims of the government when public pressure was against me and there I was taken away in a police car,

Please know you came to my rescue eventually and shut them down for me but they still have power and can enact me negatively to you.

Please know in future fight me less and them more, as I am your well-wisher and will get you there, and they will get you hellfire for remaining quiet about it, my disclamor with them in courts, church groups and the former president, somewhat, though he is calm now as we don't fight as often.

Please know the conservator was lifted in 2019 when I pursued my medical career again but they placed it on me in 2022 when they jailed me for disorderly behavior to my sister who filed charges to arrest me saying there was a tussle, while I left when she didn't give me the phone. Omar.

Please know I teach from him, my Prophet, and he tells me you have come through.

Please know in 2016 I was enacted unsafe by him in the courts as I said a local judge was unsafe,

Please know she was trying to commit me,

Please know I said she was 'dead' meaning in the spirit of things but they said I made a threat of homicide to her, which was not the case.

Please know they jailed me and there I stayed for four months then they relented and let me be and gave me the insanity plea.

Please know they did this to deride me to the community, who knew better though.

Please know they got it situated that I would be on high dose therapy in the form of monthly shots for years as I tried to get back my license to practice medicine.

Please know I lost faith during this time that I was a saint,

Please know I was forlorn and lost.

Please know eventually the conservator was lifted and I resumed my career in medicine but never practiced on my own again.

Please know I was finally taken off the high dose therapy with psychotropic medicine and I resumed teaching Islam again, something you liked in me,

Please know I was given leeway by the American people but the government was averse to my teaching again to the public at large but I had become popular with the publishing of the second edition of my book Jesus, the Messiah and the Person and I had clamor occur when they arrested me again, this time for domestic abuse, something I didn't do yet they pinned it on me though it was dropped in court proceedings late in the course,

Please know they applied the conservator again to inhibit my brain once again,

Please know America is stalwart though and protect me from them in the courts and government some.

Please know they took my Tennessee license again and I had to quit my job in Missouri when Islam became your view in things, though I was allowed to write by the American public.

Please know Muslims have become my car and I am popular there in the Mecca vicinity as saint and Messiah some to the American public,

Please know it is because I am popular now they desist some but I am harassed still and they place restraining orders on me in public places.

Please know they have resumed shots on me to medicate me again, something I don't wish for but put up for now.

Please know our Prophet is there in Heaven and knows you will protect my car now but life is fraught with difficulties, so bear not my aplomb not and get me out of situations the government creates on me, your saint Dabbat Al-Ard or Omar here. Omar.

CHAPTER NINE

SOME ARTICLES FROM MY FACEBOOK PAGE

Please know my Facebook page was viral in February of 2014 after they committed me for the first time,
Please understand what viral meant,
Please know it was all over the country,
Please know they saw it occur and decided to quell my pen,
Please know they offered me peace before and that was to practice medicine or face a trial.
Please know I chose to write on about Islamic topics,
Please know they destroyed my pen and portrayed mental disease in me again by committing me repeatedly,
Please know they arrested me in September of 2014,
Please know it was because I wrote that children were my combatants,
Please indicate disfavor as there was nothing wrong in my doing so.
Please understand me,
Please know I use figurative language,
Please know the government shut down the school because I went there to inquire about my safety as I was concerned they were going to arrest me on a false charge,
Please know they went and did that on the pretext I was a terrorist,
Please know this was unfair to an extreme and there was no arrest warrant at the time of my arrest,
Please know they arrested me on a pretext and quickly shipped me away to Western State Mental Facility in Bolivar,
Please know they kept me confined there for fifty-two days
Please know I was sent for a mental evaluation but they did not perform any tests,

Please know this is their scheme to put me away permanently.

Please know they could not as the family intervened,

Please know the American public were aghast,

Please see a requiem for me,

Please know America knows I am sane but were averse to my literature on Christ.

Please know this did not fit in with the statutes,

Please know they raised hue and cry and put pressure on the administration to release me,

Please know it was tough but I had faith I would get out.

Please see some of my literature that I post on the web,

Please know it is modified somewhat as the link is not available for review,

Please see this article about my page as a prologue to you.

Please see the following verses from the chapter of Bani-Israel.

The end is there for people who demand miracles like the way people asked our Prophet Muhammad, on him be peace.

Yours truly is a saint that has this book on my Facebook page as a miracle.

The end occurs to those who say there is nothing substantive here. It is full of advice and wisdom. It is a gift to you from Him. I am only a servant of His who cannot do anything on his own accord.

Please see the following caption there.

Please know we know Omar is a saint as he writes, then revises once or twice for minor irregularities, then posts the comments.

Please know this is different from a writer who revises what he has written after pondering about the contents of the article or comment.

Please know they know the comma door is mine in that I can write an article without break or comma,

Please know miracle,

It is to write like I do without flaw or revision in it,

Please understand the Quran was magnificent and far more comprehensive and energetic.

Yours truly has a quran as a metaphor, similar to other saints before me.

Please realize I write in a unique style arising the interest of the reader. They know hidden door or facts come through on my page to you.

It is no Quran as this book is a mercy for mankind and my aim is to emulate its style but not to write a book to compete with it.

The end is there for people who think it is not a miracle. It is, and it has captured the hearts and minds of people here in this land. In this there is certainty that there is a huge following of my Facebook page which the authorities do not care for.

Please see a requiem for me.

Please know Omar did it through his Facebook page, capturing the hearts of a generation of people in this country.

The end came for those who denied the beauty of the Quran. Eventually the nation of Arabia became Muslims, revering the Book. Omar.

Bani-Israel.

17:89 And certainly We have made clear for men in this Qur'an every kind of description, but most men consent to naught save denying.

17:90 And they say: We will by no means believe in thee, till thou cause a spring to gush forth from the earth for us,

17:91 Or thou have a garden of palms and grapes in the midst of which thou cause rivers to flow forth abundantly,

17:92 Or thou cause the heaven to come down upon us in pieces, as thou thinkest, or bring Allah and the angels face to face (with us),

17:93 Or thou have a house of gold, or thou ascend into heaven. And we will not believe in thy ascending till thou bring down to us a book we can read. Say: Glory to my Lord! am I aught but a mortal messenger?

Please know some Muslim scholar aside most of them find me coherent but different so don't ascribe me as one of them who believe scholarship is to believe in hadith.

Please know this is about a Muslim scholar who has aptitude to teach but lacks veracity from Him like I have from the Prophet's words to me.

Please know this about us- please know when you insult us you insult his personage who is Muhammad.

Please know this heretic issue is beyond me.

Please know I'm a simple man who takes people on their face value.

Please understand when they insult my mentor as a heretic I know they are doomed.

Please know why,

Please understand I have explained the metaphor and explained it is a communication we have from him, our Prophet, that gives us his prophethood and the words we write are his.

Please understand it is an analogy of being Allah that when we walk, we walk with His legs and when we talk, we speak His words.

Please know it is in the same way when we walk and talk we do so with him in mind,

Please know we do not attribute prophethood in our entity but only his spirit which comes to us and teaches his words of wisdom which we impart to you.

Please know this is not really prophethood in us but we appear as prophets because our words carry the same convictions as a prophet's would.

Please know it is as if the Prophet has come down to earth and vocalizes to you through our body.

Please know you don't see him like we do.

Please know this is a bodily incarnation of his spirit in us.

Please know this is peace for you to know I am his image.

Please know when you talk to me you do so but the answer I give you comes from heaven on occasion.

Please understand besides these issues I am as normal as you are and wish to portray to you my Muslimhood is no different than people like some in Islam who deride us.

Please know they know the caliber of our intellect and if they can't come to terms with our superiority it is because they have jealousy issues as on face value our intellect is with him, our Prophet.

Please know they should respect me. I am not a scholar like some who memorize words from our Book but I have goodness in me that is rare to find.

Please know the same applies to my mentor Mirza there and Maulana Muhammad Ali.

Please know some scholars in Islam,
Please know they come through as I am a Messiah here to you folks but before they were averse to my literature,
Please know some are like me.
Please understand we have wit.
Please know they serves Islam as I do.
Please know yet he is willing to call me a heretic because I support him, my mentor,
Please know why,
Please know I refuse to call some Muslim man a Non-Muslim whether it be him or others though I do allow the hadith to give the verdict that if you call a Muslim a heretic then it applies to you.
Please know it gives me no pleasure to do this as I would prefer to be on good terms with them but if I had to make a choice between him and the truth of my mentor's person I would choose the latter. Omar.

Please know bondage knows love everlasting.
Please know this article encompasses me.
Please know we love our child but that disappears as we grow older,
Please know don't worry there,
Please know it will be written for us to love them again.
Please know the source of love is our Creator.
Please know when we sin against Him the flow of the love stops and we are bereft.
Please understand this,
Please know when we are small the love does not stop.
Please know when we gain majority then a sin against Him will cause us to hate.
Please know we grow distant in our youth for this reason,
I know when we marry and have stability in our lives the love recurs if we are good to Him,
Please know this is the spiritual aspect of love between a parent and child.
Please know this is true.
Please understand we are uncommonly beautiful people to some.

Please know what this means,
Please know our parents value us for what we are.
Please know we are kind to them as they were kind to us,
Please understand this,
Please know our parents love us when we are small.
Please know this is kind of them,
Please know we are their loved ones and will always be so in the Hereafter.
Please understand they are kind and intervene for us there,
Please understand this,
Please know their destination may be better than ours but their love for us will draw us to them,
Please know we love our parents when we are small.
Please know this love continues for some,
Please know our love will reappear when there is peace for us and them,
Please know when love is curtailed it is because of some sin. Omar.

Please know beauty is skin deep, and the heart falters then amends, so its beauty is preserved for the penitent one.
Please know we appreciate a beautiful heart and dislike something not worthy in it.
Please see the heart when you see the person.
Please know the heart is the repository of faith. I know it sounds trite but the heart is the fashioner of the soul.
Please know our soul will be judged on the Day we are questioned.
I know the heart learns from life and amends itself.
Please know each of us unique.
Please know we have a different path but one destination.
Please understand what is our destination? It is our abode in the Hereafter.
Please learn life.
Please know we come to the reality of truth from our hardships.
Please know what truth is.
Please know it is what was conveyed to us by God.

Therefore please amend before we are taken away.
The heart can amend only in this state.
Please know what that state is.
It is life.
Please know beauty is skin deep.
Please understand beauty to Him is figment that is here today and gone tomorrow.
Please understand beauty of the heart persists and is captured in our life's lens forever.
Please know we all appreciate a beautiful heart.
Please understand it is our heart that takes us to Paradise where beauty is eternal. Omar.

Please know our testimony will be asked about when it incurs wrath from us who are defendants as I have been in my conservator case and elsewhere where I have been committed by you and jailed in unison with law enforcement who concur it is necessary to lie in court documents.

Please know the false testimony about me is something I will ask about.
Please know we are weak because we sin with ease.
Please understand we cannot feel remorse for our acts of sin unless we know the law and have empathy for other's feelings.
Please know I am empathy for you in this day and age and I feel for your community that is doing these sins without realizing it.
Please know they know not the enormity of a lie in court,
Please know we are asked about our sins that we commit in ignorance.
Please know that just as in this country that there is no excuse for not knowing the law, so it is with Him. We have to inculcate in our children that values taught to us in churches and mosques have to followed and obeyed.
Please know we must serve our child and gain them entry into Paradise as that is our role as caregivers.
Please see the common adage come through.

We are weak and our Creator is powerful and there is no power but in Him.

I am sad as your people think you are strong. When you lie in court it a power you wield that is not permitted by our Creator and thus this power is your end,

Please know this is a good adage to think before we speak.

Please understand we are weak and when we say something that is not correct for us to say then we lose faith with Him.

Please know we must be careful of what we say as it is written for us and a word spoken is like an arrow that has left the bow.

Please know we must know we cannot lie and it behooves us to tell the truth in court settings of mankind unless we are being abused by telling the truth. In this there is certainty that this goes on courts here in this country. I hope people will realize that false testimony is the death of an individual and he will be punished according his testimony or acts that take away the rights of others.

Please know to lie under oath is the death of a person and those who lie about me being unwell are going to see it, Hell there,

Please know a Muslim who does it is not one and his testimony is not acceptable again,

Please know in the conservatorship they lie I am unwell and need help in things of the nature I don't.

Please know similarly when they commit me it is based on a lie in court,

Please know I am well for all practical purposes and am not suicidal, an avenue they use routinely in court settings to inhibit me in jail of commitments,

Please know they have committed me eleven times by subterfuge and jailed me on three occasions based upon this lie that I am violent while nothing occurred in each case.

Please see the following caption there.

Please know I will take away their right of entry into Paradise for doing this. Omar.

Please know the law of apostasy from us and know those who do not submit to truth there are apostates in heart's endeavors and will be categorized by man as such.

Please know pious Muslims refrain from calling my mentor and myself Non-Muslims as they have realized my mentor's words were taken in an out of context manner when he discussed apostasy and prophethood in man. I know his views are similar to mine that our prophethood is the teachings of our Prophet coming through in dreams and relayed to you verbatim in myself and others like us. It is not true prophethood and should be viewed as his views whom you call Prophet of God. There is sadness for those who call us false as our words are his.

Please know myself and my mentor are examples of people who are called apostates by some.

Please know my mentor Mirza Ghulam Ahmad said that it was those who fought us who will be in hellfire.

Please know I agree with this sentiment. I have explained here how calling a saint an apostate makes you one in your heart. I know you know the hadith for this but to clarify if you call a Muslim man who prays to the same God in the direction of other Muslims in their prayer service an apostate the sin of apostasy is upon you.

Please understand I can count the examples of people who do this and then get involved in worldly pursuits, away from the spirit of Islam, much like the present-day Jews and Muslims.

Please know Pakistan,

Please know they have this nature because they sign edicts to this effect that piety reigns with them and not Mirza and myself or Muhammad the scholar.

Please know these people have left Islam,

Please know some of them are the worst people on the face of planet earth,

Please know the reason is simple. They are not true Muslims who submit not to the authority of our Creator where He states 'be not aggressive in warfare' and our Prophet who denied men the killing of women and children.

In this there is certainty that ISIS-like groups are many and all of them have the ideology of hate to people who are pious Muslims thereby bringing apostasy into their hearts.

Please know I know only an apostate would ignore the Quran and saying of the Prophet Muhammad, on him be peace.

Yours truly is an apostate to some but know my peace exists as these people will be shown to be the worst of humanity. I know it was similar to what our Prophet faced when he was admonished by someone in his community and he observed that he was with a group that the Quran would not settle in the hearts of them or not going below their necks.

Please know I am sad as there are many who indulge in apostasy but it those who fight me that are actually the ones in hellfire.

Please know these men are not true Muslims. You can call them false Muslims or apostates by my leave as they have left Islam. In this there is certainty that their actions show them be Non-Muslims or those who do not submit to Him. Omar.

Please know truth self-annihilates us if we have the repose to let it.

Please know this saying that we all dismantle ourselves when truth occurs tells us that truth can be used as a weapon while it is meant to dismantle willingly the person subject to it,

Please know we all see truth as a means to educate one,

Please know we are all answerable if we listen to it and don't apply it.

Please know we self-annihilate willingly when we know our reward is written.

Please understand this,

Please know this is true we self-annihilate when the truth occurs and we dismantle ourselves.

Please know what the truth is,

Please understand it is the dagger our Creator uses to remove a disease from our innards and our heart repairs after it is used.

The end comes when you use it as a weapon.

Please know it is meant to self-annihilate and is not forced on someone.

Please know peace.
Please know it is to self-annihilate willingly.
Please know this truth,
Please know that we cannot bear the truth.
Please understand why?
Please know it is because you will have to dismantle yourself and reassemble, like I did.
Please know we must admire those who teach us things.
Please know they are the gems of the universe.
Please understand how?
Please know it is because they give in to the truth until they self-annihilate, then reconstruct.
Please know it is because they give in to Him that they have this gemhood state.
Please know that is what truth does to us.
Please know eventually we develop traits of Him, the Creat, like our Prophet had,
Please know I indicate our Prophet's car and those who loved him. In this there is certainty that this world is a figment there.
Please know we must live like him to be him in the hereafter. Omar.

Please know the way to your Prophet is the teacher assigned by him to lead you there.
Please know a requiem for me,
Please know I am a saint who will change world history and I must have a pledge so that the work can be undertaken.
Please know the words,
Please understand you cannot come to Him without him refers to a specific time in the history of that nation.
Please know it is similar for me and unless you pledge allegiance to my cause or the cause of my mentor then you will not find the way to Him or him, my Prophet.
Please know we are guides for you today.
Please understand this,

Please know it is essential to pledge allegiance to the teacher who guides. If you deny him peace you will not be able to gain Paradise with Him and your destination will be one who is lost.

Please know there is no pride in this; only hardship.

Please know this is clear.

Please know the prophets are the representatives of God on earth. In a sense if they are rejected then the path to God is lost. In this there is certainty that the prophet will show them the path.

Please understand this,

Please know they are there for a purpose and that is to correct them in their misdeeds.

In the final analysis if you forsake the prophet your worship will amount to nothing.

The end occurs that people think this is especially for Jesus. Our Prophet said the same thing about himself. In this there is certainty that prophets are sent for reform and if you don't do that then you are lost.

Please see the following requiem there at his gravesite who is your prophet, Jesus there.

Please know they take my words in an out of context way and destroy my message. Omar.

Please know a liar never prospers and his destination is hellfire, eventual, to come to him.

Please understand our Prophet never told a lie and that is the reason he received the Quran in revelation.

Please know it is easy to lie when we are young and as we grow older we gain awareness of the sin.

Please know we all have lied in our youth.

The end is near for those who think that there are others who have not lied in their life.

Please know there is no one else who has made the statement that our Prophet has that he had never lied.

Please know the trait that despoils a person is a lie that is repeated without compunction.

MUHAMMAD THE PROPHET

Please know the liar never prospers and a liar can be known from his face when he lies.

Please understand that the lies lead one to Hell and truth-telling takes one to Paradise.

Please know initially it is easy to lie but with the passage of time it becomes more difficult and people repent the act.

Please know it is abnormal to lie and truth-telling is our norm.

Please know it is a sin the Quran deters,

Please know a liar is one who lies about me that I am an apostate while I am teaching the Quran to you. Omar.

Please know extinction occurs in many ways and dissolution of humanitarian principles is the reason we are extinct in world history.

Please know we weep for what has become of earth. I am sad that we lose a great treasure.

Please understand when we lose animals created by Him we lose resources of science as well.

Please see the following caption there.

Please know we are created but for how long.

Please know there are discoveries that science has to make about these plants and animals that are going extinct.

Please understand when we study them we actually study our Creator.

Please try to fathom the amount of despair we have at the death of earth.

Please know we are extinct as well.

Please understand we have gone the way of the criminal.

Please understand we are a corrupt people on earth with very little humanity left in us except for a few of us who hold humanitarian principles to be sacrosanct, like our prophets did. Our great savior Muhammad whose life history I will be embarking on soon was a man who listened to and cared for humans. He was the most pliant of men who invariable would give in to people's requests unless they were doing something He, our Creator, expressly forbid.

Please know I am pleased with him who gave me a firm handle to hold onto.

Please understand when we are faced with a certain situation we look towards the Quran and his conduct for guidance.

Please see the following caption there in his home.

Please know we are in awe of this man.

Please see the immense character and personality of this humanitarian who always did the right thing except in some cases when he was corrected by his Creator. This does not mean he did not make mistakes but he was always corrected by Him after he achieved prophethood.

Please know he came close to sinning as well since he was human but as he was meant to be a savior for mankind he was protected in this regard and did not commit a major sin overtly.

Please know he is my savior and my hero and I know that we need to be like him in order to save the world from human extinction where humanitarian principles are applied not by us to others. Omar.

Please know we yearn for our partner in fondness and love when apart from them.

Please see if man or woman yearn,

Please know he or she yearns for someone they admire.

Please know a partner is one that one admires in some respects.

Please see if you can love someone and then yearn for them when they are apart.

Please know this occurs when they are married or engaged.

Please know if sex has occurred before marriage the yearning is replaced by desire for them and love doesn't result.

Please know I know our God reserves love in a relationship if they follow Him.

Please know this is correct.

Please understand love,

Please know it is to love someone you are quiet with. I know love is companionship with the heart quiet about it.

Please understand it is a closeness of the hearts in that they agree on things, for the most part.

Please know the apart state is when the yearning occurs. Omar.

Please know a taser is a weapon they use arbitrarily in police force in this country.

Please see me,

Please know I am taser to some but I taffarraqoo it.

Please know what taffarraqoo is.

Please know it is to divide people.

Please know I bring a unified view though.

Please know some people taser me by calling me bipolar.

Please know I am not in the least bit it.

Please know I am very stable, pleasant, kind taffarraqoo man.

Please know the police are taser in reality and hurt me inordinately.

Please know it is over though and they have been caught in their tactics they brought from Israel where they suppress the population with it.

Please know what it is.

Please know it is brutality and the populace is scared of them,

Please know they are a police state as they are brutal to them in prisons.

Please know they are kind to some but the majority hurt.

Please know a prison is for reform only for some like minor criminals,

Please know it is the hardened criminals that are kept away.

Please know reform is necessary for many but punishment must be light.

Please know it is not right to use taser technology.

Please know it hurts unnecessarily and is part and parcel of brutality.

Please know this is a police state we live in as you saw on my page with you.

Please know the police have overreaching powers to arrest arbitrarily and take you there,

Please Him,
Please bring about reform gradual but thorough.
Please see the following caption on the person's face.
Please know I am not violent.
Please see if we can stop the violence coming forth from the police force to its people.
Please understand a taser is a crime for some yet the police are allowed to use it.
Please understand there has to be a need to subdue an individual with force.
Please know this gun is overused by our police force and it hurts people unnecessarily.
Please try to use caution when approached by the police as they have leeway to use this weapon for their protection.
Please see the caption there in their headquarters.
Please know we use it but it does hurt us and we are admonished by them whom we use it on.
Please know the police have a reputation they have to protect and not be considered weak.
Please know I was tased in prison and it was not pleasant,
Please know there was no need but still they did it,
Please know police brutality,
Please know they have it in them to be brutal to people like myself who love piety. Omar.

Please know it is not man's worth to respect someone in the way of bowing or prostrate themselves to them.
Please know the following comment was written on watching a video of people bowing in prostration to a man.
Please know it was filmed in Pakistan,
Please know this is a land where people have lost touch with Him,
Please know they will be punished for this act of prostrating in front of man.
Please know on occasion the Prophet would be bowed to.
Please know he decried it,

Please know he was averse to having the head bent with respect,
Please know our Creator will not forgive this,
Please know they will be raised on the Day of Judgment with their head bent,
Please know bowing is not permitted in Islam,
Please try to maintain upright and bow only to Him Who creates as He is without blemish and cannot be improved,
Please know a wife should improve her husband and people should improve their leader,
Please know no one's respect should be that they are not answerable to others,
Please know in this country much leeway is given to others in authority.
Please know this is despondency for some,
Please know I feel sick when I see this,
Please know it is not for man to bow down like this to another man,
Please know it is commonplace in Muslim countries to see this,
Please know our Prophet decried it,
Please know there are limits to showing respect,
Please know he does not like to be bowed to by men,
Please know our Prophet prevented it from happening in his community,
Please know he said that Allah does not allow this respect to men or women,
Please know we all have evil in us,
Please know He is wholly good and deserves this,
Please know a woman is not allowed to bow down to her husband,
Please know He would not allow it. Omar.

Please know a saint brings the light of his prophet to them.
Please understand we have a message to propagate after the Prophet perfected the light for the world religion to come forth in its perfected state.
Please know that we are only utensils that show the world the way we are filled by religious knowledge.

Please understand that the Prophet is the source of truth or light in the world.

Please understand we saints are similar but do not have the quality of prophets that keeps them intact and allows the message to propagate unaltered.

Please know there are various lights and each has a quality that is different from others.

Please know to appreciate saints like us who bring the Prophet to you and clarify religious belief.

Please know we have a light,

Please learn from us truth of him, our Prophet there. Omar.

Please know it is incumbent on us to teach what we know is correct in Islam to you who have peace with us.

Please see the following caption on my heart,

Please know I am a Muslim by definition.

Please understand when we teach people we see it enter their heart.

Please know some will rebel and some will advocate you.

Please understand this,

Please know after the Prophet passed away he left you in the earth to follow his footsteps and be a daee or teacher.

Please know our careers will be safe. Have courage and be a daee openly with pride that you have a Muslim heart that submits.

Please know this is true to a certain extent but dawah has to be done actively for it to be a benefit.

Please know they have failed who think it is enough to have good manners as this is not important in a country where they maintain this as a habit.

Please know dawah and nasiah or advice are advocating Islam to the Non-Muslim.

Please know we protect our career here when we tell you to be Muslim advocates of me as I am the daee you follow.

Please know Islam on a whole has slept away the last century.

Please know why,

Please know it was because they took the last Imam for a Non-Muslim and hid his book.
Please know he is rekindled.
Please see my teachings bring him forth.
Please see the following caption there,
Please know we must try to assimilate him,
Please know we must try to bring Islam to people with our tongues. I mean we should advocate its values.
Please know Islam is asleep.
Please know that Islam will awaken when the West advocates it openly. Omar.

Please know Him from the perfecture He created.
Please know we know Him from the creation He creates.
Please know how,
Please know it is because when we study nature we realize its perfection.
Please know that pride to deny Him is blindness in us.
Please understand the universe is similar.
Please know perfection in it.
Please know perfection in man.
Please see it.
Please know we study man for years in school yet we do not see.
Please see the complexity of mankind's body.
Please see it cannot create itself.
Please understand this,
Please know we love each other for the sake of Allah.
Please know we cry for our loved ones for His sake as well.
Please know how?
Please understand it is mercy that He has given us.
Please know we are kind to each other by His Grace.
Please know I am sane and realize that we have it because we stay observant of His truth.
Please know when we love one another it is His kindness through which we do so.

Please know when we disregard Him turmoil occurs here.
Please understand it occurs so we can recur with Him.
Please know I know we are grateful when we are happy.
Please understand this,
Please realize when we possess peace we can be grateful to Him.
Please don't be ingrate though when sadness afflicts you,
Please know this,
Please know we have peace when we see Him.
Please know we see Him eventually but we know Him here in our lives on earth.
Please know I know Him as I cannot fathom anything without the brain He gave us.
Please know it did not create itself.
Please see Him as a metaphor as everything is from Him.
Please know when we see Him it is through our faculties He gives us and to be grateful is sane for us. Omar.

Please know happiness with your end is a sign you will have a good outcome.
Please know an eternity is forever,
Please forsake war with yourself and follow Him,
Please know your culture was blind,
Please see the requiem,
Please know we tried to care for you,
Please know we care that you see that this life is not eternity,
Please know eternity,
Please know it knows no death, nor decay,
Please know the reality,
Please know it is not your frivolous pursuits but it is submission to Him,
Please know your law is the Old Testament,
Please submit,
Please know there is a law of the Hereafter,
Please know it is similar to the one here.
Please know there is no cage there,

Please know free,
It is there,
Please wait for Paradise though to make it occur, your freedom,
Please know here we are in a cage gained by sanity principles by law of His,
Please know this is true,
Please know negativity hurts people around you,
Please understand it,
Please know it creates an atmosphere of discord and disharmony,
Please avoid it,
Please be happy if you are to have a good outcome,
Please know how you know?
Please know it is when you have peace and you don't mind the end excessively,
Please know our happiness is our tranquility,
Please know it is not being happy in a material sense,
Please know tranquility,
Please know it is peace that will become joy for an eternity,
Please know the transition is hard but the ease occurs there for the righteous and happy ones. Omar.

Please know love for a child is a sign you have peace with Him.

Please see the following caption there in the house of those who love the child.

Please see that we love children and our children will love us as well.

Please know a child pirouetting is the sign that the world smiles with him or her.

Please know in this there is certainty that the peace of our existence comes from the child as we see them grow with us.

Please know we are responsible for their upbringing and their upkeep but they reward us with smiles and love that we don't experience otherwise.

Please see the following caption on their heart.
I love them.

Please know a child brings with him or her a great love that stems from our Creator.

Please know if we are pleased with Him then we will be pleased with them who are under our care and we will have happiness and peace.

The end is there for those who cannot fathom this fact that if we misbehave with our Creator our life is unhappy as He is the motherlode for us.

Please see the finding of fact on their face there in the child.

Please know I am happy as I love Him.

Please see the family that prays together that will have peace in their homes.

Please know that when we pray to Him we ask forgiveness for ourselves and this makes us soft-hearted and compassionate. Omar.

Please know the law of the handicapped is misused in this country.

Please know the law for the handicapped is severe in this country.

Please understand that the handicapped may or may not be disabled.

Please know that money given to them when their need can be circumvented by another vocation serves them with discredit and does not serve them in the long run.

Please know we are handicapped if we wish to be.

Please understand we are endowed with gifts from our Creator that allow us peace, no matter what the circumstances may be. Omar.

Please know you are the Antichrist the way you train your soldier to fight the innocent in the streets of the cities you conquer.

Please try to see reason and thus be decent. In what way can you justify the killing of innocents as occur in war when your homeland is not at threat.

Please know we are judged for our acts of violence.

The end occurs when you fight rather than pursue peace talks with people you are against.

Please know our Prophet would like to negotiate peace agreements with his enemies.

Please know you have the might economically and other nations will not be able to stand against you for long.

Please know if they do they will see abject poverty of its people.

Please know there is a prediction of this time by our Prophet.

The end occurs if I tell you that your nation is the one predicted that has in its right hand heaven to those it befriends and in its left hand hell to those it sanctions.

Please know it is the character of the Antichrist to do this.

Please know it's head will be in the heavens which is what you understand of space and its feet will be in the deep sea which is where you will harvest its resources. It is clear it fits your nation.

Please know it will be blind in its right eye which is the eye that sees the spirit and its left eye will shine forth like a light. I know this to be the light of materialism. I know you have great factories that produce the finest of science and technology however your insight into religion is little.

Please know movies like American Sniper make me sick. It is a propaganda machine that you use to disarm the youth of their reason.

Please know there is no glory in killing.

Please understand there is only dismay in your hearts when you have killed the enemy.

Please know I grieve at the American soldier as before they are indoctrinated they are decent and like to have fun.

Please understand the psyche at the armed forces can be understood by the picture of a young girl wearing the headdress who was used as a target for their soldiers. In this way they are taught to hate others.

Please know ure son in repose to Him knows that you cannot justify acts like these to your people and to the world. Omar.

Please know corporal punishment is permitted in the child if indecency is found trying in him or her.

Please know our child is like a flower to us but when he misbehaves he must be punished, like all children should.

Please know punishment exacts response and no one should be above it if they commit the crime of it.

Please know our Creator wants us to be violent as well as loving parents.

Please know the age of majority is when the child is able to differentiate right from wrong in his or her conception of things.

Please know this,

Please know a child is always trying to get away with crime with the nature of evil in it,

Please know they don't understand the difference between right and wrong until it is beaten into them.

Please know a child is like a flower and the punishment should be mild in most cases.

Please know our Creator fashioned the child such.

Please know schools have the ability to enforce corporal punishment in this state and it should be maintained in my view as misbehavior requires immediate action and other disciplinary enforcements.

Please see a requiem,

Please know children are our beloved and we want them to be good citizens and people.

Please know truant behavior is evil with us.

Please understand this,

Please know children are raw creatures with little understanding of implications of disorderly conduct except that they will be punished.

Please know if children are not hit for misconduct we do them a disservice and they will know the repercussions will be easy to bear,

Please know our Prophet allowed corporal punishment for them,

Please know why?

Please know it is the fear of painful repercussions that keep them at bay,

Please know he kept a whip for this purpose,

Please know he never used it but allowed his companions to do so when their child crossed the limits.

Please know he did not recommend the corporal punishment over the age of majority. Omar.

Please see we all have a destiny known to Him and not known to man himself.

Please see this verse in Ibrahim where the Creator is the owner of everything.

Please know He controls everything in His dominion.

Please know humans are no exception though some may think they are as they have free will to do things as they please but they don't actually as God controls them as well, though they think not.

Please know God allows things to happen by the will of the people.

Please know they may kill or maim, whatever they wish, but God will call them to account of it.

Please know we have free will, true, but God allows us to do certain things and disallows us many things as well.

Please know in any eventuality we will come to know our deeds have consequences we can't avoid and we will be punished accordingly or He may wish to forgive some things we do in haste.

Please see it occur we are early in Islam as we live by the law for the most part.

Please know those of other faiths are judged according to their deeds.

Please know there is leeway in Islam for many things.

Please know the Prophet said we will get wet when we wade through it, water I mean here.

Please know so it is with sins.

Please know there many who have killed millions.

Please know it is with permit they do.

Please know it was their will to do it.

Please know they are accounted for in the Hereafter.

Please know it is time for moderation you say of him.

Please know there are many miscreants still who wish to maim and kill.

Please know it is civilized to prevent this.

Please know China is an example currently where it occurs, genocide I mean.

Please know they are accountable for it and will be punished.

Please know other countries do it but less.

Please know it is our world to stop this genocide of them. Omar. Ibrahim.

14:1 I, Allah, am the Seer. A Book which We have revealed to thee that thou mayest bring forth men, by their Lord's permission, from darkness into light, to the way of the Mighty, the Praised One,

14:2 Of Allah, Whose is whatever is in the heavens and whatever is in the earth. And woe to the disbelievers for the severe chastisement!

14:3 Those who love this world's life more than the Hereafter, and turn away from Allah's path, and would have it crooked. Those are far astray.

14:4 And We sent no messenger but with the language of his people, so that he might explain to them clearly. Then Allah leaves in error whom He pleases and He guides whom He pleases. And He is the Mighty, the Wise.

Conclusion for you here is to be kind to me as I bring you his teachings in a format you can understand and read.

Please know this book is to know you as a friend of mine,

Please know to befriend me and not call me things which bring you solace not.

Please know there is nothing wrong in significance in me and what they say is contrived as it is easy to do to one.

Please know I am a Muslim and that is the issue for you.

Please know you have found in it solace and what your heart desired to know.

Please know it is now for you to adopt it in your lives and live a life of upbearing with Him.

Please know I am kind to you as I bring this upbearing from Him to you and you will find my Prophet thereby in your homes from where light will emanate from. Omar.

EPILOGUE HERE

ABOUT THE AUTHOR
OMAR AHMAD

Please know the author is myself, Omar Ahmad and I am based in Tennessee and as a result of my writings have faced discrimination from government and church authorities where my license has been suspended and have faced jail and commitment processes since I state I am a saint of the hereafter Dabbat Al-Ard who has communication from his Prophet, amongst others as well.

Please know I am an accomplished author you know from my works on the internet page I have and my first book 'Jesus, the Messiah and the Person.' the first and second edition included.

Please know he is the bringer of no god but Allah to your realm, who is Muhammad, who writes his page to you on Facebook among others as well where you understand One God precepts from his page and somewhat from his writings, like this book is his claim to be in authorship and not mine in essence of things I have here.

Please know we are kind here and know you publish me in a format which would not be allowed in any country in our realm as I am open about the abuse I face. Omar.

ABOUT THE BOOK

Please know this book has an author other than myself and I say in this treatise Muhammad is the author, I am the pen he uses.

Please know I am a Christian missionary to you in the sense I bring Christ's views to your realm as the Islam I serve here.

Please know I am a Christian saint in outlook and Muslim as well as Islam has that perspective as well that mercy encompasses all His creatures which you have in your faith but was lost with dogma from him, your Christ, as you take him, who is Paul, to be your Christ.

Please know this is a collection of works that is Muhammad's where he has delineated his role in ending Christian acclaim of him as Him, the Creator, which he is not in your views now.

Please know he is kind to give me credit but I wrote not a farthing, as we say in the English sense of word here,

Please know my role as an author is to transcribe from him in the sainthood I possess today as you recognize me as saint in this realm of ours where Muhammad is Prophet to you as your teacher and mine too.

Please know there is no God in your outlook however until you recognize Him as the law-giver to you, unless you want law of your own, where he is god to you, your president and government at large,

Please know you understand that concept so I won't belabor you on the issue and let you realize your law has to contravene Him until you realize the statutes must fall in place with the shariah He creates through the teachings of Prophet Muhammad to you on my page to you in Islam of the West here in United States.

Please know the credit goes to him for this works of his and I am the assimilator of facts and I learn from him just as you do, firsthand here.

Please know there is 'no god but Allah' in these works, try them, and see for yourself the appetite they create for the Hereafter.

Omar,
March 2023.
Jackson, Tennessee.

www.ingramcontent.com/pod-product-compliance
Lightning Source LLC
LaVergne TN
LVHW091701070526
838199LV00050B/2237